QuickBooks for Contractors
Guide Setting up and Running your Contractor's Business

Cristie Will

Copyright © 2016 by Cristie Will
All rights reserved. This book or any portion thereof
may not be reproduced or used in any manner whatsoever
without the express written permission of the publisher
except for the use of brief quotations in a book review.
Printed in the United States of America

First Printing, 2016

ISBN-13:1516845447
ISBN-10:**9781516845446**

WillWrite Productions Inc.
www.cbwill.com
www.soswill.com

Trademark Acknowledgments
QuickBooks® and QuickBooks Pro® are registered trademarks of Intuit, Inc. All the software images include in this book are from QuickBooks Premier®.

Disclaimer
This book/guide was written using QuickBooks Premier 2015 and 2016. This is to help you get started using QuickBooks. Be sure to check with your CPA to make sure your accounts are correct.

Introduction

This book was written to help Subcontractors with Their Accounting. This QuickBooks for Contractors book is a detailed step by step guide from setting up your Company File to Running your Business.
No Matter if you are a Plumber, Electrician, Construction Company or a Handyman business.

Setting you your business is like building a home. You need a good solid sturdy foundation or you will have all kinds of problems correcting issues when building your new home and the same thing will happen building your QuickBooks Company file.

Why should you believe me and my capabilities? I grew up in the Construction Industry all my life for one. I have been using QuickBooks for the last 17 years, have set up lots of clients, trained and held QuickBooks Classes. I have worked with or setup just about every kind of contracting business.

Some contractors have special payroll requirements and I will go over those things in this Book.

I will cover estimating and job costing as well, since that is just as important in most contracting businesses.

I suggest starting out with QuickBooks Premier Contractor edition instead of going with Pro. Pro is a little cheaper and doesn't offer as many features as the Premier Contractor Edition, but you will have the other features handy that are not available in QuickBooks Pro.

Here's what I will go over in this book
- Setting up your Company File
- Setting Preferences
- Setting up your Chart of Accounts
- Setup, Edit and Use Classes, Customers & Jobs
- Setup Vendors and subcontractors
- Setup Employee Payroll
- Setup current balances
- Create and use estimates
- Setup Job cost
- Create and send Invoices and Statements
- Enter Vendor Bills, Pay Bills and write checks
- Process Payroll and expenses into job cost reports.
- Go over job costing
- Run Worker's Comps reports plus many more reports along with Financial Statements
- Go over and set up month end and year end accounting procedures.

At the end of the day you will learn pretty much what a Construction Company needs and Make your CPA's job a whole lot easier.

Table of Contents

Chapter 1	Getting Started	5
Chapter 2	Company File Activities	32
Chapter 3	Setting Preferences	44
Chapter 4	Chart of Accounts	74
Chapter 5	Loan Manager, Mileage	81
Chapter 6	Lists, Items & Prices	88
Chapter 7	Customers	120
Chapter 8	Vendors	139
Chapter 9	Inventory	147
Chapter 10	Employees, Payroll Items	152
Chapter 11	Banking	196
Chapter 12	Print & Send Forms	211
Chapter 13	Reports	225
Chapter 14	Opening Balances	238
Chapter 15	Payables	242
Chapter 16	Receivables	254
Chapter 17	Estimating	276
Chapter 18	Month & Year End	282
	Handy Cheat Sheets, Tips & Shortcuts	283
	Blank Note Pages	318
	About Cristie	323
	Other Resources	324

Chapter 1
Getting Started

This chapter is a little bit of everything, such as installing QuickBooks, terms used, Setting up your company file, setting preferences and passwords along with backing up your data just to name a few.

Installing QuickBooks

Follow the directions on installing your QuickBooks software. One thing is or certain before opening the box make sure your computer system has all the requirements. This is important especially if your computer system is a little older and you just purchased a new QuickBooks Software Program.
QuickBooks has multi user versions available for you if more than one user and computer will be used in your Practice.

Before Setting Your Company File and Using QuickBooks

You need to have your Federal and State Account numbers. Have your Bank accounts with beginning balances. The beginning balance needs to be the balance that you want to start from. If this is the month of July and if you want the beginning of the year then you will need to start with the Bank Statements showing the beginning balance as of January 1. The same thing for Credit Cards, you will need the beginning of the year Statements, or if you have a year end March 31 and want to start April 1, then that would be the Statements you need. Here's a quick run-down what you need:

- Company Information like address, phone numbers your Fed and State ID's
- Federal Account Numbers
- State Account Numbers
- All Banking Account Numbers (Main Checking, Petty Cash, Savings, Payroll just to name a few)
- Customers/Receivables that you are doing business with or even ones you want entered.
- Vendors/Payables/Bill Pay that you owe and do business with
- Services/Products you offer

Main QuickBooks Terms

You may already be familiar with these terms and that's one step closer for those that know the terms. Here is a summary of what the main terms are and meaning.

Chart of Accounts

This is the heart of your Company basically. The chart of accounts is a complete list of a company's accounts and their balances. To open the chart of accounts, choose Lists > Chart of Accounts.

When you set up your company file, QuickBooks automatically created a chart of accounts. QuickBooks uses the chart of accounts to track how much money your company has, how much money it owes, how much money is coming in, and how much is going out. Because QuickBooks handles most of the accounting behind the scenes, you may not have to use the chart of accounts very often. Even so, it's helpful to understand how the chart of accounts works.

Item List

The item list is what your Company sells and resells in your business. QuickBooks items represent everything that can be a line item on a sale or purchase form-for example, services and products you sell, things you buy, discounts you offer, and assets you own. You use items when you create invoices, fill out checks, create purchase orders, or buy new equipment.

While they provide a quick means of data entry, a much more important role for items is to handle the behind-the-scenes accounting. When you create an item, you link it to an account; when the item is used on a form, it posts an entry to that account and another entry to the appropriate accounts receivable, accounts payable, checking, fixed asset, or other account.

While items are easy to set up, you should spend some time deciding how they can best work for you before you start setting them up and using them. Use your current list of services and products as a starting point. Consider how much detail you want on your invoices or statements and set up your items with that level of detail in mind.

Class

In QuickBooks, you can create classes that you assign to transactions. This lets you track account balances by department, business office or location, separate properties you own, or any other meaningful breakdown of your business.

Many business owners have certain segments of their business that they want to keep a close eye on. By using the class tracking feature, you can define these segments and track their associated account balances on invoices, bills, and other documents.

Businesses with different departments or locations can use classes to report account balances for each department.

Customer

The Customers are who you work for. Customers hire you for a job or purchase products from you. In QuickBooks, a **customer** is anyone who pays you for goods or services.

Vendors

Vendors are your suppliers and anyone you do business with that you pay for their products and/or services. One example would be if you are leasing your office space you would write a check for Rent or the phone company or office supply place just to name a few.

Jobs

Job is a specific project or scope of work that you want to track.

If you do only 1 job for each customer, you can store job information with the rest of the information for each customer. In that case, your Customers & Jobs list will contain only entries for customers.

However, if you do multiple jobs for a customer, or if you want to keep track of your income and expenses on a job-by-job basis, you should create subentries for your customers, each containing information about a job that you want to track. In this case, your Customers & Jobs list will be a hierarchical list of both customers and their jobs.

Ok let's get started!

Creating Your Company File

You can have lots of companies within QuickBooks, so it's a good idea to make your own sample company to follow along in this book to get the hang of everything. After getting the hang of it all go back and make your company file, however if you feel comfortable enough make your company file from the get go.

1. Click on the File button from the top Main Menu Bar.
2. Select and Click on New Company.
3. Next you will see the following screen and then click Detailed Start.
4. You will be asked about your company, so have your information ready to enter.

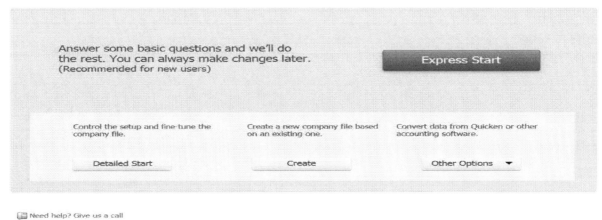

Enter your company information

1. You will be asked to enter your Company Information, see below in the screen.
2. Once you fill in your information click the next button. (if you don't have all the information setting up you can always enter later.

Select your Industry

For this book and setup we are choosing Construction General Contractor then click the next button. Click Next.

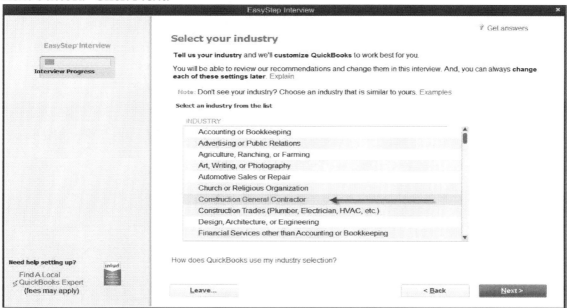

How is your company organized?

Notice I chose LLC. There is a drop down list and you can choose either Single-Member LLC (Form 1040) or Multi-member LLC (Form 1065). After making your selection click on the next button. Note: If you are not set up you will need to get setup. I would contact a CPA to get their recommendation as to what would be best for you and your Company.

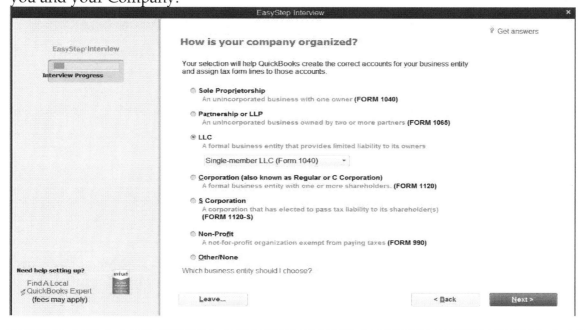

Select the first month of your fiscal year

A fiscal year (also known as a **fiscal year**) is a 12-month period used for calculating your company's yearly financial reports. Some states require financial reports once every 12 months, and don't require that the twelve months constitute a calendar year (i.e., January to December).

Many businesses use **January** as the first month of their fiscal year to coincide with their income tax year, which makes it easier to prepare their company's income tax statement. Your accountant can advise you if you decide to use a month other than January. For this setup I will choose January then click Next.

Set up your Administrator password.

This is optional, but I recommend setting it up. You can setup later as well and change your password too. Click Next when you are done.

Create your company file

This is the next screen and as you can see you are getting ready to save your new company file and ask for location.

If you're not sharing your QuickBooks Company file with other users, we recommend you save your company file on the same computer as QuickBooks. You can use the default location—the QuickBooks Company Files folder—or you can select a different location. If you choose to save your company file in a different location you should save it in its own folder. As you use QuickBooks you'll create other files that will be saved to the same location as the company file.

If you use QuickBooks Pro or Premier in multi-user mode, where you save your company file can affect performance. Click Next.

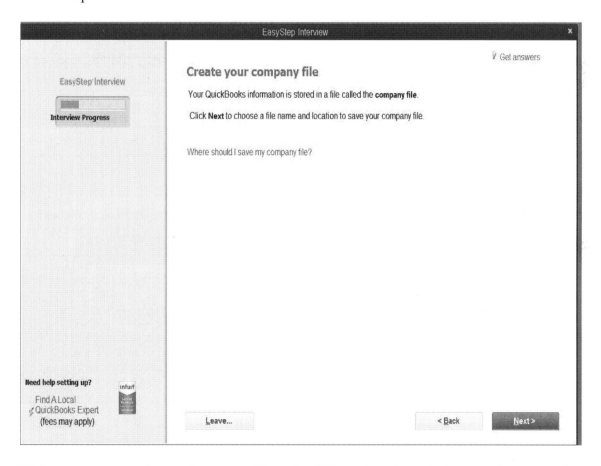

We have now created your Company file and will be going through the Easy Step Interview to personalize your Company File.

EasyStep Interview

The next section of the EasyStep Interview will ask you questions about your business. QuickBooks will use your answers to enable features you will need. Equally important, QuickBooks will disable features you do not need. By enabling and disabling features, QuickBooks will be customized **just for your business**. You won't have to search through features you don't need to be able to complete your tasks.

Need some guidance? QuickBooks will give you recommendations about features that best suits your business needs. For example, QuickBooks will advise a retail-based business to charge sales tax.

You can always change your feature selection. If your business needs change or you realize you're missing a key feature you need, simply go to the Preferences window to change which features are enabled for your business. Click Next.

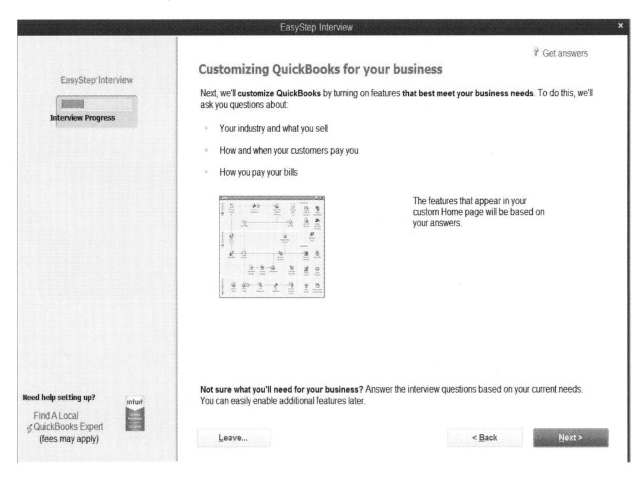

What do you sell?

QuickBooks will use information about what you sell to tailor the rest of the EasyStep interview to your needs. For example, if you sell products, you will have the opportunity to set up inventory. I chose Both services and Products. Click Next.

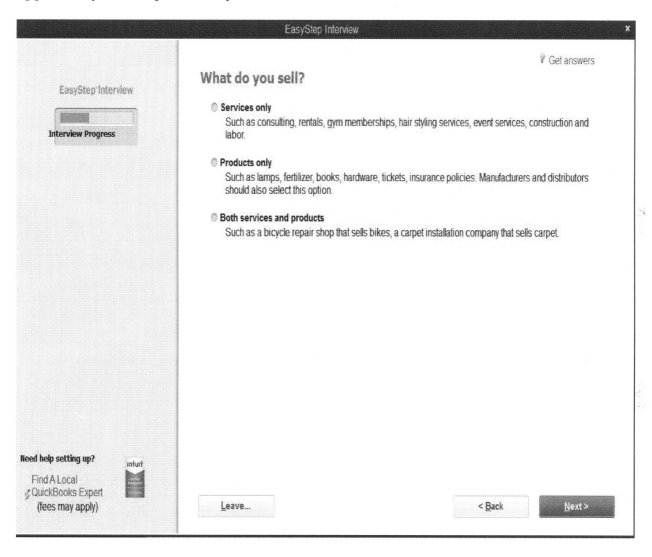

Do you Charge Sales Tax?

If you charge sales tax for the products or services you sell, you pay your collected sales tax to a sales tax agency on a regular schedule. QuickBooks helps automate your sales tax-related tasks so you can keep accurate information about the sales tax you collect and pay.

When you set up QuickBooks to track sales tax for your business, you can mark individual charges as taxable. QuickBooks will figure out the total sales tax on your forms, such as estimates, invoices, sales receipts, refunds, and credit memos. QuickBooks will total the sales tax you collect, compute what you owe, and track what taxes you've paid—even if you collect and owe sales tax at different rates, in different states, or to different agencies.

I am staying with the Default for this industry and keeping it No. Click Next.

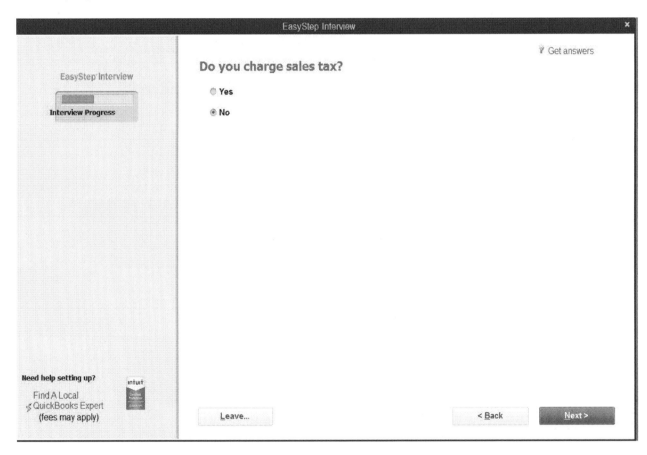

Do you want to create Estimates in QuickBooks?

If you provide estimates, bids, or quotes to your customers, you can use the QuickBooks estimates form. By creating estimates in QuickBooks, you can track your proposals and easily turn each estimate into an invoice. You can create multiple invoices to bill for the portions of estimates that have been completed.

I am staying with the Default selection for this industry. It is necessary. Click Next.

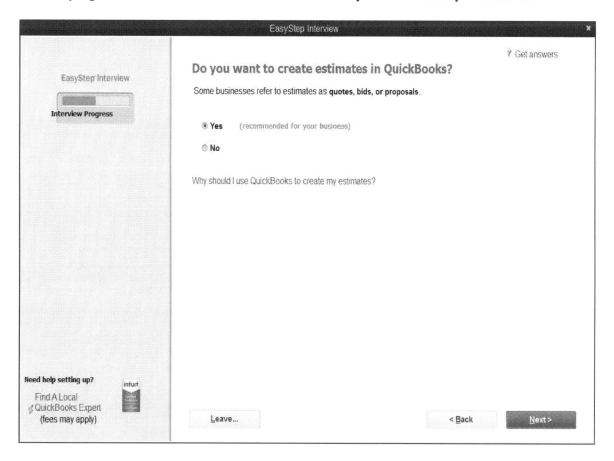

QuickBooks For Contractors

Tracking customer order in QuickBooks

Sales orders are used to track customer orders or pre-sales orders for items that you don't have in stock or are not yet ready to invoice for. This is especially useful for out-of-stock items, items that you build to order, or special order items.

Sales orders can be based on other sales information entered into QuickBooks. You can also use sales orders to create other information in QuickBooks, such as generating invoices. Specifically:

- **You can create a sales order from an estimate.** After providing an estimate to a customer, you can then create a sales order to show a sales commitment.
- **You can create an invoice from a partial or complete sales order.** You can bill your customers when the entire order is fulfilled or as you fulfill portions of the order.
- **You can create a purchase order from a sales order.** You can use the purchase order to purchase items from vendors to fulfill the sales order.

Every business is different, but have many same things to follow. In the Construction Industry you generally won't use sales order, but there are those occasions you might, so if you fit in that category then click yes.

I am staying with the default choice of No. Click Next.

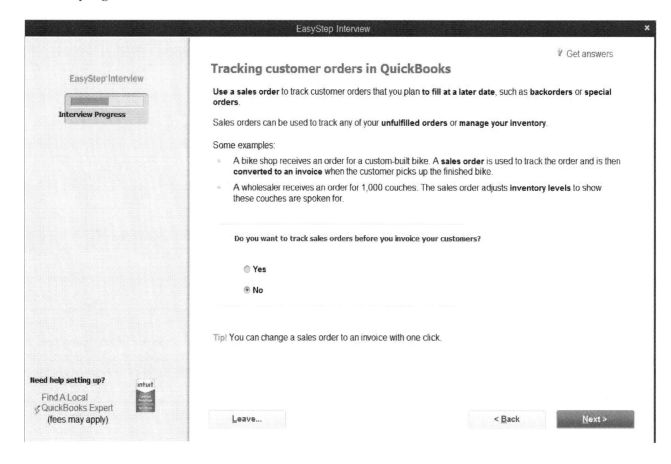

Using Statements in QuickBooks

Statements are used when you allow a customer to accumulate charges before requesting payment, or if you assess a regular monthly charge. When you're ready, such as at the end of the month or when you've accumulated charges, you can print a **billing statement** to send to your customers.

For example, you can use a billing statement to:

- bill your customers on a regular basis, such as monthly.
- send a customer a reminder of past-due charges.
- charge your customers for a regular service.

I am staying with the Default choice of Yes on this. Click Next.

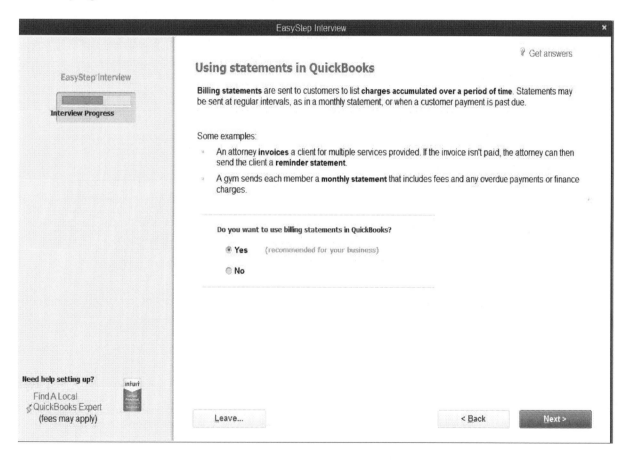

Using progress invoicing

Use a progress invoice to bill your customers based on the progress of a job, such as phases of work.

A progress invoice is billed on progress against an estimate. If you'd like to bill your customers on progress, such as phases of work, first create an estimate. You don't need to give it to your customer, but you'll use it to invoice your customer on progress against the estimate.

By creating estimates in QuickBooks, you'll be able to run reports on both progress invoices and estimates. You'll also be able to keep track of any outstanding estimates you have with customers.

I am staying with the default choice of yes and this is not only a must really, but highly recommended. Click Next.

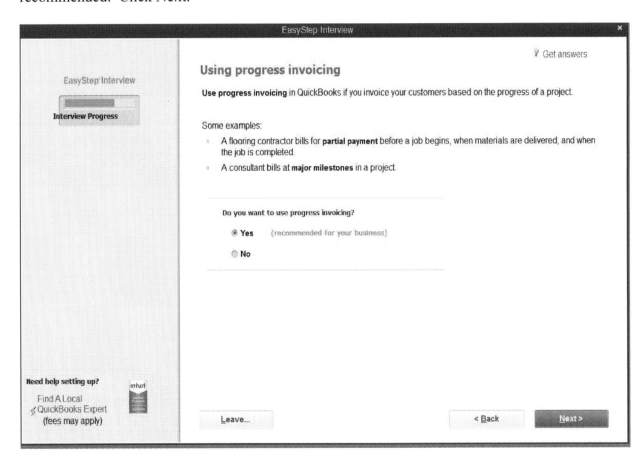

Managing bills you owe

QuickBooks can help you manage your bills that you owe. Managing your bills in QuickBooks will help you keep track of **what** you owe, **who** you owe it to, and **how much** you owe.

- **Do you pay your bills as soon as you get them?** If you do and you don't care about keeping track of how much you currently owe, you don't need to track your bills. Simply write a check to record your payment in QuickBooks.
- **Do you want help managing your bills?** By managing your bills in QuickBooks you can:
    - See the total of all your outstanding bills, as well as a breakdown by payee or vendor.
    - Have QuickBooks remind you when your bills are due
    - Make an informed decision about which bills to pay first. You can decide based on information such as who you owe the most money to, which vendors you want to treat more cautiously, or which bills are most overdue.
    - Manage your cash flow with clear visibility into your spending.

You definitely need this, so I am staying with the Default answer Yes. Click Next.

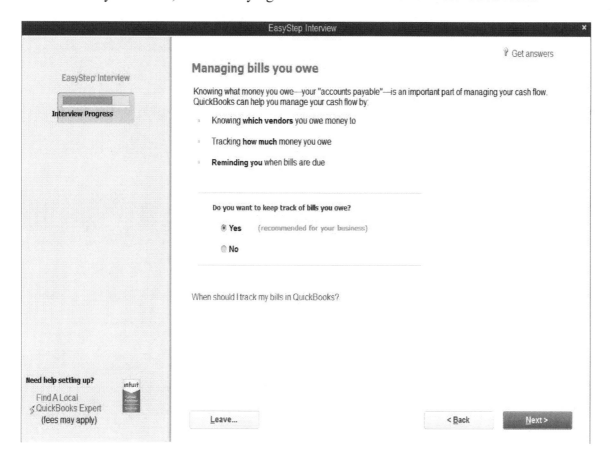

QuickBooks For Contractors

Tracking inventory in QuickBooks

If your company sells products to customers, you may want to track inventory. QuickBooks can track inventory levels, decrease inventory quantity automatically when you make a sale, and prompt you to reorder inventory when your levels are low.

I am going to change the Default to yes this time. You may stock pipe or other parts and need this and for purposes of training I chose this. Click Next.

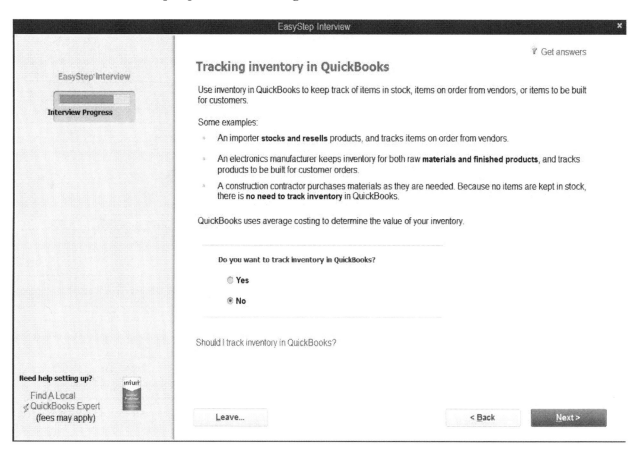

Tracking time in QuickBooks

Tracking time in QuickBooks can help you:

- **See how much time you spent on a project**. This can help you calculate your costs and decide if you are charging appropriately.
- **Track hours worked by employees**. You can then create accurate paychecks and bill customers for actual hours worked.

QuickBooks includes **three tools for tracking time**:

- A **Stopwatch** that you can use to time an activity while you' performing it.
- **Weekly timesheets** or activity-by-activity timesheets where you can enter time data manually.
- The **Timer**—a separate program that can run on its own without QuickBooks. When you use the Timer, you can:
    - Automatically track time spent on a task (you click the Start button when you begin an activity and click the Stop button when you stop work). Alternatively, you can enter the time worked after you have done the work.
    - Track time without running QuickBooks.
    - Give a copy of the Timer program to people whose work you want to track in QuickBooks (for example, owners, partners, employees, or subcontractors).

This is an important feature and you do need this, so I stayed with the Default answer of yes. Click Next.

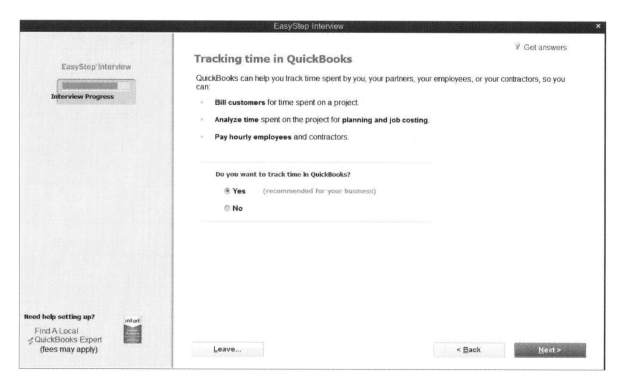

Do you have employees?

You can use QuickBooks to track contact information about all your employees, manage your payroll, track employees' hours, and manage sick and vacation time.

The default on this choice is blank, so for training I chose yes we have employees and contractors. Click Next.

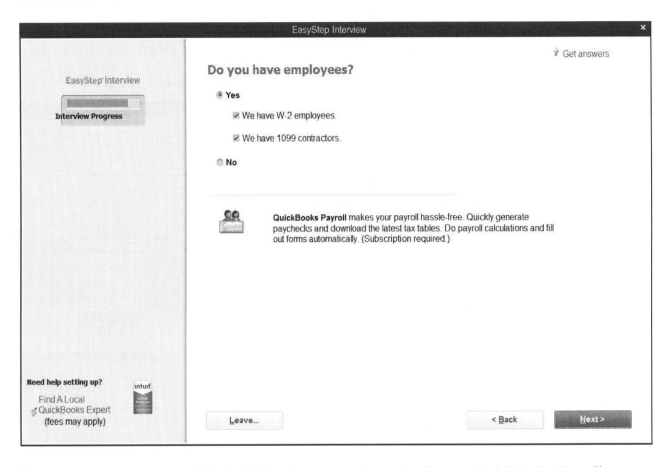

If you want to process payroll in QuickBooks, you need to subscribe to a QuickBooks Payroll service. With a QuickBooks Payroll subscription, you can:

- Easily print paychecks right from your PC.
- Get automatic tax table updates and automatic calculations to save you time and improve accuracy.
- Just print, sign, and mail payroll tax filings, or let QuickBooks Payroll do it for you.

We will go step by step through payroll in the Payroll Chapter.

Using accounts in QuickBooks

Next we will guide you through creating the bank accounts, expense accounts and income accounts that make up your **chart of accounts**.

The chart of accounts is the backbone of your accounting system. That's why it's so important to understand how it works. Think of a chart of accounts as a file cabinet, with a file for each type of accounting information you want to track. For example, if you need to know how much money you spend on postage, you'll set up a file (an account in the chart of accounts) for Postage Expense.

We will go over this in the Chart of Accounts chapter. Click Next.

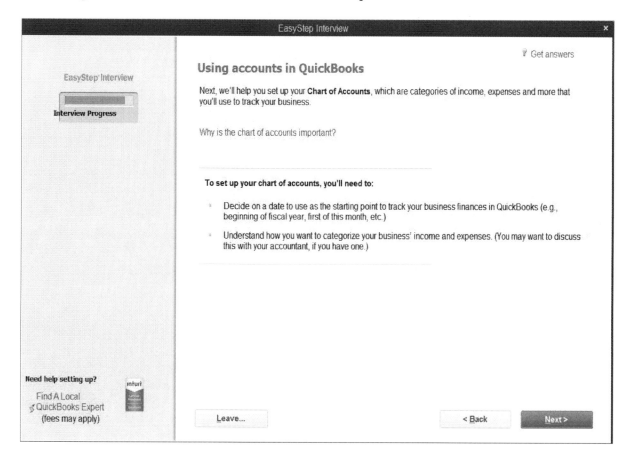

Select a date to start tracking your finances

The start date is a date you choose as the **starting point for your financial records in QuickBooks**—similar to starting a new register for a checking account.

Important: Once you choose a start date you'll need to enter the balances for your accounts as of your start date. Once you start using QuickBooks, you'll enter details for any transactions—such as bill payments, invoices, and payments from customers—that have occurred between your start date and today's date.

For this exercise and training I am using Beginning of this fiscal year. Click Next.

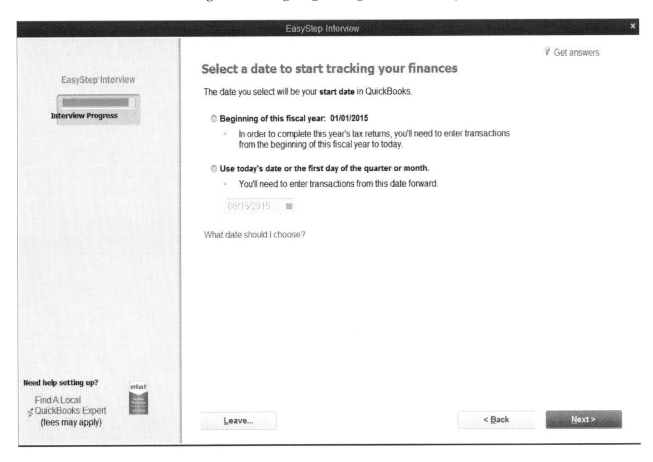

Review income and expense accounts

This portion of the EasyStep Interview will guide you through creating income and expense accounts. Based on your industry selection, QuickBooks will recommend a set of income and expense accounts to use. You can start with these accounts or create new ones later. You can also delete or rename these accounts later.

This is your Chart of Accounts. Go through and see if this looks like you want. If you see an account you know you will use and it's doesn't have a check mark then place a check mark next to it so you don't have to go back and add it. When finished Click Next.

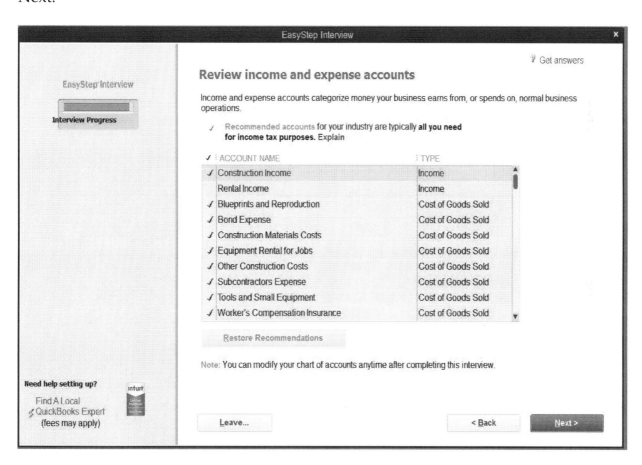

Congratulations!

Now we'll help you get up-and-running in no time.

What happens next?

First, we'll help you get your critical info (like the people you do business with and the products and services you sell) into QuickBooks using the QuickBooks Setup wizard.

Then, we'll show you how to get started with key tasks like creating invoices and sales receipts, entering bills, and more. Click Go to Setup button.

QuickBooks Setup Wizard

Since Bank Accounts is at the top of the Chart of Accounts I like to Start with Bank Accounts. Have your bank account information ready and Click on the Add button to add your bank accounts.

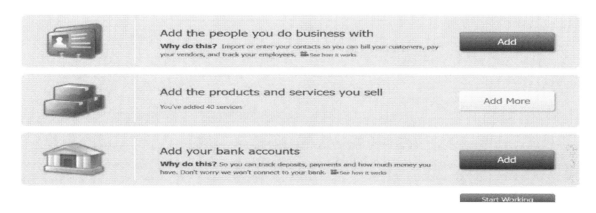

Add your bank accounts screen

I added five accounts and depends if you have a separate payroll checking etc. The five I just entered are Main Checking, Adjustment bank account, Savings Account, Payroll and Petty Cash Accounts. Click Continue when done. Click Start Working. We add the rest in the next few screens see next page.

QuickBooks For Contractors

Add the People you do business with

Instead of going through the next two screens before working I have you go through the add edit Multiple Entries, this is faster and easier.

Here's your Home Page

1. Click Lists at the top Main Menu Bar (see red arrow)
2. Select Add/Edit Multiple List Entries

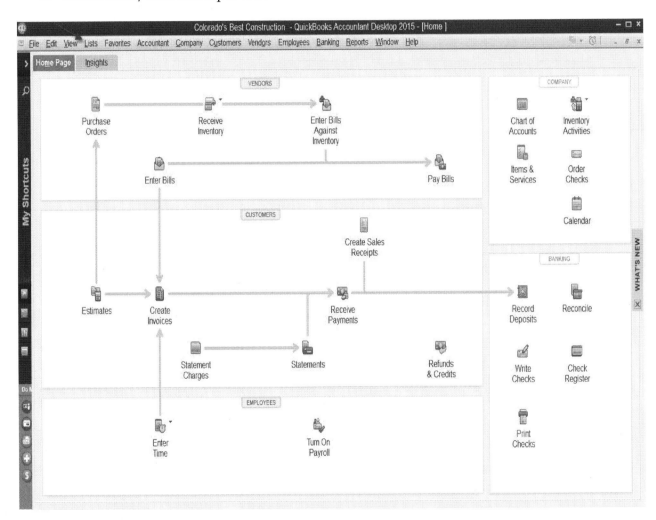

Here's the Add/Edit Multiple List Entries

In this window you can add multiple entries for

- Customers
- Vendors
- Service items
- Inventory Parts
- Non-Inventory Parts
- Inventory Assemblies

See the red arrow? This is where you will enter multiple customers and when you are done you will click the Save Changes button at the bottom of the screen

You will then click on the drop-down list arrow under List and select Vendors next to add your vendors. Click Save Changes when ready to go to the next list.

I will take you through each of these with screenshots to give you a feel. We will go over all of these in detail in the following chapters.

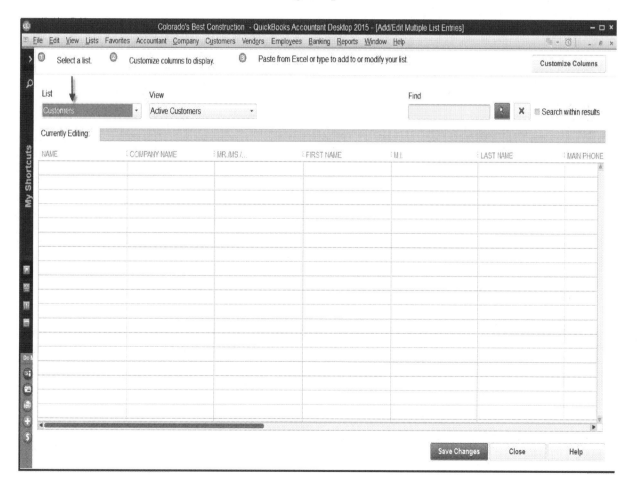

Adding Multiple Customers

Here I've added a few customers. This is just to get you going. We will need to go in and setup the Preferences once we are done with this. You will need to tweak your lists probably some since some features may not be turned on that you will use. Click Save Changes.

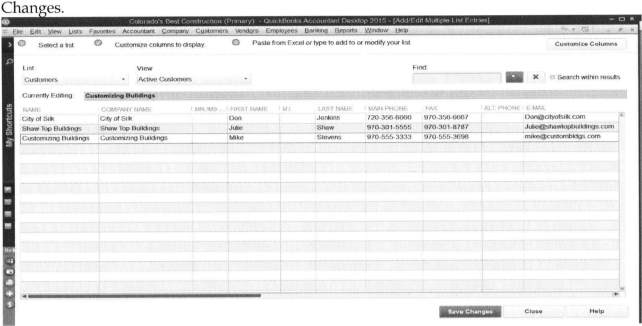

Adding Vendors

Click on the drop-down arrow located under List and choose Vendors to start entering Vendors. When finished click Save Changes.

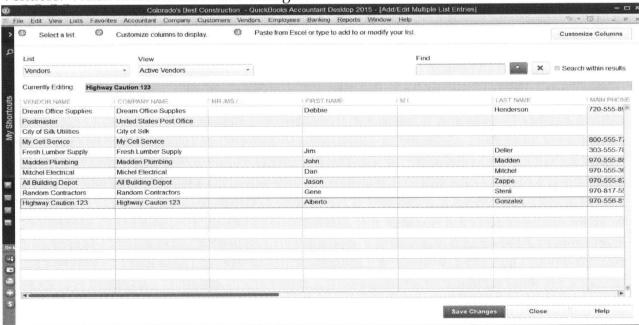

Inventory Items/Service Items

These items were alreay set up during the company setup. We have a whole chapter discussing items and will go over and add more then.

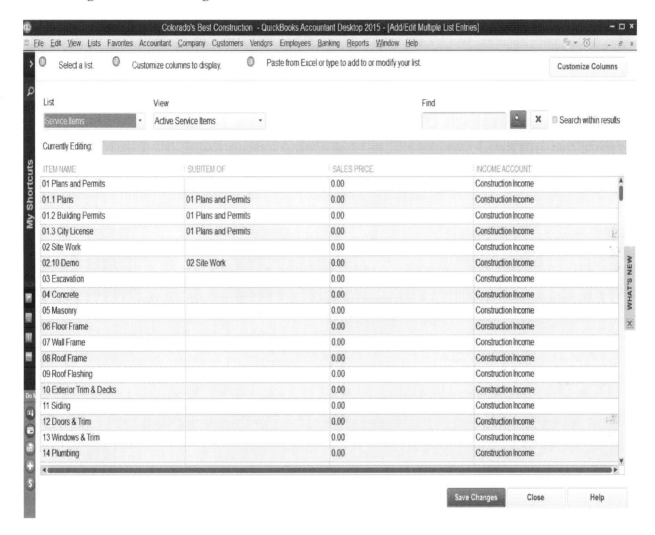

We are now done with setup. The next Chapter we will go over daily, weekly, and monthly company file activities including upgrading, restoring and backing up your Company file. Your Company File is like the Golden Egg you need and better protect it.

QuickBooks For Contractors

Chapter 2
Company File Activities
Backup, Restore, Updates & Upgrades

Backups

The backup file (.qbb) contains copies of all of the data you need to re-create your company file (.qbw) and QuickBooks environment, including your supporting files (such as templates, letters, images, and so on).

I cannot stress how important backing up your data is. I have dropped the ball along with many of my clients on backing up, so I can speak from many mistakes we have all made not backing up. If you aren't sure when you backed up and then lost your files it's a bigger mess, so if you have regular backups you know pretty much what you have to reenter. We will go over scheduling your backups to help you avoid this kind of problem.

How to make a backup

1. Click File from the top of the Main Menu Bar
2. Select Backup Company
3. Select from the slide out menu Create Local Backup I will save to desktop, but it's best to have a flash drive or CD.
4. Click Next.

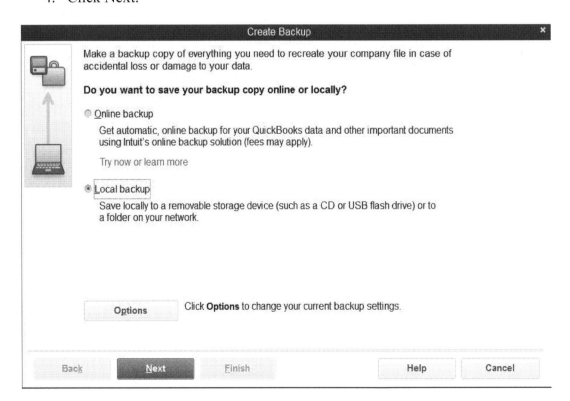

This is the next screen where you are given options like where to save the backup. Notice the boxes check to have the date and time to the file and recommended along with limit the number of backup copies in this folder, you set the number.

Next is the online and local backup. The box remind me to back up when I close my company file every 4 times, here you can choose the times as well. You don't have to check this option either. We will get into scheduling backups in this chapter. Once you have made your choices click ok.

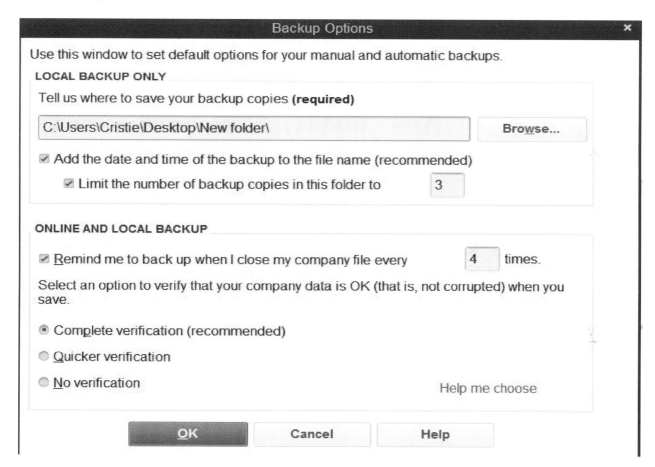

Since I chose to save to my desktop this is the next screen prompting you to think about saving to your desktop, I chose use this location this time.

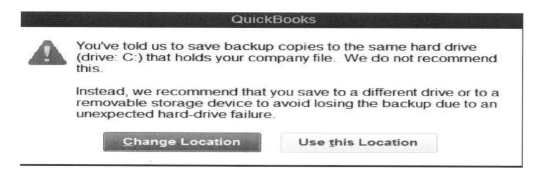

This screen is next asking when you want to sve your backup copy? I clicked save it now. Notice it ask about schedule backups. We are going to schedule some. For this exercise select Save it now and click Next.

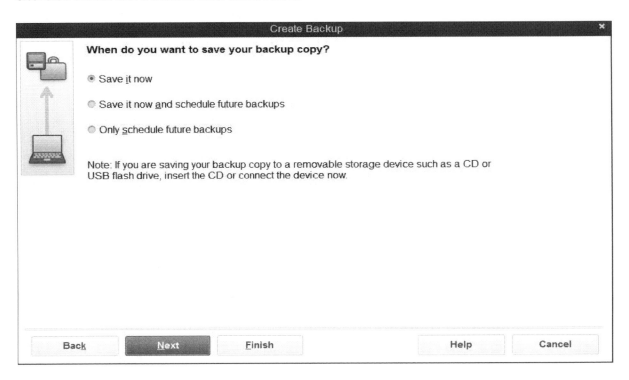

This screen will be the next screen prompting to let you know where you are saving the backup file. Click save.

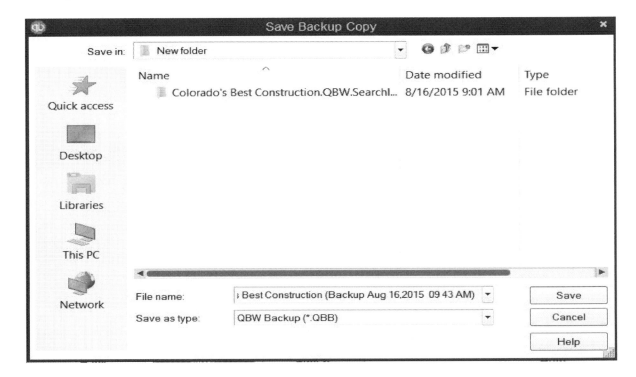

Restore your company file

The backup file (.qbb) contains copies of all of the data you need to re-create your company file (.qbw) and QuickBooks environment, including your supporting files (such as templates, letters, images, and so on). Your backup file contains your company data up to the date the backup was made. Make sure you restore the most recent file.

Follow these steps to restore a local backup from a CD, USB flash drive, local hard drive, network folder, or other media.

If you backed up your company file using Intuit Data Protect, you must restore it through that same service. Intuit Data Protect is a subscription service that automatically backs up your company file and other important data. When you back up your QuickBooks Company file with Intuit Data Protect everything you need to re-create your company file and QuickBooks environment is backed up as well.

Each backup is stored for 45 days, so you always have the most recent 45 days' worth of data available to restore, if you ever need it. You can choose to restore the most recent backup, or you can select an earlier backup if needed.

1. Click File at the top of the Main Menu Bar
2. Select Open or Restore Company
3. Select Restore a backup copy
4. Click Next.

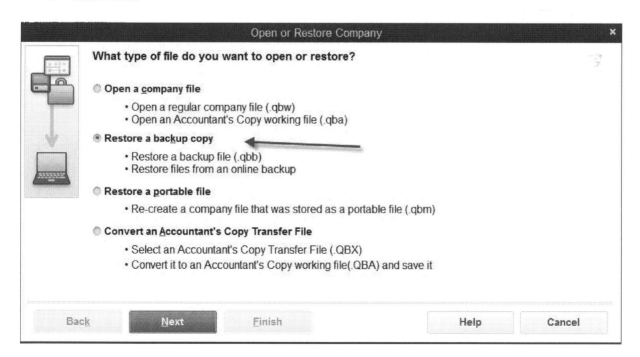

Notice the other options? We will cover those next. We are going to restore from the backup file we just made.

This is the next screen, choose Local backup and Click Next.

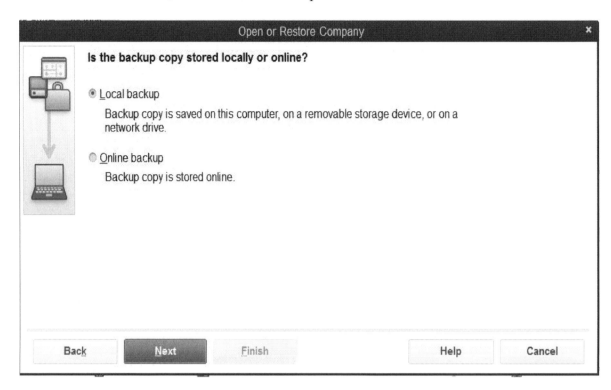

This is the next screen. This is the file we just backed up and now we are going to restore it. Click open.

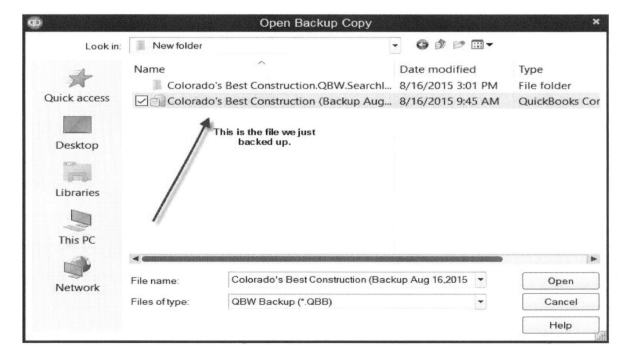

This is the next screen asking where you want to restore the file? You want to overwrite the current company file, this is usually the case. The reason for restore is probably either from a huge amount of wrong entries, lost data for some reason, but normally you want to restore to a certain point to move forward. click next.

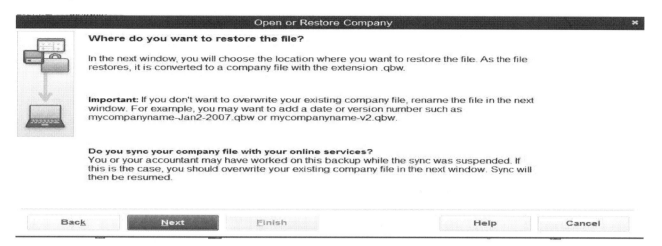

This is the next screen showing where you are saving and the name click save.

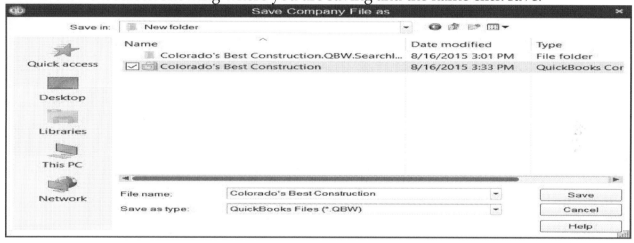

Click yes to Confirm Save As then the next screen, Delete Entire File pops up as a precautionary step asking you to type YES to confirm, so type YES and click OK. This is just overwriting the current file with the backup file.

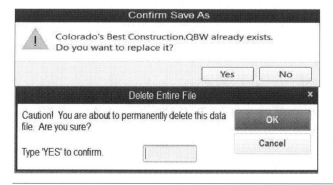

Portable Company File

A portable company file is a compact version of your company file containing only financial data, and is small enough to be sent by email or saved to portable media. You can use a portable company file whenever you need to move your company financial data to another location or send it to another person.

How to make a Portable Company File

1. Click File at the top of the Main Menu Bar
2. Select Send Company File
3. Next choose Portable File Company

Click on to learn why Cloud storage is safer than email. Even though they recommend to go the cloud way you can still email file, of course at your own risk. Having said that I have always emailed the file with a password and no problems, but doesn't mean you won't have problems. I would say to be safe to go by QuickBooks recommendations. Make your choice where to send your portable file and click send.

Open or Restore Company File

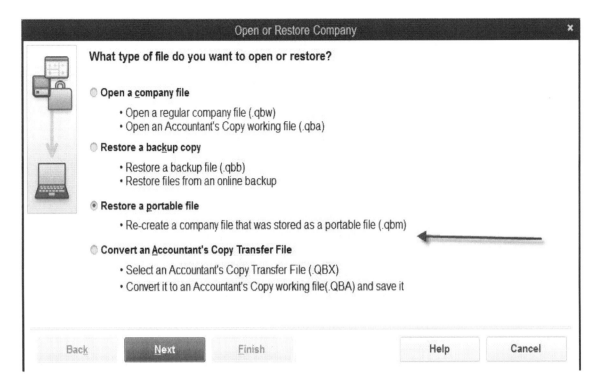

Click on File on the top Main Menu Bar and Click on Open or Restore Company File and select Restore a portable file as shown above and click next.

Click on the portable file where you have the file saved. Like the example above with the red arrow pointing to it. The click Open.

Click Next.

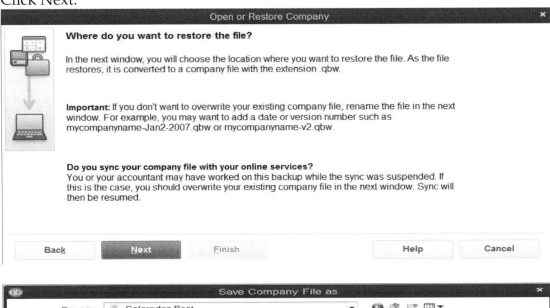

Click Save. Click yes to replace the other file.

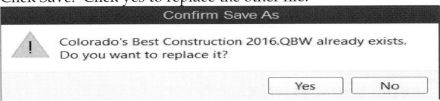

Type YES and Click ok. It looks like you will delete your file, but it's just overwriting your other file and this is just precaution. It's always best to have another backup file on a thumb drive just in case of an accident.

Updates

To update your QuickBooks automatically you need to set the updates up.

1. Click on Help at the top of the Main Menu Bar.
2. Select Update QuickBooks

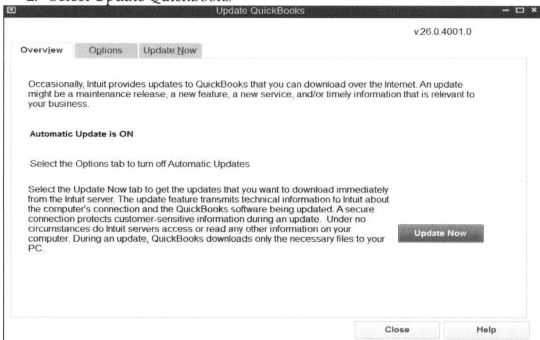

Click on Options tab and make sure Automatic Update is set to Yes. Click on the button Mark All below and Save to update everything.

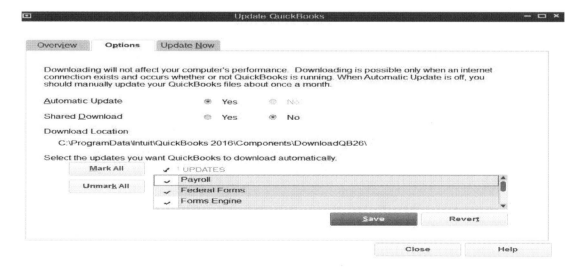

If you have not updated QuickBooks at all you may want to run update now and to do that click on the tab Update Now. See Example on the next page.

QuickBooks For Contractors

To get your updates right now click on the button get updates. When you do this you have to wait for the updates to finish.

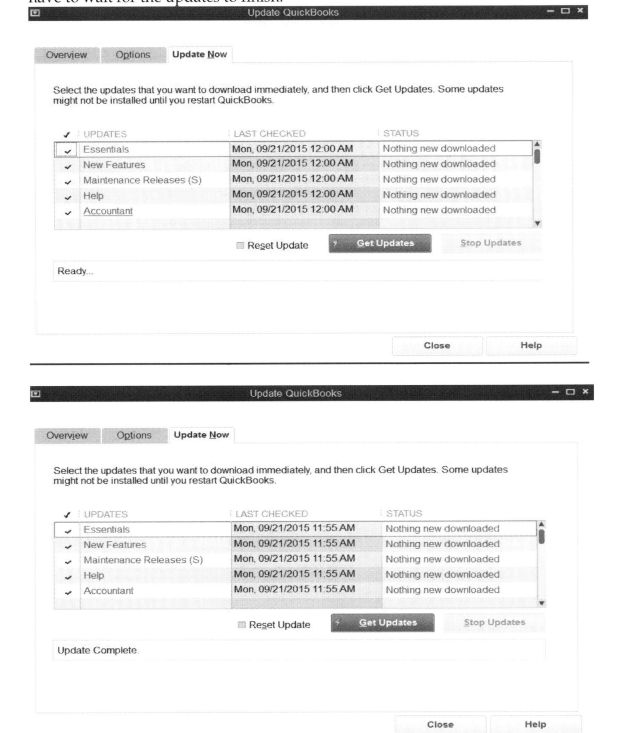

The QuickBooks finished updating. It says update complete. Click the Close button.

QuickBooks Upgrades

The upgrade rules can change, so check out upgrading before you do so. The experience I have had in the past with clients if they wait too many years/version upgrades then its problematic upgrading your company file, but can be done.

Example of waiting too long to upgrade. Client A did not use payroll for their personal accounting file. Since they did not use QuickBooks for payroll it wasn't necessary to upgrade, although QuickBooks quit servicing a version that out of date. To upgrade this client to use their file and not lose any data we had to take baby steps. I upgraded them in three year sequences until they had a company file that would upgrade to the newest upgrade.

I would suggest not to wait more than four years if not using payroll for the reason's I mentioned. They didn't save any money waiting that long since they had to pay me to obtain QuickBooks versions that old and spend the time upgrading every three years until it was correct. The truth be known it probably cost them more. If you are in this position an accountant can help you or Intuit/QuickBooks can help as well.

If you are using QuickBooks Payroll you have to upgrade every three years because QuickBooks requires it. They only maintain three years of the latest versions of QuickBooks, unless you pay the monthly fee to use QuickBooks online. You can also pay this annually as well.

I love QuickBooks payroll no matter if you are doing it yourself and it's so simple once its set up I would probably never outsource mine. You can also hand over to QuickBooks to handle all aspects of payroll or your accountant.

Using QuickBooks online has its Pros and Cons as everything in life does. I am old school and have a problem with my books being in the Cloud. Having said that I have read that it's supposed to be safer and more secure. This is something everyone has to come to their own conclusion and decision which way to go.

Pros of using the online version is the convenience of accessing your books anywhere you have an internet connection. Having said that you might not be able to access your books if their system is down for maintenance or any reason or if you do not have an internet connection.

Depending on the choice you were to make for the online version you might be paying more or less then you would if you upgraded every year or every couple of years.

The online version does not have near the features, in my opinion, as the Premier desktop editions have. When it is all said and done choose what is best for you.

QuickBooks For Contractors

Chapter 3
Setting Preferences

Setting your Preferences is like laying the foundation of your home. If not set up properly it could result in issues. I will take you through each Preference and what they typically should be. Preferences are used to customize your features like if you use payroll or not. Little things like automatically adding a decimal point so you don't have to remember to do so and at the same time if you prefer adding the decimal point then you will leave that unchecked. Let's get started.

Accounting Preferences

1. Click on Edit at the top main menu bar
2. Select Preferences
3. click on the first one, Accounting
4. The tab my Preferences is checked autofill memo in general journal entry. Leave checked. There are no other Preferences under My Preferences, so click on Company Preferences tab.

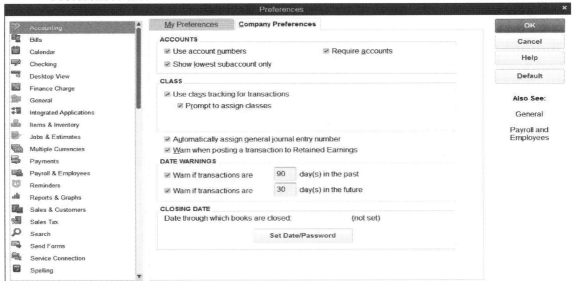

Use account numbers for your Chart of Accounts is highly recommended and I will explain in Chapter 4 pertaining to Chart of Accounts. In chapter 4 you will be able to see plenty of screen shots of Chart of Accounts.

Show lowest subaccount only is to display the subaccount only instead of displaying the main account and other subaccounts. This allows you to zero in and view the exact account when viewing transactions.

Require Accounts will warn and force you to allocate every transaction to an account and that's good. This will help especially at year end for your CPA along with correct reports too.

Use Class Tracking is used to classify and track locations, services, labor, materials, subcontractors, rentals and more. The sky is just about the limit on things you want to track. I will have more in depth information later in the book under Class chapter.

Prompt to Assign Classes will prompt you if you require classes and didn't assign a transaction a class. I highly recommend this to be checked.

Automatically Assign General Journal Entry Number is automatically assigned by QuickBooks. I highly recommend this to make it much easier than to remember the right number you would assign.

Warn when posting a transaction to Retained Earnings. I highly recommend checking this option. By selecting this option it will help you from getting out of balance with your books. The Retained Earnings account is what your business has made or lost since the beginning of your business. Every year QuickBooks closes out your income and expenses and sends the difference into your Retained Earnings account. If one year you made a profit and the next year you had a loss then the balance would be the result of your profit year minus your loss year and so on.

Date Warnings will warn you if you enter a wrong date. This is invaluable and highly recommend you checking this option. I know there are times you may post an out of date transaction and that's ok, but when you don't want to this is when it's invaluable. You set the time frames to what works for you.

Closing Date is the date through which books are closed for year end. Click on the button Set Date/Password. The screen shot below is what pops up. You can see I set the closing date as of the last day of year end. You can still add things in, but you will be prompted to enter a password and that helps keep unauthorized people out and it helps you avoid an unnecessary mistake. After setting dates and password click ok.

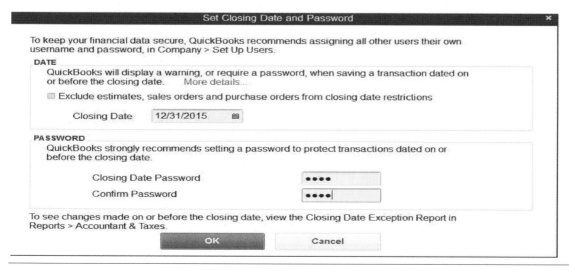

Bills Preferences

There are no Preferences under My Preferences in the Bills Preferences, so click on the Company Preferences tab. If you don't have your Preferences window open do the following:

1. Click on Edit at the top Main Menu Bar
2. Select Preferences
3. Click on Bills in the column to the left under Accounting.

Entering Bills is simple but yet necessary and a part of every person's life whether it be for business or personal. You want to set up for every possible discount to take advantage of and use any credits as well. As you can see I left the default of 10 days for bills being due after receipt, this is QuickBooks default. You can set this to whatever days applies to you.

Bills are Due typically is 30 days, but you can set this to whatever is best for you. If you don't change it then it will default to 10 days.

Warn about duplicate bill numbers from same vendor prevents you from entering the same bill and paying the same bill multiple times. I highly recommend this feature.

Paying Bills

Automatically use credits this allows you to use any credits against what you will pay your creditors and will automatically apply for you. I highly recommend this so that you don't overlook losing a credit.

Automatically use Discounts if you have the opportunity to use discounts then I would highly recommend this and this feature will automatically apply for you as well. If you do use this you will need to set up a discount account, but check first you may have an account already.

Calendar

This Preference is unlike most of them and it has no Company Preferences, but it has My Preferences. If the Preference's window is not open then do the following.

1. Click on Edit at the top Main Menu Bar
2. Select Preferences
3. Click on Calendar in the column to the left under Bills.

I left this on QuickBooks default. As you can see its items to help you and pertain to your business.

Calendar View can be set to Default, Remember Last View or change to one of the other settings, daily, weekly or monthly view.

Weekly View is set to Variable (5/7 days) the default or you can change to fixed 5 days or fixed 7 days.

Show is set to all Transactions QuickBooks default and personally I would leave that. It shows you can change it to many different things such as To Do, Transactions Due, Deposit, Estimate and Invoice just to name a few. If you leave to all Transactions you can see everything at once.

Upcoming & Past Due Settings this is as it shows to allow you to view everything you have that is due or past due or will be due. This would be what works for you as well.

Checking

The Checking Preferences has My Preferences and Company Preferences that need to be set up. We will start with My Preferences.

1. Click on Edit at the top Main Menu Bar
2. Select Preferences.
3. Click on Checking in the column to the left under Calendar.
4. My Preferences tab is up first. Select Default Accounts as shown below.

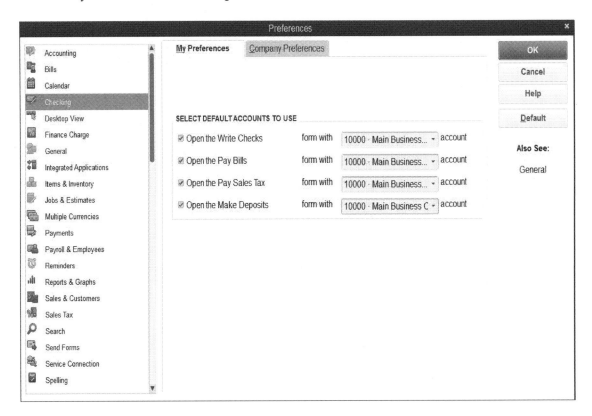

Checking Company Preferences

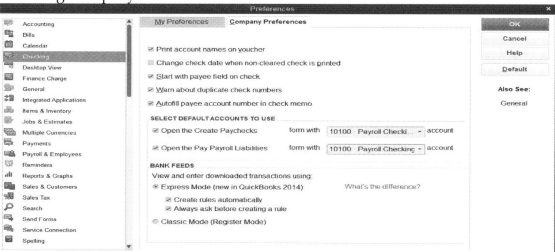

Print account names on voucher if you use voucher checks with attachments where the payee, date, account name, memo, amount and total will appear on the voucher. If you don't select this QuickBooks will omit just the Account name, but the rest of the information will appear.

Change check date when non-cleared check is printed this shows the date the check was printed not the date it was created in QuickBooks. You would want to check this if you enter your checks on a different day than you print or send checks out.

Start with payee field on check this option lets you skip the check number and date and go right to the payee field. This is a good option since QuickBooks fills in the date and next check number, however you want to always check those fields to be sure check numbers are right and didn't get off someway.

Warn about duplicate check numbers this is just what it says. If you enter a check already used QuickBooks will warn you that the number has already been used. This is highly recommended to use.

Autofill payee account number in check memo if you choose this option the vender account will print on the memo field on the check. This is nice not to have to remember to do that if you enter account numbers.

Select Default Accounts to Use as you can see that you need to fill in the checking account to create and pay payroll liabilities out of. This is of course if you use the payroll feature in QuickBooks.

Bank Feeds is for downloading transactions from your Financial Institution/bank. The settings in the example are QuickBooks Default mode and I recommend leaving it on that even if you don't download transactions.

QuickBooks For Contractors

Desktop View

The Desktop View Preferences has options to choose under My Preference and Company Preferences. We will start with my Preferences first.

1. Click on Edit at the top Main Menu Bar
2. Select Preferences.
3. Click on Desktop View in the column to the left under Checking.
4. My Preferences tab is up first. The screen shot below is Default settings. I am fine with these settings under My Preferences, but you can change to what you like.
5. When you have finished click the Company Preferences tab.

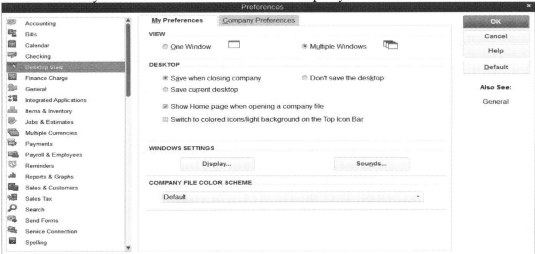

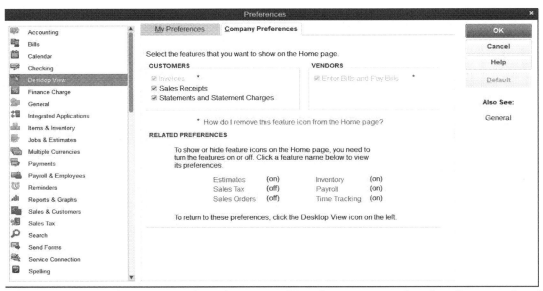

These are turned on as to what the typical Preferences are for the Contracting business, which is if you use Payroll for example. I left my choices as shown. If you need to change them then do so as to what meets your needs.

Finance Charge

There are no Preference's under My Preference's under this feature, so we will go over the Company Preferences.

1. Click on Edit at the top Main Menu Bar
2. Select Preferences.
3. Click on Finance Charge in the column to the left under Desktop View.
4. Click on Company Preference's tab.

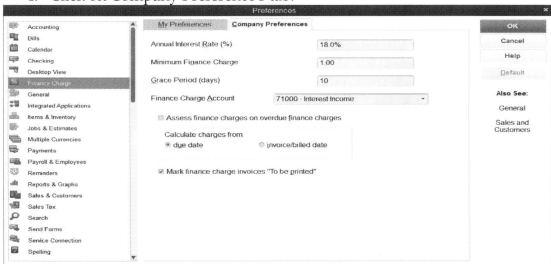

The settings in the screen shot above for finance charges is pretty typical. It is up to you whether you want to charge your customers fees for late payments. Companies charge this often times just to keep their customers paying on time. More often than not the customers don't pay these late fees. You can change any of the fields to your business needs. You may need to set up the interest Income account to collect the finance charges. This account is classified as other Income. See below.

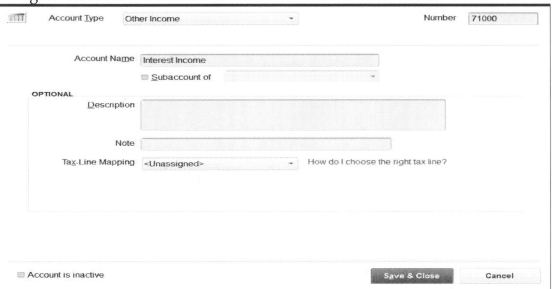

General

The General tab has features to choose under My Preferences and Company Preferences, so we will start with My Preferences.

1. Click on Edit at the top Main Menu Bar
2. Select Preferences.
3. Click on General in the column to the left under Finance Charge.
4. My Preferences tab is up first. I set features the way I like.
5. When you have finished click the Company Preferences tab.

This is pretty self-explanatory. The General is mainly to help you move around in QuickBooks. For example I clicked on automatically place decimal point. I have clients that had rather place the decimal point, so they did not check this feature. Set these features as to what you like. Remember this can always be changed anytime if you decide you don't like something or want to come back and choose a feature you didn't choose now.

The Company Preferences are default and it works perfect for the contracting business. These can be changed anytime to meet your needs as well.

Integrated Applications

Integrated application preferences govern the rights integrated applications have to access the current QuickBooks company file. The preferences set in this window apply to all integrated applications seeking to access this company file. You can permit or deny access to individual applications by clicking in the Allow Access column of the "Applications that have previously requested access" table. You can set other preferences for individual applications using the Properties window. As you can see I don't have any integrated applications here.

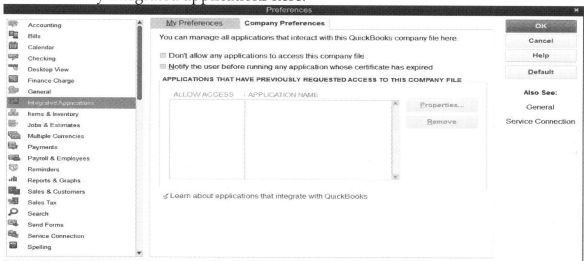

The screen shot below is some of the integrated applications you could use/buy for QuickBooks. There are more to choose from. You don't have to have any of these extra applications, but they are available if you find a need.

Items & Inventory

There are no Preference's under My Preference's under this feature, so we will go over the Company Preferences.

1. Click on Edit at the top Main Menu Bar
2. Select Preferences.
3. Click on Items & Inventory in the column to the left under Integrated Applications.
4. Click on Company Preference's tab. This screen shot is typical for the contracting business that sells parts/inventory with some of their services. We will discuss in further detail later in the book on Items and Inventory.

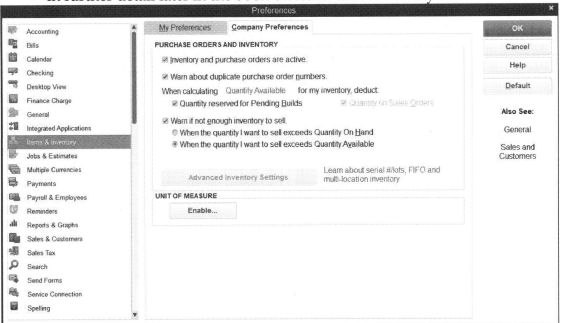

Inventory and purchase orders are active, you would choose this if you plan to use purchase orders to track which materials are on order, when you ordered them and from the vendor you ordered them from along with if you plan to use purchase orders to track costs.

Warn about duplicate purchase order numbers. This feature will warn you if you have a duplicate purchase order. I recommend this to help keep job materials straight.

When calculating Quantity Available for my inventory, deduct either Quantity reserved for Pending Builds or Quantity on Sales Orders. If you are unsure on this one you can come back to it after we go over in detail about Items & Inventory.

Warn if not enough inventory to sell this is another feature I would check because it would let you know you need more on hand and/or you need to build more of the item you are needing and wanting to sell.

Unit of Measure

As you can see from the screen shot on the previous page I do not have the Unit of Measure enabled. It is not too typical for the contracting business, but sometimes it is needed. The screen shot below explains in summary the Unit of Measure with QuickBooks. I will go over in more detail in Items and Inventory chapter.

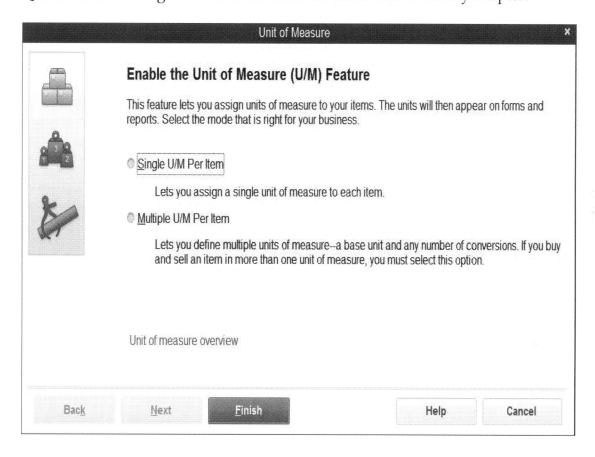

QuickBooks For Contractors

Jobs & Estimates

There are no Preference's under My Preference's under this feature, so we will go over the Company Preferences.

1. Click on Edit at the top Main Menu Bar
2. Select Preferences.
3. Click on Jobs & Estimates in the column to the left under Items & Inventory.
4. Click on Company Preference's tab. This screen shot is typical for the contracting business. We will discuss in further detail later in the book.

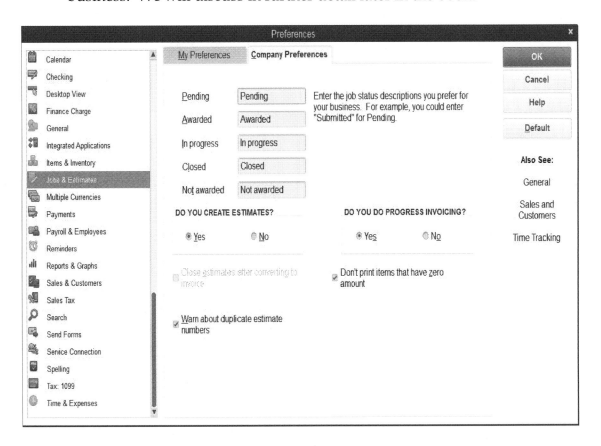

These are typical Company Preference's and can be changed to meet your needs. These settings also depends if you create estimates and are you going to implement progress invoicing. If you make any changes click ok.

Multiple Currencies

There are no Preference's under My Preference's under this feature, so we will go over the Company Preferences.

1. Click on Edit at the top Main Menu Bar
2. Select Preferences.
3. Click on Multiple Currencies in the column to the left under Jobs & Estimates.
4. Click on Company Preference's tab.

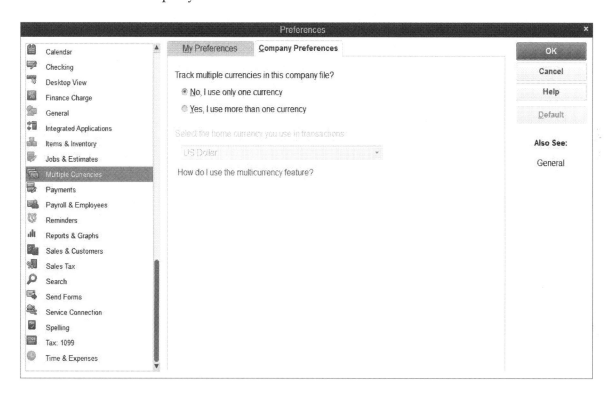

As you can see only one currency is checked, but QuickBooks does have the capabilities to use more than one currency.

Payments

There are no Preference's under My Preference's under this feature, so we will go over the Company Preferences.

1. Click on Edit at the top Main Menu Bar
2. Select Preferences.
3. Click on Payments in the column to the left under Multiple Currencies.
4. Click on Company Preference's tab.

These features are the default features. You can add online payments to pay with credit card or bank transfer from a bank account.

Payroll & Employees

There are no Preference's under My Preference's under this feature, so we will go over the Company Preferences. Payroll & Employees is an extremely important feature and will cover in more detail in the book. The way you set these preferences will determine how QuickBooks will handle payroll costs to job cost reports.

1. Click on Edit at the top Main Menu Bar
2. Select Preferences.
3. Click on Payroll & Employees in the column to the left under Payments.
4. Click on Company Preference's tab.

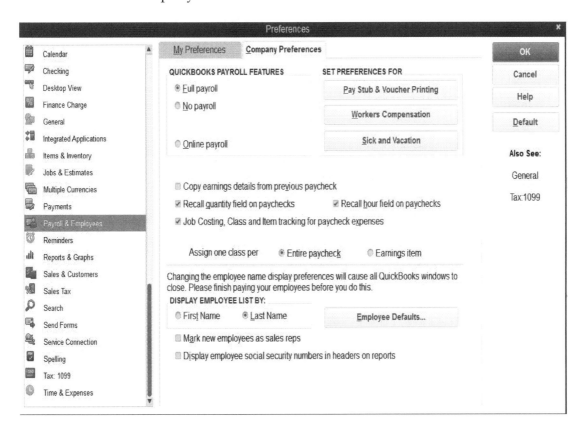

Full Payroll is where you do all your payroll in house, but use QuickBooks service. Choose this feature even if you outsource your payroll. I will discuss this more in the Payroll Chapter.

Recall quantity field on paychecks and recall hour field on paychecks. I recommend this because more often than not you have many employees with the exact same hours and other items the same. This just makes payroll easier and less mistakes made, however you will have those employees that change each pay period as well.

Job costing, Class and Item tracking for paycheck expenses is important to select. By selecting this it will automatically disburse the appropriate items pertaining to payroll to the right job, job phase and class.

Assign one class per paycheck. You will want to select Entire Paycheck since we are using one class, labor, for all the transactions on the timecards. This will save you time when entering timecards and processing payroll.

Employee Defaults

The defaults you see here will appear on the New Employee, Payroll Info Tab window each time you enter a new employee. Click ok to save the template. This is kept simple and can customize each employee.

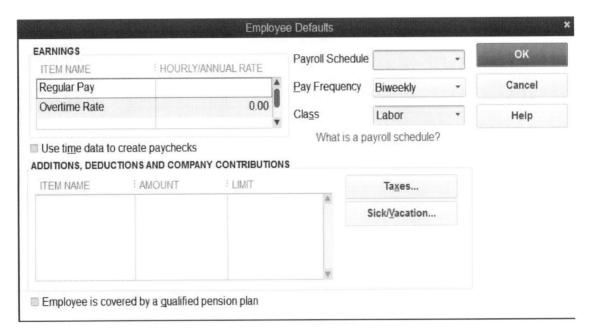

If you want to track Workers Comp be sure to set this up in the Payroll & Employee Preferences.

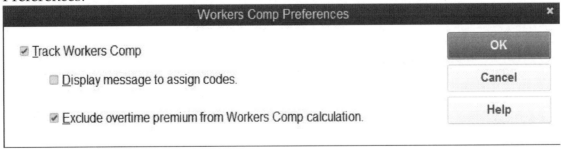

Sick and Vacation

Click on the Sick and Vacation button in the Payroll & Employees defaults to set up.

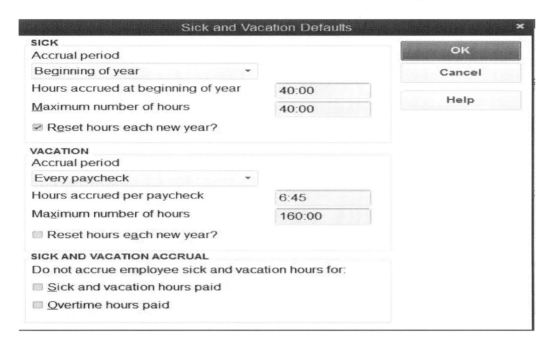

Click on the pay stub and voucher printing the Payroll & Employee's default page. Set to your needs.

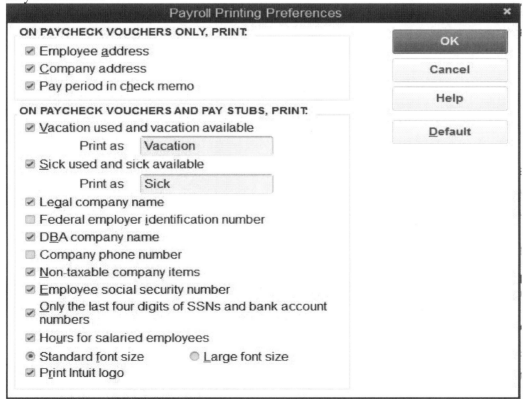

Reminders

QuickBooks gives you a fairly vast set of Reminders to do list, such as print checks, payroll, invoices, deposits or pay bills just to name a few. If you have a schedule in place that you go by you may not want or need this. I checked to be reminded.

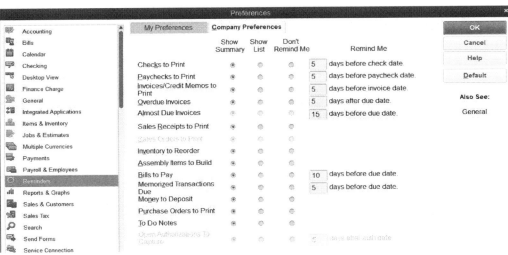

The screen shot above is Company Preferences. As you can see QuickBooks gives you three options for each task. Also, you have the option to set the number of days to be reminded. Set this to your needs.

If you chose to be reminded this screen will pop up when you login to QuickBooks.

Reports & Graphs

The General tab has features to choose under My Preferences and Company Preferences, so we will start with My Preferences.

1. Click on Edit at the top Main Menu Bar
2. Select Preferences.
3. Click on Reports & Graphs in the column to the left under Reminders.
4. My Preferences tab is up first. Set these features for you needs.
5. When you have finished click the Company Preferences tab.

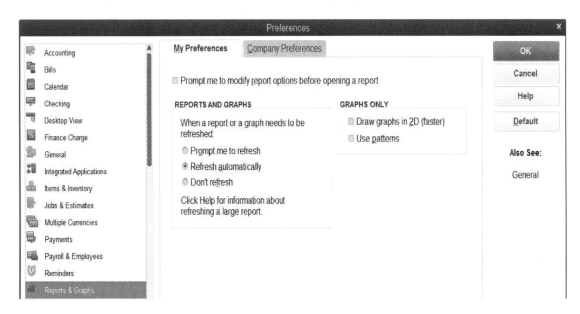

The Company Preferences in the screenshot below are the Default settings. I left them as is because this is what I need and is most typical.

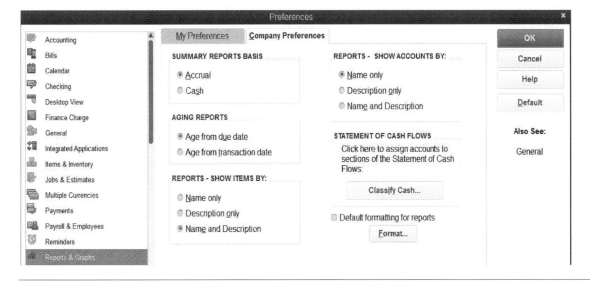

QuickBooks For Contractors

Sales & Customers

The Sales & Customers tab has features to choose under My Preferences and Company Preferences, so we will start with My Preferences.

1. Click on Edit at the top Main Menu Bar
2. Select Preferences.
3. Click on Sales & Customers in the column to the left under Reports & Graphs.
4. My Preferences tab is up first. Set these features for you needs.
5. When you have finished click the Company Preferences tab.

This screenshot is set to Default settings for my Preferences and I left this as is since this setting works for me. Change if you need a different setting.

This is not the default setting. The sales orders option has been unmarked. This is a typical setting for Contractors. If you have a need for sales orders then you would want to check that option. Once you have made changes then click ok.

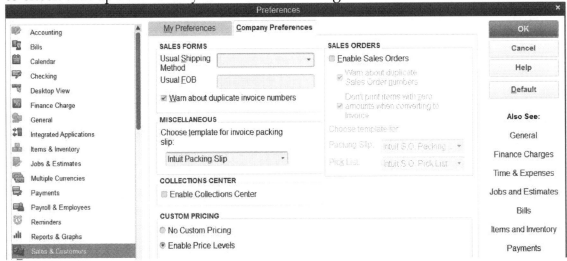

Sales Tax

The Sales Tax Preference does not have any options under My Preference, so click on Company Preferences.

1. Click on Edit at the top Main Menu Bar
2. Select Preferences.
3. Click on Sales Tax in the column to the left under Sales & Customers.

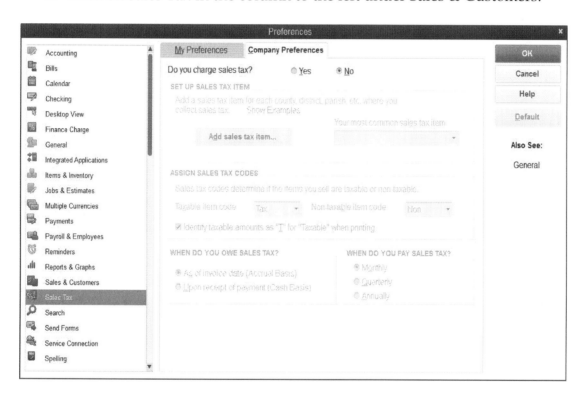

As you can see from the screenshot above this company does not charge sales tax. How you set these settings will depend on the requirements of your state and are pretty easy to follow, so first check out your state requirements.

Search

The Search Preference under My Preferences is shown below. This is the default and I left it as is. The Search Field is automatic in the 2016 version.

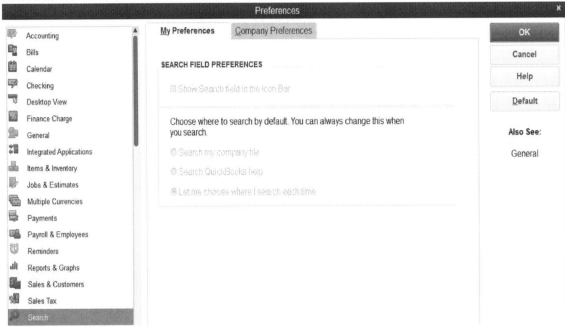

This is QuickBooks default setting and as you can see 60 mins recommended. This too can be changed to your needs.

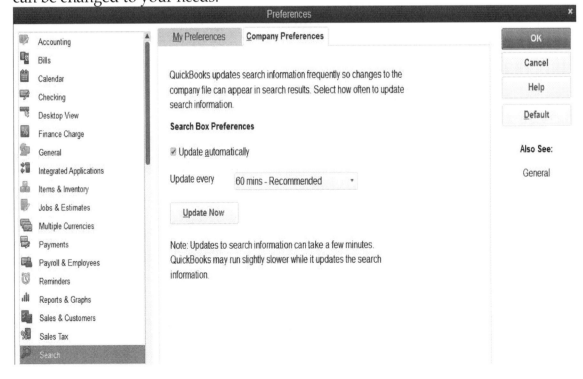

Send Forms

The Send Forms tab has features to choose under My Preferences and Company Preferences, so we will start with My Preferences.

1. Click on Edit at the top Main Menu Bar
2. Select Preferences.
3. Click on Send Forms in the column to the left under Search.
4. My Preferences tab is up first.

I set mine to outlook since that is the email program I use and I like the Auto-check the Email Later checkbox. Set the options to your needs and click on the Company Preferences tab.

If you are going to send forms through email the form will have a basic letter with the email.

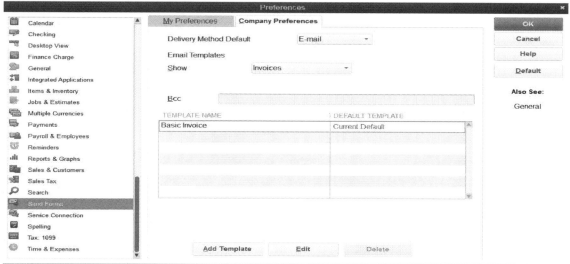

See the screenshot on the next page of the letter attached to this basic invoice.

Edit Email Template

This is the email Template and as you can see this needs to be edited to at least say my company name instead of Twice Right Construction. Other than the name change this may be fine. After making necessary changes click Save to save your changes.

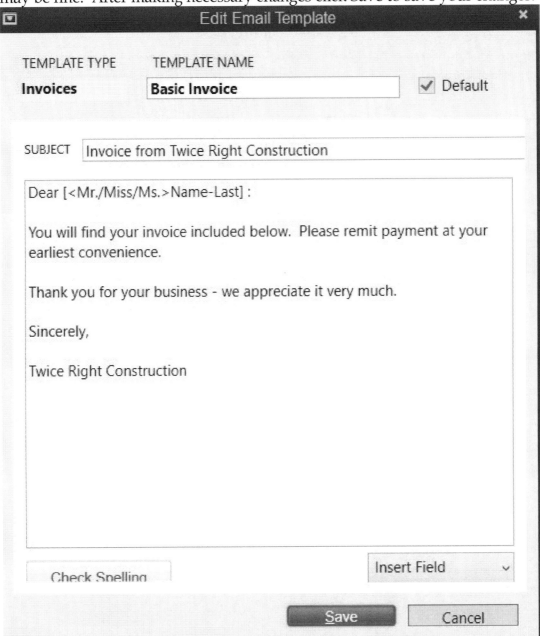

Note: depending on the version you are using you will want to add template to make it your own. Some versions will not allow you to make and save changes.

Service Connection

The Send Forms tab has features to choose under My Preferences and Company Preferences, so we will start with My Preferences.

1. Click on Edit at the top Main Menu Bar
2. Select Preferences.
3. Click on Service Connection in the column to the left under Send Forms.
4. My Preferences tab is up first.

This screenshot is My Preferences default and for now I am leaving at the default settings. After making your choices and click on Company Preferences.

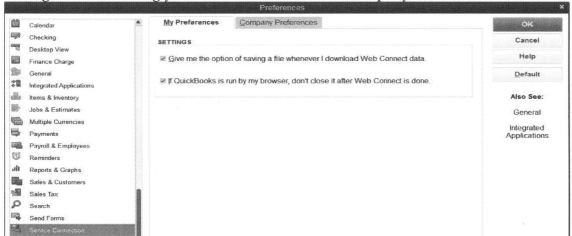

This screenshot of Company Preferences is QuickBooks default setting. I am leaving these settings at the default settings. After making your changes click ok.

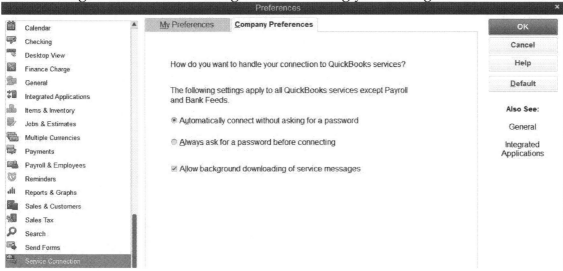

If you are just setting up your QuickBooks you probably not using any services yet and you may not in the future.

Spelling

The Spelling Preference does not have any options under My Preference, so click on Company Preferences.

1. Click on Edit at the top Main Menu Bar
2. Select Preferences.
3. Click on Spelling in the column to the left under Service Connection.

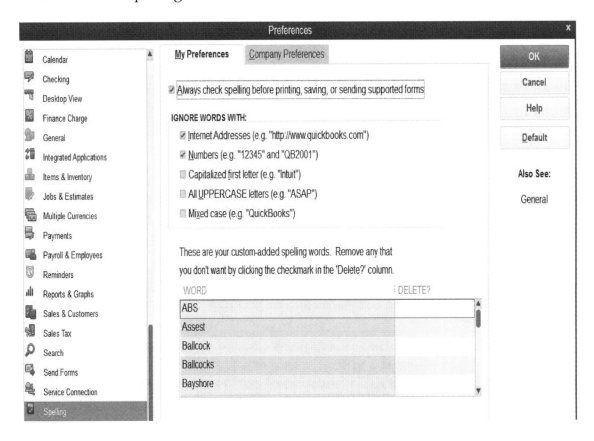

These settings are my settings. The only thing I marked that wasn't marked was the option "Internet Address (e.g. "http://www.quickbooks.com"). Make the changes, if any, for your needs and click ok.

Tax: 1099

1099s are forms that your business files with the IRS for reporting the total amount paid to each of your vendors and/or subcontractors each year. You have to file a 1099 for each vendor or subcontractor who has been paid over $600 of labor during the year. You will want to click yes if you work with subcontractors or vendors that you send 1099 forms to. QuickBooks can be set up to track all 1099 related transactions. At the year-end QuickBooks can print your 1099 forms. You are not required to send 1099 forms to material suppliers/vendors from whom you purchase materials from.

The Tax: 1099 Preference does not have any options under My Preference, so click on Company Preferences.

1. Click on Edit at the top Main Menu Bar
2. Select Preferences.
3. Click on Tax: 1099 in the column to the left under Spelling.

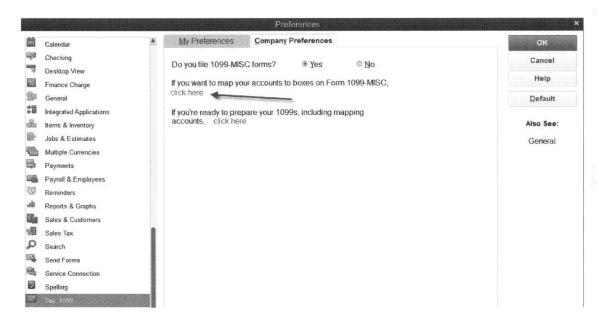

Before completing this section you need to have your Chart of Accounts set up, so if you don't have that done come back to this feature later after finishing your Chart of Accounts.

If you file 1099-Misc forms you need to link the correct accounts with each 1099 category. Most construction businesses report amounts in Box 7: Nonemployee compensation. Check with your CPA on this to be sure you get it setup as they like.

Click where the red arrow is pointing at click here in the screenshot above. See Screenshot on next page.

This is the screen that appears when you clicked on click here. This is where you will link your 1099 accounts to Box 7. As you can see under Tip most companies map the accounts they use to pay 1099 vendors to Box 7: Nonemployee Compensation on Form 1099-MISC.

Each 1099 category must have a unique account, such as if you report Nonemployee Compensation (Box 7) and you have a cost of goods sold named job related costs, you can choose this account for Box 7, but once you do you cannot use it to track any of the other 1099 categories. Be sure to check with your CPA on how he/she wants you to track them.

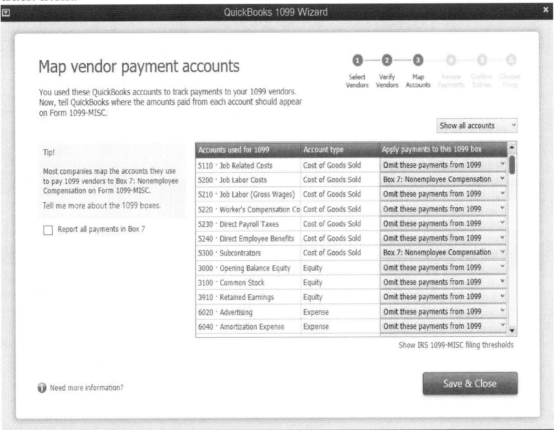

When you set this up and finish click Save & Close.

Time & Expenses

The Time & Expenses Preference does not have any options under My Preference, so click on Company Preferences.

1. Click on Edit at the top Main Menu Bar
2. Select Preferences.
3. Click on Time & Expenses in the column to the left under Tax: 1099.

This screenshot is of QuickBooks default settings. It's really easy to track time on a job using the time tracking feature that is set up right. Let's go over the features.

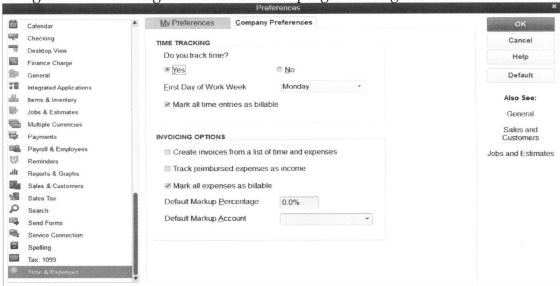

If you are tracking time then you click yes.

First Day of Work Week you would choose the day that is always the first day of your work week or you can go by your printed timecards. Let's say if you start your week on Wednesday and end on Thursday then you would select Wednesday as your first day of work week. If you pay biweekly, the 1st or the 15th then choose the day you've been using on your timecards.

Create Invoices from a list of Time & Expenses. You can invoice customers with unbilled time and expenses directly from a single list. You can use the list to quickly view subtotals of your unbilled time and expenses for each customer, filter the list by date, sort your results, and select which customers to bill. When you select a customer to bill, the outstanding billables are transferred directly to an invoice.

Track reimbursed expenses as income. I recommend not selecting this option because you will bet reports showing customer invoices as income and bills as job costs. If you do choose this, QuickBooks records the income and expense into and out of the same account.

Chapter 4
Chart of Accounts

The Chart of Accounts to a business is like the foundation to a home. If you build your home on a faulty foundation you will most likely always have problems. If your Chart of Accounts is not set up right then you will most likely have issues, so let's do this right to begin with.

QuickBooks does not require you to use account numbers with your chart of accounts, but I highly recommend it. By numbering your Chart of Accounts it helps keep accounts grouped in the right group and easier for your CPA as well. See the standard numbering system below and the summary of each account to follow.

1000-1999	Assets
2000-2999	Liabilities
3000-3999	Capital
4000-4999	Income or Revenue
5000-5999	Job Costs
6000-6999	Overhead Costs
7000-7999	Other Income
8000-8999	Other Expense

Assets

Assets are things your company owns and are divided into two groups. The two groups are current assets and fixed assets.

Current assets are usually in the number range of 1000 to 1499 and they typically would be all your bank accounts, accounts receivable and inventory.

Fixed assets are usually in the number range of 1500 to 1999 and these are items that you would typically have to sell to turn into cash. Vehicles, Equipment and Land/Property are examples of fixed assets.

Liabilities

Liabilities are debts your company owes for. This can be any kind of Bank Loan, Credit Cards, Vehicle, Equipment and Property are the main liabilities/debts. An example would be you go to the bank and get a $50,000 bank loan and the bank deposits it in your account. You would record the $50,000 as a liability not as income such as Construction Revenue or whatever you name your Revenue account.

Capital

Capital all depends on how your business is structured, such as LLC, corporation or Sole Proprietor. I will give a run-down of the different types, but check with your CPA to see what is best for you and your business.

A company ownership of a single member LLC or a sole proprietor will need an Owner's Investment account along with an Owner's drawing account. The investment account is to keep track of the money the owner has invested in the business plus or minus the net profit or loss each year. The Owner's drawing account would be used for money taken out by the owner for personal use. Under this structure keep in mind the owner doesn't get a payroll check like an employee, instead the owner takes draws and pays quarterly estimated taxes and should always be allocated to the Owner's Drawing account.

If a company is a general or limited liability partnership, or a limited liability company filing as a partnership you need to have a Capital and Drawing Accounts for each partner.

If a company is an S-Corporation, C-Corporation or an LLC filing as a Corporation they will have a Common Stock and could have a Preferred Stock account. They are representing the total amount of stock the company has issued.

Income and/or Revenue

Income/Revenue is the money coming in from your business services you do every day such as building a structure brought into your Construction Revenue account. You can have other income from say rent from property you may own and that would go into a separate account called Rent Income under other income accounts in the number range of 7000 to 7999.

Job Costs

Job Costs, also known as, Cost of Goods Sold are the costs of building your product/and or Service. I say service, because you may supply all labor to build r make something for a client and the client provides all materials if any. If you are a builder, whether it be commercial buildings or homes the costs are everything it costs you to build that structure from labor, materials to permits.

Overhead Costs

Overhead Costs are costs that you pay no matter if you have work or no work if you have a business. These costs are things such as telephone, insurance, utilities, or rent just to name a few.

Other Income

Other Income is other sources of income other than your business revenue/income. This could be Rental income, interest income from an investment or maybe a stock sale.

Other Expense

Other Expense is an expense outside your regular business expenses, such as selling an asset and taking a loss or maybe the fees from the stock you sold.

Using a premade/sample chart of accounts

Going through your company setup we chose the General Contractor industry and by doing that a premade chart of accounts was setup. What I recommend is taking that chart of accounts and fine tuning it. Adding, deleting or renaming accounts you need or don't need until you have it solid and correct.

If you want to have that super solid foundation for your Chart of Accounts I recommend you running it by your CPA.

I have enclosed my Contractor Chart of Accounts for you to see and compare on the next two pages.

Remember you can change the type, number, name, description, note, tax-related information, or opening balance for any existing account in the chart of accounts Edit account window.

Take the time to look over your chart of accounts against mine to see if you think you need to make any changes before moving on.

Colorados Best Construction
Account Listing
December 15, 2020

Account	Type
1110 · Company Checking Account	Bank
1111 · Adjustment Register	Bank
1120 · Company Savings Account	Bank
1130 · Payroll Checking Account	Bank
1140 · Petty Cash Account	Bank
1210 · Accounts Receivable	Accounts Receivable
1310 · Employee Advances	Other Current Asset
1320 · Retentions Receivable	Other Current Asset
1330 · Security Deposit	Other Current Asset
1340 · Vendor Deposits	Other Current Asset
1390 · Undeposited Funds	Other Current Asset
1400 · Refundable Workers Comp Deposit	Other Current Asset
1560 · Escrow Deposit	Other Current Asset
1570 · Land Purchase	Other Current Asset
1571 · Land Interest/Closing Costs	Other Current Asset
1580 · WIP - Land Development	Other Current Asset
1590 · WIP - Construction	Other Current Asset
1510 · Automobiles & Trucks	Fixed Asset
1520 · Computer & Office Equipment	Fixed Asset
1530 · Machinery & Equipment	Fixed Asset
1540 · Accumulated Depreciation	Fixed Asset
2010 · Accounts Payable	Accounts Payable
2050 · Mastercard Payable	Credit Card
2060 · Visa Card Payable	Credit Card
2100 · Payroll Liabilities	Other Current Liability
2200 · Customer Deposits	Other Current Liability
2240 · Worker's Comp Payable	Other Current Liability
2300 · Loans Payable	Other Current Liability
2310 · Loan - Dale Olsen	Other Current Liability
2400 · Land Aquisition Loan	Other Current Liability
2405 · Land Development Loan	Other Current Liability
2410 · Construction Loan	Long Term Liability
2460 · Truck Loan	Long Term Liability
3000 · Opening Balance Equity	Equity
3100 · Common Stock	Equity
3910 · Retained Earnings	Equity
4110 · Construction Income	Income
4810 · Vendor Refunds	Income
4910 · Workers' Comp Dividend	Income
5110 · Job Related Costs	Cost of Goods Sold
5200 · Job Labor Costs	Cost of Goods Sold
5210 · Job Labor (Gross Wages)	Cost of Goods Sold
5220 · Worker's Compensation Costs	Cost of Goods Sold
5230 · Direct Payroll Taxes	Cost of Goods Sold
5240 · Direct Employee Benefits	Cost of Goods Sold
5300 · Subcontrators	Cost of Goods Sold
6020 · Advertising	Expense
6040 · Amortization Expense	Expense
6050 · Bad Debt	Expense
6060 · Bank Service Charges	Expense
6070 · Bid Deposit	Expense
6075 · Bond Expense	Expense
6090 · Business License & Fees	Expense
6100 · Car/Truck Expense	Expense
6101 · Gas & Oil	Expense
6103 · Repairs & Maintenance	Expense
6105 · Registration & License	Expense
6107 · Insurance-Auto	Expense
6130 · Cleaning/Janitorial	Expense
6135 · Computer Supplies/Equipment	Expense
6140 · Contributions	Expense
6150 · Depreciation Expense	Expense
6160 · Dues and Subscriptions	Expense
6180 · Insurance	Expense
6181 · Disability Insurance	Expense
6182 · Liability Insurance	Expense
6185 · Worker's Comp	Expense
6200 · Interest Expense	Expense

Colorados Best Construction
Account Listing
December 15, 2020

Account	Type
6201 · Finance Charge	Expense
6202 · Loan Interest	Expense
6203 · Credit Card Interest	Expense
6230 · Licenses and Permits	Expense
6240 · Miscellaneous	Expense
6490 · Office Supplies	Expense
6500 · Payroll Expenses (office)	Expense
6501 · Payroll (office staff)	Expense
6502 · Payroll tax expense	Expense
6503 · Officer's Labor	Expense
6504 · Designer's Wages	Expense
6508 · Vac/Holiday/Sick Pay	Expense
6509 · Employee Bonus	Expense
6510 · Employee Benefits	Expense
6570 · Professional Fees	Expense
6571 · Accounting	Expense
6572 · Legal Fees	Expense
6573 · Computer Consultants	Expense
6610 · Postage and Delivery	Expense
6650 · Rent	Expense
6670 · Repairs	Expense
6671 · Building Repairs	Expense
6672 · Computer Repairs	Expense
6673 · Equipment Repairs	Expense
6800 · Telephone	Expense
6820 · Taxes	Expense
6830 · Training and Conferences	Expense
6900 · Meals and Entertainment	Expense
6910 · Travel	Expense
6920 · Tools & Machinery (under $500)	Expense
6970 · Utilities	Expense
7010 · Interest Income	Other Income
7030 · Other Income	Other Income
7800 · Trade Discount	Other Income
8010 · Other Expenses	Other Expense
2 · Purchase Orders	Non-Posting
4 · Estimates	Non-Posting

New, Add, Change, Edit and Print Chart of Accounts

Adding a New Account

1. Go to Menu Bar at the top of the screen, click on lists then click on Chart of Accounts
2. Click on the Account button at the bottom left of the screen and choose New.
3. Choose the Account type that you are wanting to set up and click continue.
4. Enter account information and when done click save and close.

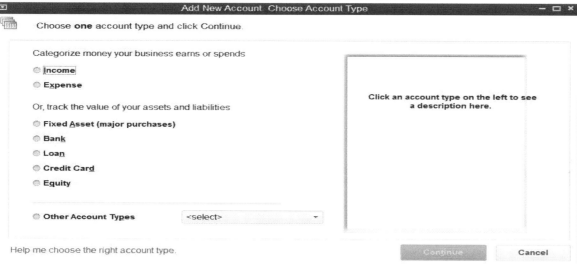

Adding a New Sub-Account

1. Go to Menu Bar at the top of the screen, click on lists then click on Chart of Accounts
2. Click on the Account button at the bottom left of the screen and choose New.
3. Choose the Account type that you are wanting to set up and click continue.
4. Enter account information and when done click save and close.

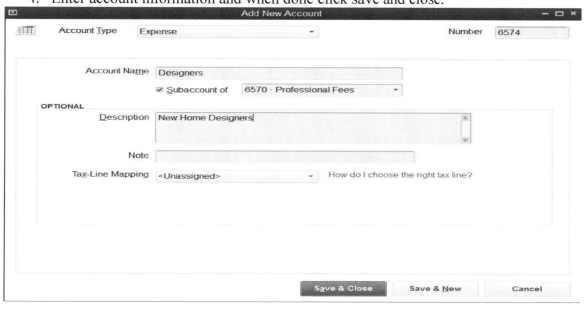

Editing an Account

1. Go to Menu Bar at the top of the screen, click on lists then click on Chart of Accounts.
2. Click once on the account you want to edit to highlight the account.
3. Click on the Account button at the bottom left of the screen and choose Edit Account.
4. The account you had highlighted to edit opens up. Edit the information then click save and close.

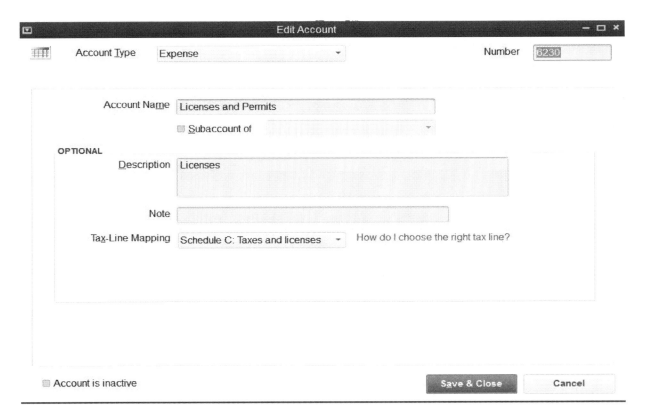

Delete or Inactivate an Account

1. Go to Menu Bar at the top of the screen, click on lists then click on Chart of Accounts.
2. Click once on the account you want to delete or inactivate to highlight the account.
3. Click on the Account button at the bottom left of the screen and click on Delete Account or Make Account Inactive.
4. Click OK to confirm any deleted account. If you chose to make account Inactive it will just disappear from your list, but it's just inactive and can be made active again anytime.

Print Chart of Accounts listing

1. Have your chart of accounts open
2. Go to the bottom of the screen click on Reports button
3. Select Account Listing
4. Select Print at the top of the report. You can adjust this report, I will go over customizing reports in the Reports Chapter.

Chapter 5
Loan Manager, Mileage, & Asset Tracking

Loan Manager

Before setting up the Loan Manager payments, but sure to have your loan documents at hand. Next we need to set up three chart of accounts.

1. Click on Lists at the Top of the Main Menu Bar
2. Select Chart of Accounts
3. Click the Account Button at the bottom of the Screen on the Chart of Accounts window.
4. Select New, Click Fixed Asset and Click Continue
5. Enter Name of County Line Road Land, Enter the opening balance and date
6. Click Save and New
7. Change the Account Type to Long Term Liability
8. Enter the name Land Payment & enter the opening balance and date, Click Save & New.
9. Change Account Type to Expense
10. Enter Name as Land Interest. Click save and Close

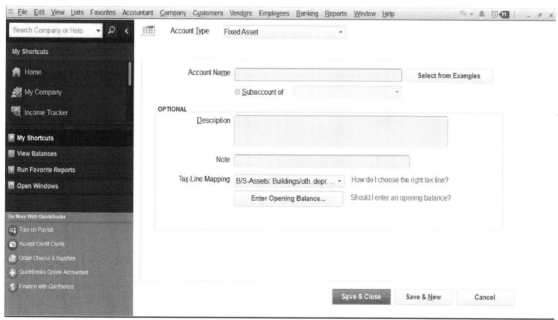

Ok we have now set up the three accounts to make your new Loan payment. Each loan payment will be different, depending on what the loan is for. The example I am setting up is for Land Acquisition to build a new office building on. The loan is just for the land right now. Remember when you set the chart of account up for this loan you entered the loan amount in the beginning balance, so in the loan manager you won't have to enter that nor will you have to set up a journal enter by entering the beginning balances.

QuickBooks For Contractors

Adding Loan to Loan Manager

1. Adding a Loan to the Loan Manager, click Banking, choose Loan Manager from the top Menu Bar.
2. Click the Add a Loan button.
3. Enter the loan information on each screen and click next until the wizard is completed.
4. Click the Finish button when done.
5. See each screenshot for more explanation.

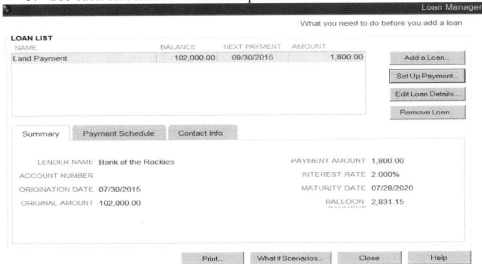

As you can see I entered, amount, lender, date and term of loan. Click Next

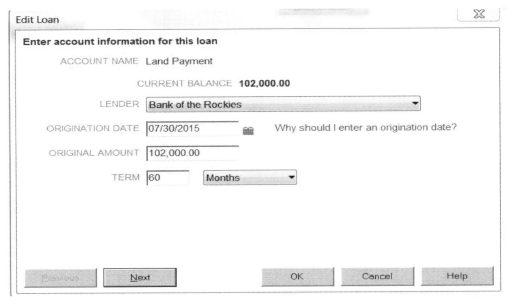

Here it has the next payment due date, payment amount with principal and interest. Click next.

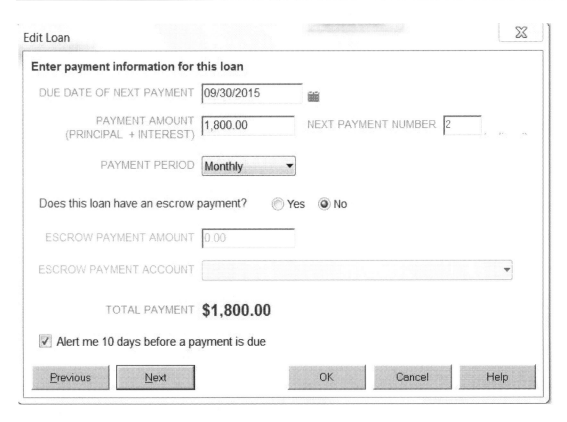

This screen has the interest rate, payment account, Interest Expense Account, Fees Acct. Click ok.

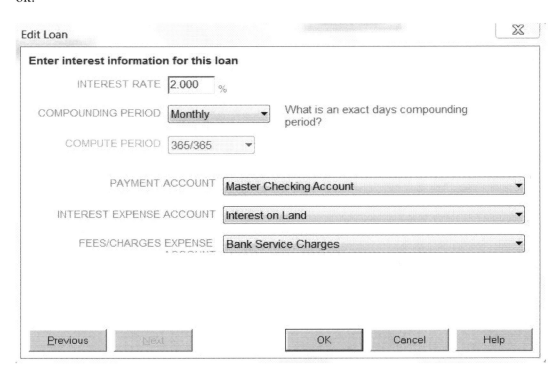

This screen shows you the payment schedule that includes principal and interest and a running balance as it gets paid down. You can print this as well.

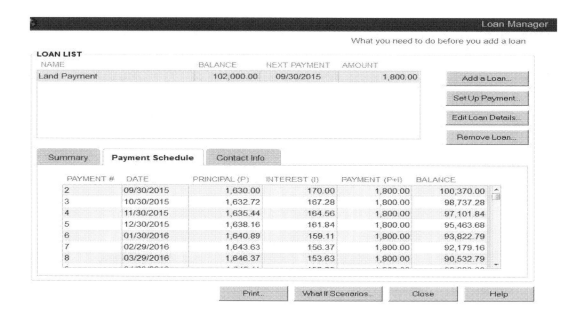

Editing a Loan in Loan Manager
1. Click Banking, choose Loan Manager from the top Menu Bar.
2. Click the loan name in the Loan List.
3. Click the Edit Loan Details button to return to the wizard to edit the loan or click the Remove Loan Button and Yes to remove if wanting to delete loan.

Setting up Payment

Click on Set up Payment in the Loan Manger screen. Make sure the loan you are setting up for a payment is highlighted. Click ok.

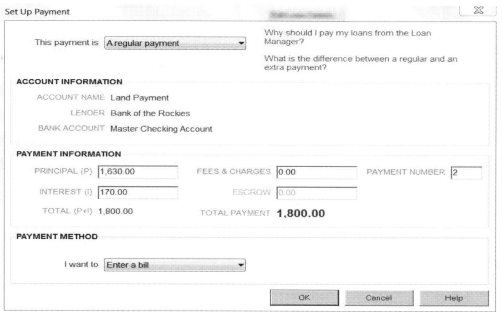

By setting up the payment this will enter the loan payment principal and loan interest into the correct accounts. You can enter a bill or you can choose to write a check.

Fixed Asset List

Fixed Asset Item List lets you keep track of all assets over $500. Only use this list for Assets over $500. Use this for not only property, vehicles, equipment, large tools, but for office equipment such as computers etc. The fixed asset list does not keep track of depreciation, but has great convenience to keep and locate your assets.

1. Click on Lists at the top Main Menu Bar
2. Select Fixed Asset Item List
3. Click on Item at the bottom of the Fixed Asset open screen
4. Click New and add the equipment shown in the screenshot below.

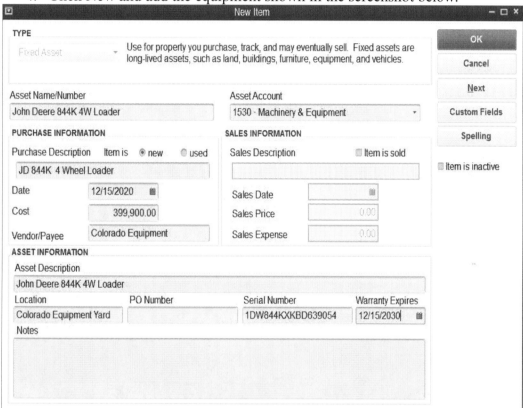

After adding the piece of equipment this is a list of assets on the Fixed Asset Item List.

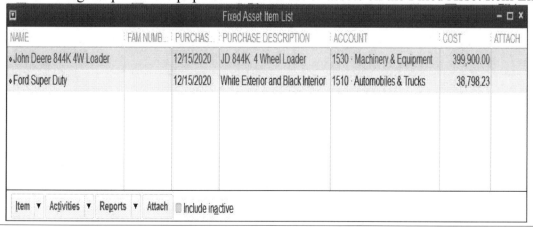

Cash Flow Projector

This report is to help you forecast how much cash you will have by projecting your cash in and cash out basically. To create this report do the following:

1. Click Company at the top Main Menu Bar
2. Click Planning & Budget
3. Select Cash Flow Projector and click Next
4. Place check marks on your accounts that you want in report and click next until you come to the button that says Finish Projection and click that button.

Colorado's Best Construction
Weekly Cash Flow Projection
September 24 through November 07, 2015

	Current Week	9/27/15	10/4/15	10/11/15	10/18/15	10/25/15	11/1/15
Cash:							
Beginning Cash		362,750	362,750	367,506	372,262	377,018	381,774	386,530
Cash Receipts	0	4,756	4,756	4,756	4,756	4,756	4,756
Adjustments	0	0	0	0	0	0	0
Total Cash	362,750	367,506	372,262	377,018	381,774	386,530	391,286
Business Expenses:							
None	0	0	0	0	0	0	0
Adjustments	0	0	0	0	0	0	0
Total Business Expenses	0	0	0	0	0	0	0
Cash Available for Disbursement	362,750	367,506	372,262	377,018	381,774	386,530	391,286
Accounts Payable:							
None	0	0	0	0	0	0	0
Adjustments	0	0	0	0	0	0	0
Total Accounts Payable	0	0	0	0	0	0	0
Ending Cash Balance	362,750	367,506	372,262	377,018	381,774	386,530	391,286

Enter Vehicle Mileage

To keep track of your vehicle mileage do the following:

1. Click Company at the top of the Main Menu Bar
2. Click Enter Vehicle Mileage
3. Enter Vehicle, add if not entered yet.
4. Enter dates
5. Enter Odometer start and End
6. Enter Cutomer Job if its for a job.
7. Enter Class
8. Enter Notes if needed.

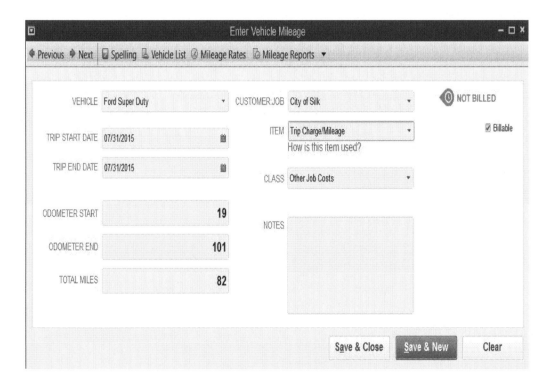

Chapter 6
Lists
Items, Prices, Class, Billing & Other

Items are another important part of the foundation of your business. The Items are what you do as a business basically. The items are your products and services that you offer customers. When a job is complete the items will show up for services and products on an invoice or receipt that you would give to your customer. We will go over the different items in this chapter along with other lists such as price list and class list.

List and Summary of all Items

Service

Service items are the work/labor you performed for a project/job that your company was hired for. To track payments and expenses the right way, be sure to create different service items for subcontracted work vs. work performed by an owner/partner or employee.

When you use service items for subcontractors, QuickBooks records expenses and income for the work in separate accounts. You can use these items on purchase forms and sales forms as well. Keep in mind if you send 1099-MISC forms to subcontractors, assign the cost of the service item to an expense account that tracks payments to 1099 vendors.

Inventory Part

An inventory part a line item you can use when you're filling out a sales form or purchase form. You use inventory items to track merchandise/products your business purchases, keeps in stock as inventory, and then resells. For every inventory item, QuickBooks tracks the current number in stock and the average value of your inventory after every purchase and sale.

Inventory Assembly

An inventory assembly item is line items you can use when you use the sales or purchase form. An assembly item allows you to combine inventory part items and other assembly items, such as (subassemblies) into a single item on a Bill of Materials, which lists the assembly item's parts. You can also include the costs with building the assembly item by including non-inventory part items, service items, and "other charge" items to the Bill of Materials.

Creating and adding assembly items to inventory is a two-step process. First you create the Bill of Materials that specifies what goes into making the assembly item, and then you build a certain quantity of the assembly item so QuickBooks can deduct the component parts from inventory and add new quantities of the assembled item. So as soon as you build an assembly item, its parts are no longer in stock as inventory because they are part of a new inventory assembly item.

Non-Inventory Part

A non-inventory part is a line item you can use when you are filling out a sales form or purchase order forms. Use non-inventory part items to track merchandise that you will purchase and do not resell or you sell but do not purchase. Also, you purchase and resell but do not stock or track in inventory. More or less you order as needed for a sale.

Other Charge

Other Charge items are items such as shipping and handling charges that you need to add to a customer's invoice. Other Charge items can be used for handling bounced checks. You can use this item type for many things like late fees, opening balance, reimbursable expenses, retainers, surcharges, gift certificates, and prepayments.

Subtotal

You can use this item on sales forms, a subtotal item totals the amounts of the items above it, up to the last subtotal.

Group

You would want to use Group if you often enter the same group of items when you record a sale or purchase. Instead of entering each item individually when you fill out a form, you enter the name of the group item, so this makes faster, easier and can help reduce mistakes.

Group items enable you to track the items that you sell in greater detail. If you track a lot of detail about your items but want to give your customers simple invoices, then you would want to use group items. Group items also give you a way to enter a great amount of line item detail fast.

Note: If you create a group item, you will not be able to change it to another type. If you need to change the only way to do this is to delete item and create a new item using the new type you want.

QuickBooks For Contractors

Discount

A discount item is used to apply a discount that's either a percentage or fixed amount to the line above the discount item on a sales form. Don't use a discount item for early payment. QuickBooks can calculate these discounts when you receive payments from customers.

Payment

Payment item subtracts the amount of a payment from the total amount of an invoice or statement. You need a payment item when you receive a partial payment toward the amount of an invoice or statement at or before the time you create the invoice or statement. If you receive full payment at the time of the sale, use a sales receipt form instead of an invoice with a payment item to make it easier. You can always use an invoice then apply the payment, but a sales receipt takes care of both at once.

Entering a New Service Item

1. Click on Lists at the top main Menu Bar.
2. Click Item Lists
3. Click on Item at the bottom of the open Items Screen
4. Select New.

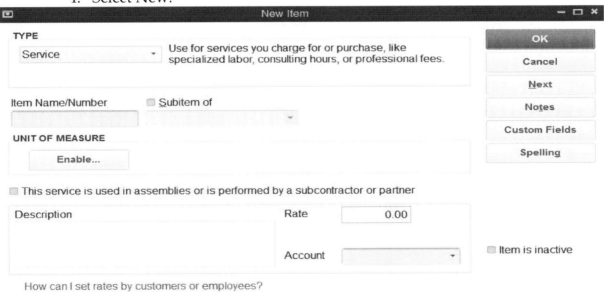

As you can see on this screenshot Type - Service is for services you charge for or purchase, like specialized labor, consulting hours, or professional fees. See Screenshot below for added service. Be sure to check this service is used in assemblies or is performed by a subcontractor or partner. This is an important box to check and choosing the correct expense and income account helps make it easier for accounting to be more accurate. This helps track estimated costs and actual costs for this item as well.

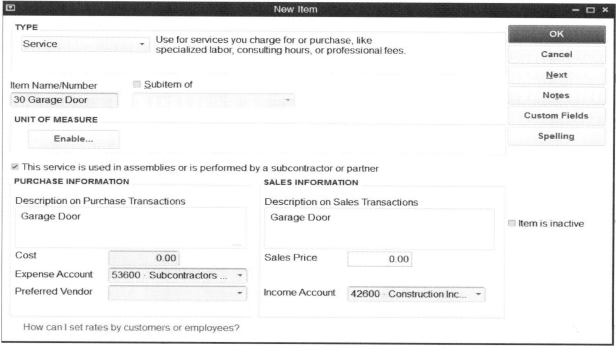

Subitem

1. Click on Lists at the top main Menu Bar.
2. Click Item Lists
3. Click on Item at the bottom of the open Items Screen
4. Select New.
5. Choose Service and click Subitem of box.
6. Click on drop down arrow to choose the item you want to add the subitem to and enter as the screenshot shows if doing sample company or enter the way for your company.

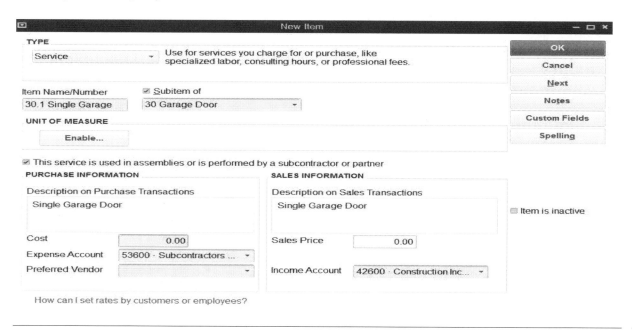

This is the second subitem for the service item of garage doors. See new items in item listing on next page. Click ok to close the new item.

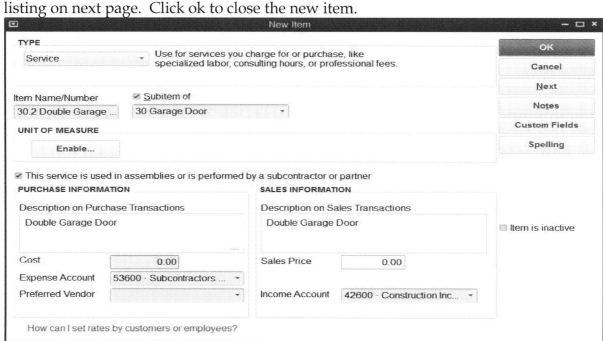

Results of new item and subitems. See items below with the red arrow.

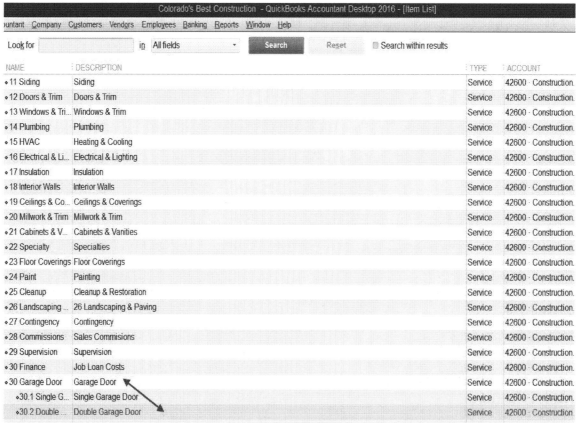

Entering Inventory Items

1. Click on Lists at the top main Menu Bar.
2. Click Item Lists
3. Click on Item at the bottom of the open Items Screen
4. Select New and click Inventory Part. This is before entering new item.

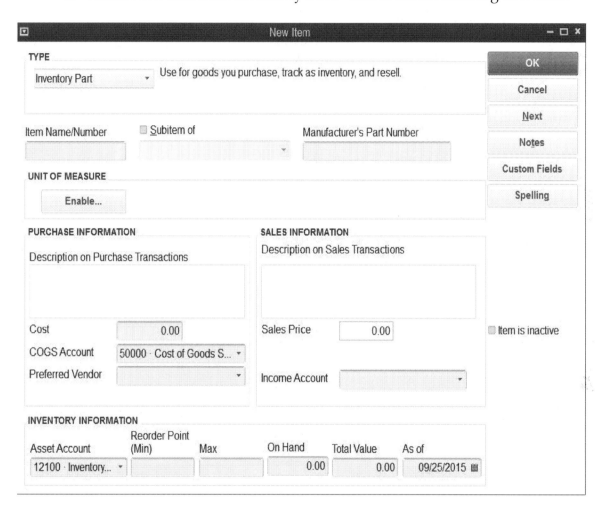

New Inventory Item entered

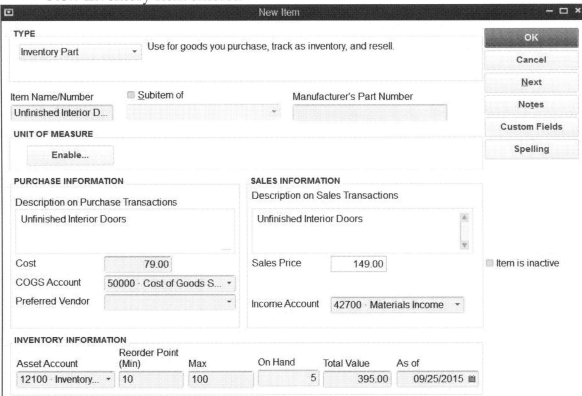

Steps to entering New Inventory Item
1. Type - enter Inventory Part
2. Item Name/Number - Enter a name, number or both.
3. Enter Manufacturer's Part Number is needed.
4. Description - Type in What the Inventory Part is
5. Cost - enter what the product cost you.
6. COGS Account - enter the correct cost of goods account.
7. Preferred Vendor - enter the vendor you usually purchase this part from or you can leave blank.
8. Description of sales will prefill and will be on your invoices. You can change it.
9. Sales price is the amount you charge the customer.
10. The Income Account - choose the right account and if you don't have the right account then create a new correct account.

Note: You can enter a unit of measure and we will go over that next and add a new item that needs unit of measure. Unite of measure is not available in QuickBooks Pro or QuickBooks Premier Retail Edition.

See Unit of Measure information with new item added on the next page.

Unit of Measure

You can turn unit of measure on and off in preferences or enable it to turn it on with Inventory Item screen open by clicking on Unit of Measure Enable button.

With unit of measure turned on, you can show what quantities, prices, rates, and costs are based on. For example, if you provide a customer with consulting and you enter 4 on an invoice as the quantity for your Consulting service item, the unit of measure can show whether that quantity means four hours, four days, or four weeks. Or, if you enter a quantity of 25 on an invoice for the Ball Point Pen item, the unit of measure can show whether that quantity means 25 individual pens, 25 boxes of 12, or 25 cases containing 120 pens each.

QuickBooks provides two different ways or modes for assigning units of measure to items. You can choose to assign only one unit of measure to each item (Single U/M Per Item mode) or more than one unit of measure to each item (Multiple U/M Per Item mode).

In Single mode you can assign different units of measure to different items, but each item can have only one unit of measure assigned to it. You should choose Single mode only if you buy, stock, and sell each item by the same unit of measure. For example, choose this mode if you buy an item by the foot, keep track of it in inventory by the foot, and sell it by the foot.

You should choose Multiple mode if you buy, stock, or sell items in different units. For example, choose this mode if you buy an inventory item by the gallon and sell it by the ounce, or if you sell consulting services by both the hour and the day.

If you choose Multiple mode, you'll need to define unit of measure sets that you can assign to items. A unit of measure set consists of a base unit (usually the smallest unit used to track a certain type of item) and any number of related units (defined as containing a certain number of base units). For example, you could create a unit of measure set called "Length by the inch" with a base unit of inch and related units of foot (containing 12 inches) and yard (containing 36 inches).

You can change or convert the unit of measure when you enter an item on a transaction form, such as an invoice or purchase order. For example, suppose you have an item called Cable that you've assigned a unit of measure set that contains the inch, foot, and yard units of measure. If you enter Cable on an invoice with a quantity of 30 feet, you could then **change** the unit of measure to yards (causing 30 feet to become 30 yards) or **convert** the unit of measure to yards (causing 30 feet to become 10 yards).

QuickBooks For Contractors

As you can see I went with Multiple U/M Per Item because of more options. Click Next.

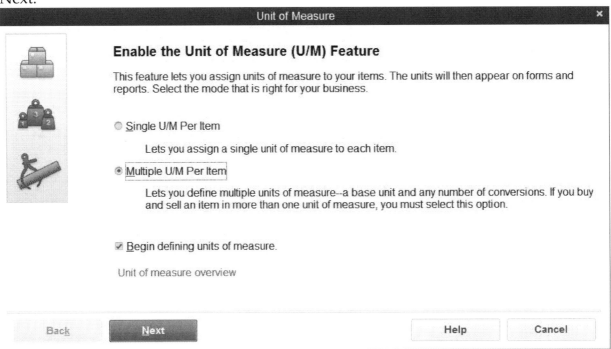

I chose count as my selection. You can only choose one unit of measure. Click next.

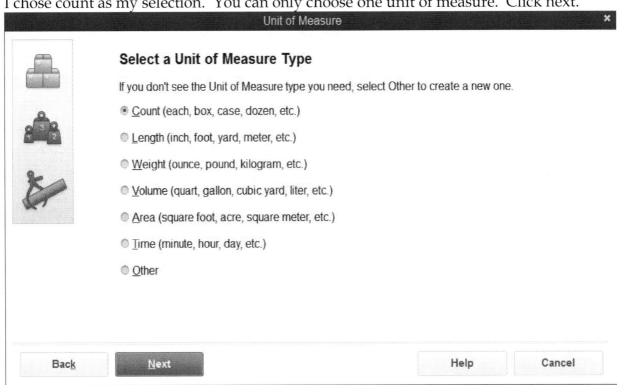

I chose each as my base Unit of Measure. You can only choose one here. Click next.

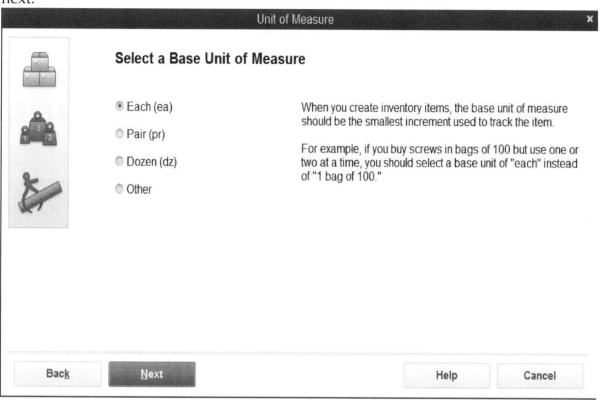

You can add Related Units as shown below. Click Next once you are done.

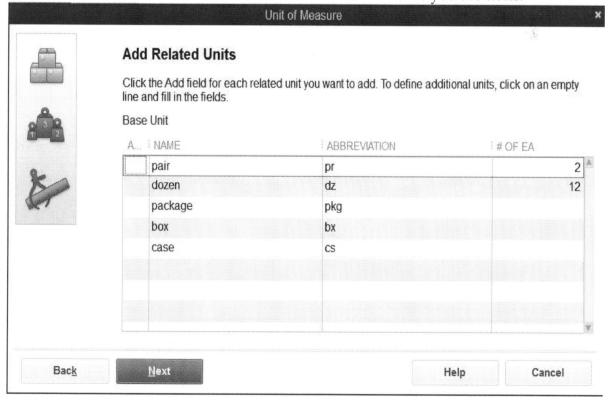

This is the next screen and each was automatically filled in. As you can see if shipping selected it overrides the unit of measure on sales orders when printing pick lists. I left as is. Click next.

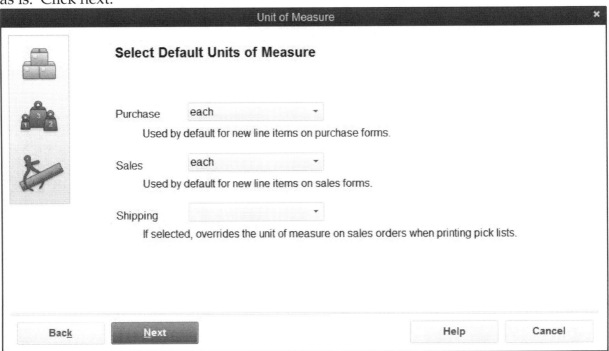

Last screen is to give your new Unit of Measure Set a Name. This is the name it came up with and I am leaving it as is. This is just a sample exercise, but know you can change the name. Click Finish.

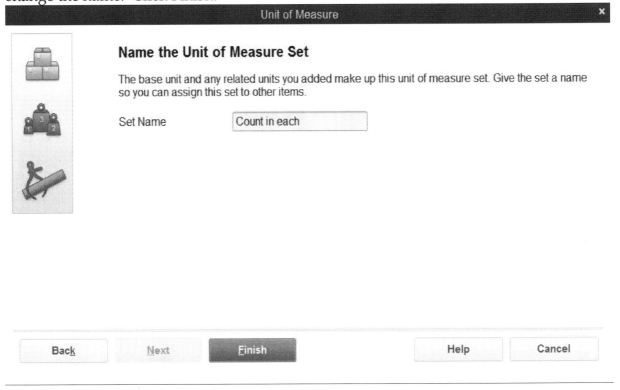

New Inventory Part with Unit of Measure Default Screen.

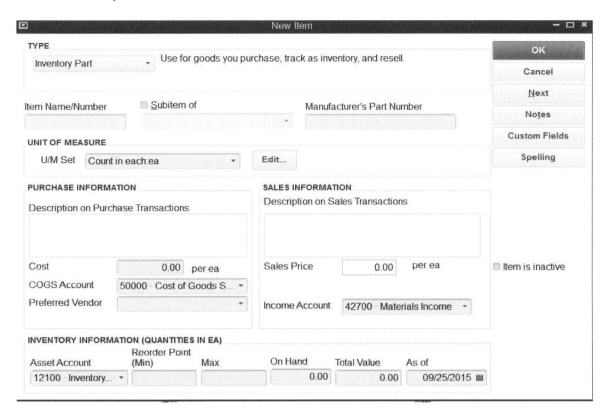

New Inventory Item with Unit of Measure, entered as subitem to new doors. See below.

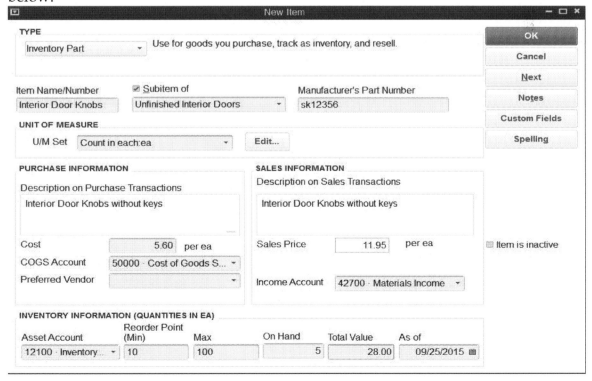

Inventory Assembly Item

To enter a new Inventory Assembly Item do the following:

1. Click on Lists at the top main Menu Bar.
2. Click Item Lists
3. Click on Item at the bottom of the open Items Screen
4. Select New and click Inventory Assembly. See new item entered below.
5. Click Ok when finished entering information.

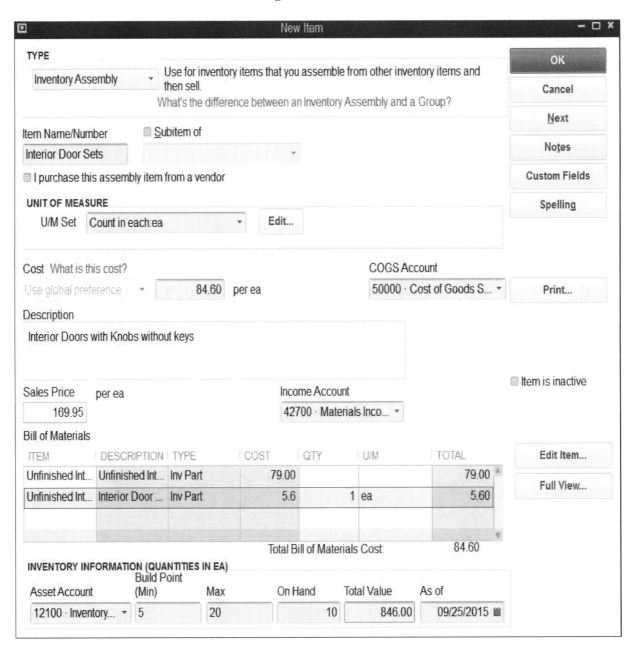

Invoice created with new Assembly Item.

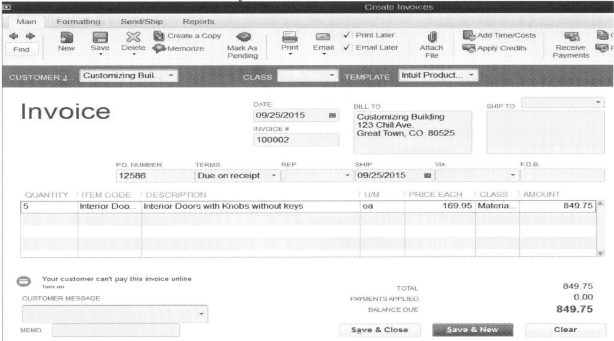

New Non-Inventory Item

Notice it for this type it says to use for goods you buy but don't track, like office supplies, or materials for a specific job that you charge back to the customer. This is being charged back to the customer. When charging back to the customer make sure the box is checked that says "this item is used in assemblies or is purchased for a specific customer job".

1. Click on Lists at the top main Menu Bar.
2. Click Item Lists
3. Click on Item at the bottom of the open Items Screen
4. Select New and click Non-Inventory Part. See new item entered below.
5. Click Ok when finished entering information.

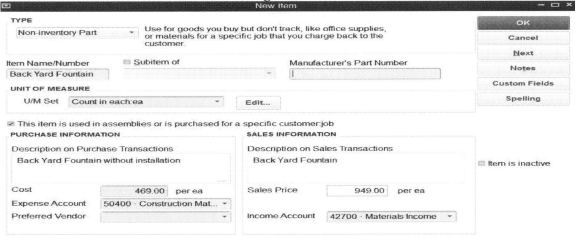

Other Charge

1. Click on Lists at the top main Menu Bar.
2. Click Item Lists
3. Click on Item at the bottom of the open Items Screen
4. Select New and click Other Charge. See new item entered below.
5. Click Ok when finished entering information.
6. The other shipping charge was set up, see below.

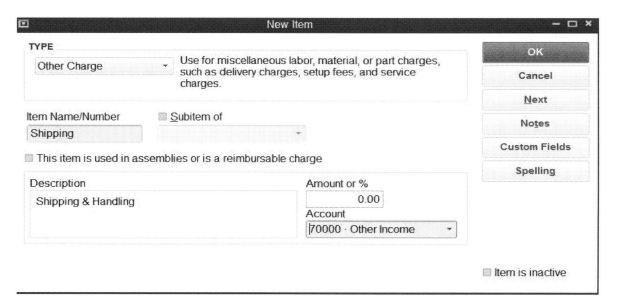

Subtotal

1. Click on Lists at the top main Menu Bar.
2. Click Item Lists
3. Click on Item at the bottom of the open Items Screen
4. Select New and click Subtotal. See new item entered below.
5. Click Ok when finished entering information.

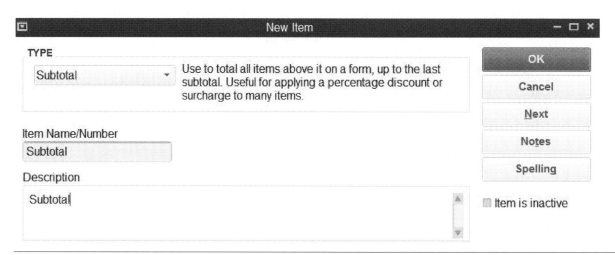

Group

1. Click on Lists at the top main Menu Bar.
2. Click Item Lists and Click on Item at the bottom of the screen.
3. Select New and click Group. See new item entered below and click ok when done.

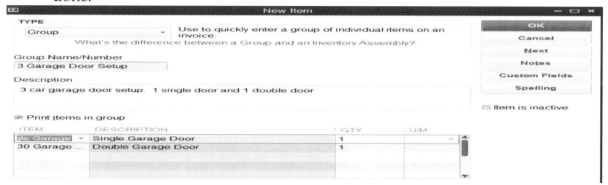

Discount

1. Click on Lists at the top main Menu Bar.
2. Click Item Lists & Click Item button on bottom of screen.
3. Select New and click Discount. See new item entered below & Click ok when done.

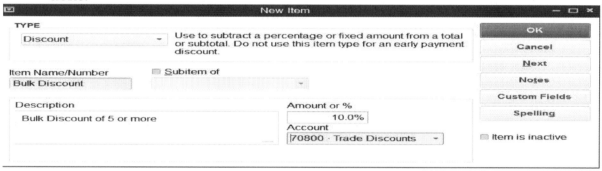

Payment

1. Click on Lists at the top main Menu Bar.
2. Click Item Lists & Click Item button on bottom of screen.
3. Select New and click Discount. See new item entered below & Click ok when done.

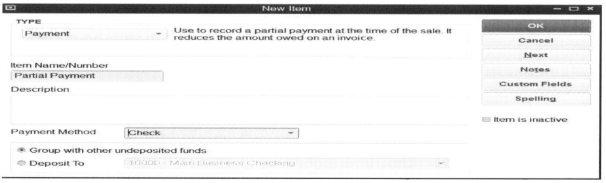

QuickBooks For Contractors

Price Level Lists

Price levels let you set custom pricing for different customers or jobs. Once you create a price level and associate it with one or more customers or jobs, each time you create an invoice, estimate, sales receipt, sales order or credit memo for those customers or jobs, QuickBooks automatically pulls up the correct custom price for a customer or job. You create price levels, then use them on sales forms to adjust the price of an item. You can also manually adjust the prices while creating a sales form.

Note: Price levels associated with customers are automatically used for billable time and reimbursable mileage items. They are not automatically used for reimbursable items and expenses from purchase transactions or invoices created from estimates.

Enter Price Level for a Customer

1. Click on Lists at the top main Menu Bar.
2. Click Price level lists and Click New.

Screenshot after implementing a New Price Level.

After Setting new Price level I entered the special price with Customer/Customizing Buildings.

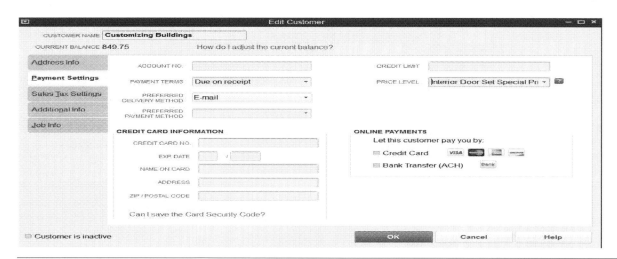

104

Notice new invoice with price level implemented. Without price level the price each would be 169.95 and it's 152.95 now.

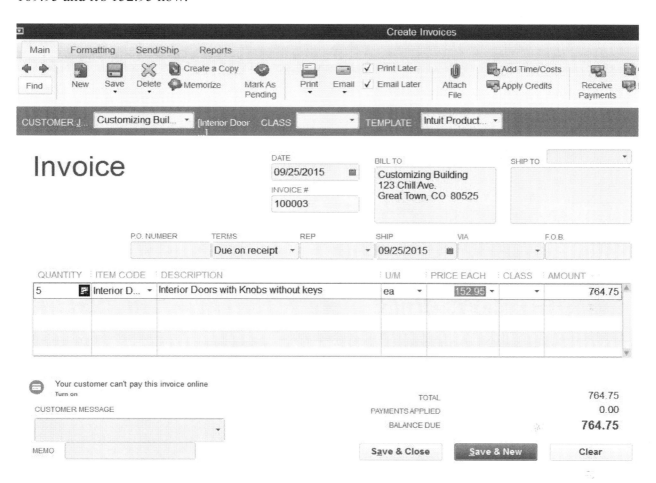

Here's the screen listing of the Price Level's setup. Right now just the one price level is set up. I hope you can see this is a nice feature.

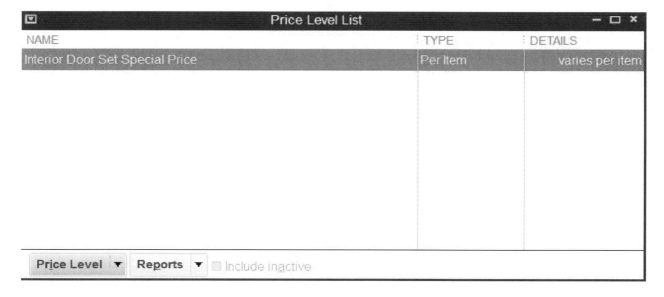

Class List

You can create classes that you assign to transactions. This allows you to track account balances by department, business office or location, or separate properties you own. By using the class tracking feature, you can track their associated account balances on invoices, bills, and other documents. For example, if you had a restaurant with three locations, you might create a North, a South, and a East class for tracking account balances by location. A farmer might create a class for each enterprise such as Corn, Hogs, and Soybeans.

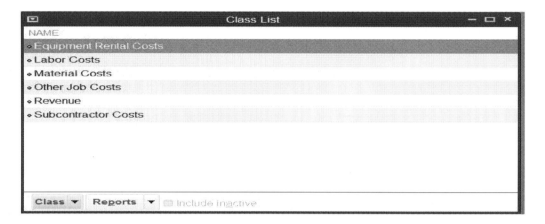

We are going to add two new classes. One is for Commercial Buildings and the other is for Single Family Homes.

1. Click Lists at the top of the main Menu Bar
2. Click Class List and Click Class at the bottom of the screen.
3. Click New and enter Commercial Buildings and Click Next.

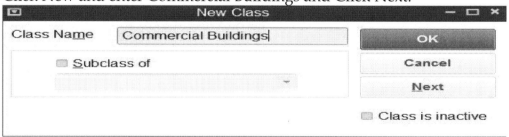

Type in Single Family Homes and Click ok.

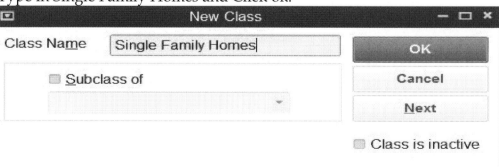

New Billing Rate Level

The Billing Rate Level list stores all the billing rate levels you create. Billing rate levels let you set custom service item rates. The name and type of each billing rate level, either fixed hourly rate or custom hourly rate per service item and you can have up to 100 billing rate levels. Also, you can add, edit, delete, rename, or duplicate billing rate levels.

1. Click on Lists at the top of the main Menu Bar.
2. Click Billing Rate Level List
3. Click Billing Rate Level at the bottom of the screen and Select New. Click ok.

Billing Rate Level List with new Special Rate.

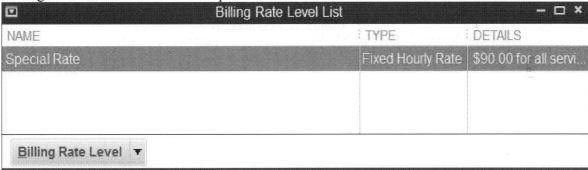

I added the special billing rate to an employee, see in screenshot below. Now when this employee is billed out he will be billed out at special rate.

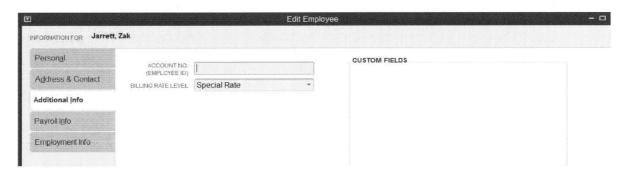

Customer & Vendor Profile Lists

Sales Rep List - Your business may need to track the income that is associated with people who have a relationship with your business. These people may or may not be employees. For example, you might track income from a partner or a 1099 vendor who is an independent contractor.

QuickBooks has a Sales Rep List that allows you to specify employees, vendors, or "other names" as sales reps. each sales rep is assigned initials. The names and initials appear on the Rep drop-down list on sales forms, allowing you to associate specific sales reps with specific sales so you can track their income.

To access Sales Rep List do the following:

1. Click Lists at the top of the Main Menu Bar
2. Select Customers & Vendor Profile Lists
3. Choose Sales Rep List
4. Click Sales Rep Button at the bottom of the screen & Choose New.
5. Add New Sales Rep information and click ok unless you have more than one then click next.
6. To edit, delete or make inactive follow this same steps and choose the option you need.

New Sales Rep input screen

Sales Rep List

Customer Type List - This list shows the customer types you've set up. In QuickBooks, you use customer types to categorize customers and jobs in ways that are meaningful to your business.

Once you've assigned a customer type to each customer, you can create reports that provide useful information about the customers you serve. For example, if you've categorized your customers by market segment, you can create a separate sales report for each segment.

To access Customer Type List do the following:

1. Click Lists at the top of the Main Menu Bar
2. Select Customers & Vendor Profile Lists
3. Choose Customer Type List
4. Click Customer Type button at the bottom of the screen & Choose New.
5. Add New Customer Type information and click ok unless you have more than one then click next.
6. To edit, delete or make inactive follow this same steps and choose the option you need.

New Customer Type Input Screen

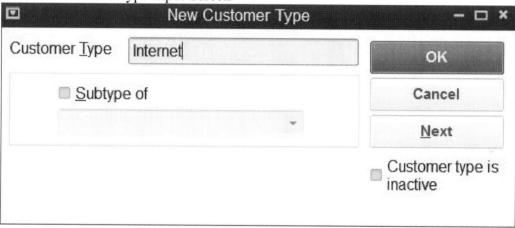

Customer Type List

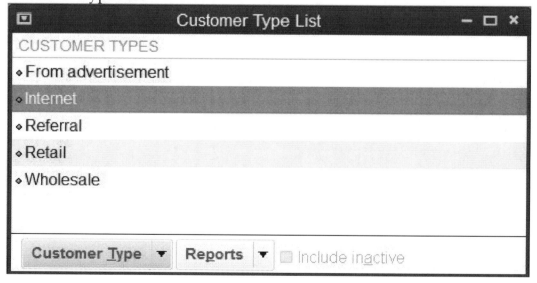

Vendor Type List - Use vendor types to categorize your vendors in ways that are meaningful to your business. For example, you could set up your vendor types so that they indicate a vendor's industry or geographic location. You can also place a vendor type as a subtype of another vendor type. For example, you might create the type Painters with the subtypes Exterior and Interior.

You can create reports and do special mailings that are based on your vendor types. For example, if you own a construction company and use subcontractors, you might want to use the ones closest to each job. You could then create a QuickBooks report that shows the subcontractors in each geographic area.

To access Vendor Type List do the following:

1. Click Lists at the top of the Main Menu Bar
2. Select Customers & Vendor Profile Lists
3. Choose Vendor Type List
4. Click Vendor Type button at the bottom of the screen & Choose New.
5. Add New Vendor Type information and click ok unless you have more than one then click next.
6. To edit, delete or make inactive follow this same steps and choose the option you need.
   New Vendor Type input screen

Vendor Type List

Job Type List - This list holds the job types you've set up for grouping and categorizing your jobs on reports. You can add new job types to this list whenever you need them.

The Job Type list is automatically available to you when you set up a job (in the New/Edit Job window) or enter job information about a customer (on the Job Info tab in the New/Edit Customer window). To add a job type, click the Job Info tab in the New/Edit Customer window and fill in the Job Type field.

To access Job Type List do the following:

1. Click Lists at the top of the Main Menu Bar
2. Select Customers & Vendor Profile Lists
3. Choose Job Type List
4. Click Job Type button at the bottom of the screen & Choose New.
5. Add New Job Type information and click ok unless you have more than one then click next.
6. To edit, delete or make inactive follow this same steps and choose the option you need.

New Job Type Input Screen

Job Type List

Terms List - A shorthand way of expressing when you expect to receive payment from a customer, or when a vendor expects to receive payment from you. Terms show the number of days (or date) by which payment is due and can include a discount for early payment.

Example: 1% 10 Net 30 This means: payment due in 30 days, 1% discount if paid within 10 days.

To access Terms List do the following:

1. Click Lists at the top of the Main Menu Bar
2. Select Customers & Vendor Profile Lists
3. Choose Terms List
4. Click Terms button at the bottom of the screen & Choose New.
5. Add New Terms information and click ok unless you have more than one then click next.
6. To edit, delete or make inactive follow this same steps and choose the option you need.

New Terms Input Screen

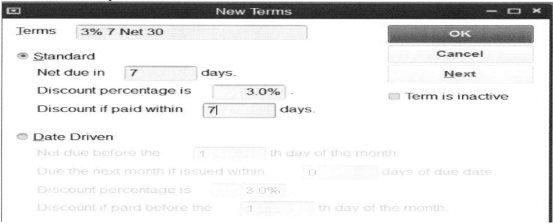

Terms List Screen

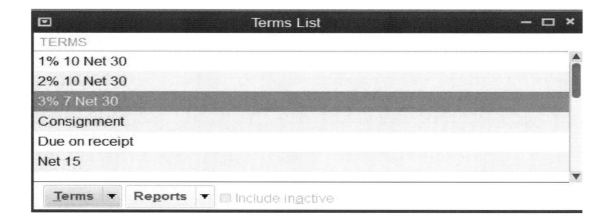

Customer Message List - The Customer Message list contains standard messages that you can include at the bottom of a printed sales form. For example, you might want to thank your customers for their business. Using the Customer Message list, you can create the "thank you" message once and include it on any invoice.

To access Customer Message List do the following:

1. Click Lists at the top of the Main Menu Bar
2. Select Customers & Vendor Profile Lists
3. Choose Customer Message List
4. Click Customer Message button at the bottom of the screen & Choose New.
5. Add New Message information and click ok unless you have more than one then click next.
6. To edit, delete or make inactive follow this same steps and choose the option you need.

New Customer Message Input Screen

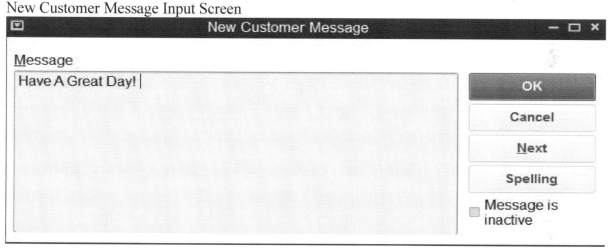

Customer Message List

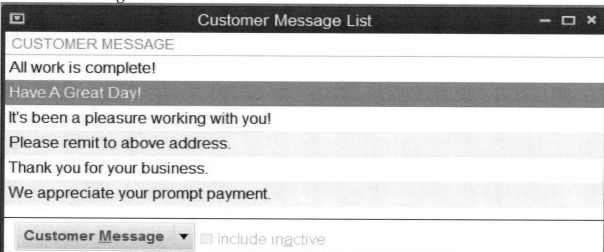

Payment Method List - Use this list to hold information about the different ways you receive payments from your customers (cash, check, Master Card, Visa, American Express, and so on). You can select a payment method from this list when you enter a customer payment. This lets you sort your deposits by payment method and create reports based on payment method.

If you don't separate deposits by payment method, you probably don't need to use payment methods.

To access Payment Method List do the following:

1. Click Lists at the top of the Main Menu Bar
2. Select Customers & Vendor Profile Lists
3. Choose Payment Method List
4. Click Payment Method button at the bottom of the screen & Choose New.
5. Add New Payment Method information and click ok unless you have more than one then click next.
6. To edit, delete or make inactive follow this same steps and choose the option you need.
   New Payment Method Input Screen

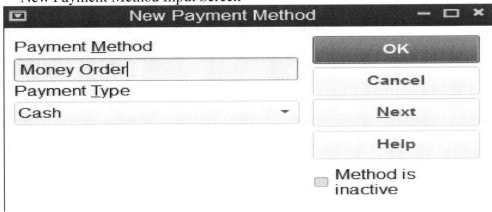

Payment Method List

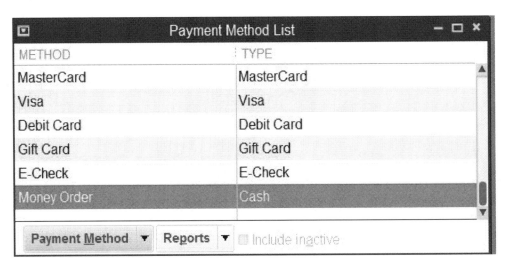

Ship Via List - Use this list to store the different shipping methods you use to send products to your customers. You can select a shipping method from this list when you write an invoice or a sales receipt.

Click the Shipping Method drop-down arrow to add, edit, or delete shipping methods. You can make a shipping method inactive, print the list, and more.

To access Ship Via List do the following:

1. Click Lists at the top of the Main Menu Bar
2. Select Customers & Vendor Profile Lists
3. Choose Ship Via List
4. Click Shipping Method button at the bottom of the screen & Choose New.
5. Add New Shipping Method information and click ok unless you have more than one then click next.
6. To edit, delete or make inactive follow this same steps and choose the option you need.

Add New Shipping Method Input Screen

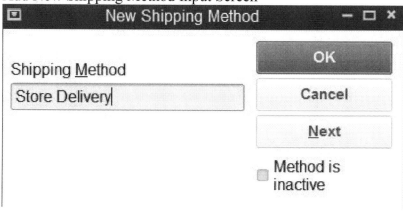

Ship Via List

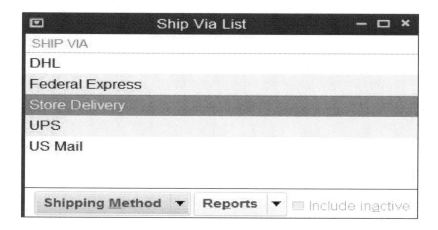

QuickBooks For Contractors

Vehicle List - The Vehicle list stores the names and descriptions of your business vehicles. To track mileage for a vehicle, the vehicle must be entered on this list. You also may want to track your business vehicles in the fixed asset tracker.

To access Vehicle List do the following:

1. Click Lists at the top of the Main Menu Bar
2. Select Customers & Vendor Profile Lists
3. Choose Vehicle List
4. Click Vehicle button at the bottom of the screen & Choose New.
5. Add New Vehicle information and click ok unless you have more than one then click next.
6. To edit, delete or make inactive follow this same steps and choose the option you need.

Add New Vehicle Input Screen

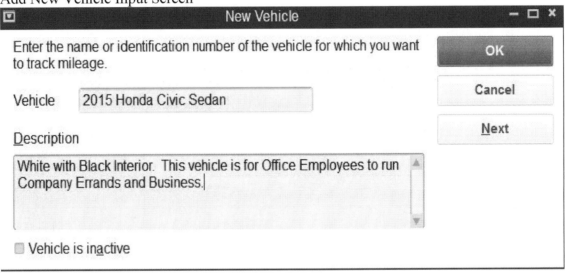

Vehicle Listing Page

Sales Tax Code List - QuickBooks uses sales tax codes to track the taxable or non-taxable status of both the items you sell (products and services) and your customers. If your tax agency requires you to report the reasons why particular sales are taxable or non-taxable (and many do), the sales tax codes that you assign to your items and customers allow you to run reports that provide this information for your sales tax return.

When you turn on sales tax, QuickBooks creates 2 sales tax codes for you. Use the taxable code (TAX) for items and customers that are taxed. Use the non-taxable code (NON) for items and customers that are not taxed, such as non-profit organizations or items that the customer plans to resell. Non-taxable sales tax codes are also used for some out-of-state sales.

For many businesses, these 2 preset sales tax codes are the only ones needed. You can add additional sales tax codes to accommodate other reasons for charging (or not charging) sales tax on your transactions. You then assign the appropriate sales tax code to each of the products and services you sell, and to each of your customers. A customer's sales tax code always overrides an item's sales tax code. For example, if you are selling a taxable item to a non-profit customer, the item would not be taxed.

To access Sales Tax Code List do the following:

1. Click Lists at the top of the Main Menu Bar
2. Select Sales Tax Code List
3. Click Sales Tax Code button at the bottom of the screen & Choose New.
4. Add New Sales Tax Code information if needed and click ok unless you have more than one then click next.
5. To edit, delete or make inactive follow this same steps and choose the option you need.
   Add New Sales Tax Code Input Screen

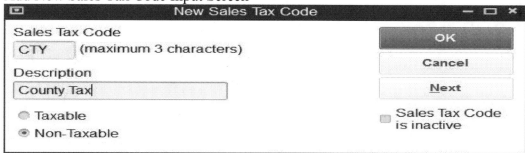

Sales Tax Code List

QuickBooks For Contractors

Other Names List - The Other Names list is for persons or companies that are neither customers, vendors, nor employees. For example, this list could include owners or partners. You can move a name from this list to the Vendor, Employees, or Customers & Jobs lists. You can also select names from the Other Names list when you write checks or enter credit card charges.

To access Other Names List do the following:

1. Click Lists at the top of the Main Menu Bar
2. Select Other Names List
3. Click Other Names button at the bottom of the screen & Choose New.
4. Add New Name information if needed and click ok unless you have more than one then click next.
   Add New Name Input Screen

Other Names List

Memorized Transaction List - This list contains the transactions you have memorized and the memorized transaction groups you have created. Individual transactions appear in normal font. The names of groups appear in bold. Transactions within a group appear indented immediately below the group name.

Click the Memorized Transaction drop-down arrow to delete a memorized transaction or edit its schedule. You can create a memorized transaction group, print the list, and more. To enter a transaction that you memorized, select the transaction in the list and then click Enter Transaction at the bottom of the window.

To memorize a check/payment have the check open and click the memorize button, see red arrow below.

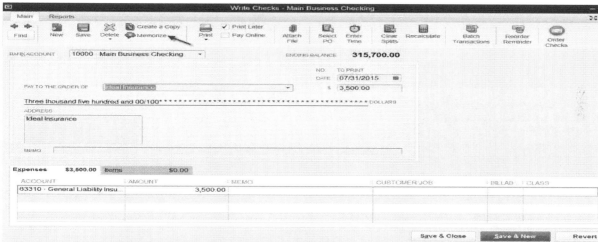

This Screen pops up next, I entered Monthly and make sure the date is correct and click ok.

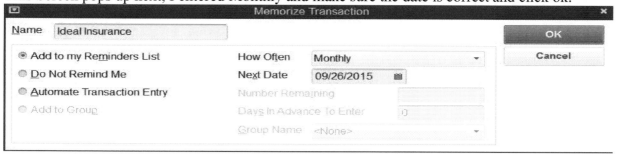

Here is the Memorized Transaction List and the Transaction that we just memorized. Click x to exit screen.

Chapter 7
Customers

I said the Chart of Accounts is your foundation and your Items are another layer of your foundation. Customers are the life of your business because without them you have no business. We will go over setting up customers and adding a job/project to that customer along with of course creating invoices along with the other important aspects of customers.

To access Customers do the following:

1. Click Customers at the top main Menu Bar
2. Select Customer Center
3. The screenshot below is the Customer Center Ribbon.
4. Click on New Customer & Job drop down arrow
5. Select New Customer

Here is the first screen of adding a new Customer. We will go down each tab and fill out the appropriate information. We will go over the Job Info, but the best way is to set the customer up then add a job unless you are pretty sure this is the only job from them. Say for example they hire you to build a home and that's it. If they hire you to build an addition or remodel chances are they will be back, providing you do a great job for them.

Address Info

When ready click on Payment settings tab just below the Address Info tab.

Payment Settings

On the payment settings tab there are a multitude of ways to send and receive payments. I chose invoice to be emailed and this customer pays by credit card. You cannot store the security code by law.

Note: the box below that says "Online Payment" you have to turn on in preferences and you have to have an account with QuickBooks to process this. Of course there are other ways to collect payments online like through you website or you can always take a credit card payment over the phone just to name a couple.

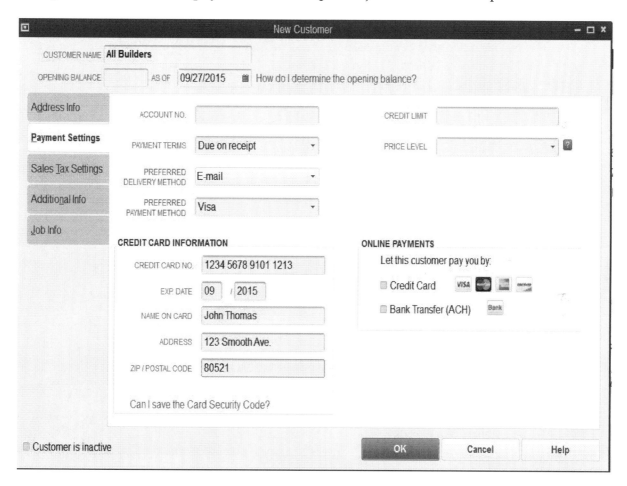

As you can see I left the account number blank, the credit limit and price level blank. As you know you fill in and use what works for you. When you are done with the payment settings screen click on the sales tax settings tab just below the payment settings tab.

Sales Tax Settings

Sales tax Settings is a simple setting as you can see in the screenshot below. You either charge the client tax or you don't depending on your state rules. For this customer I selected not tax code because this customer builds homes and supplies his own materials. This customer hired this company out as a labor Subcontractor. You may have a customer that sometimes you tax them and sometimes you don't depending on the job/project you were hired to do for them.

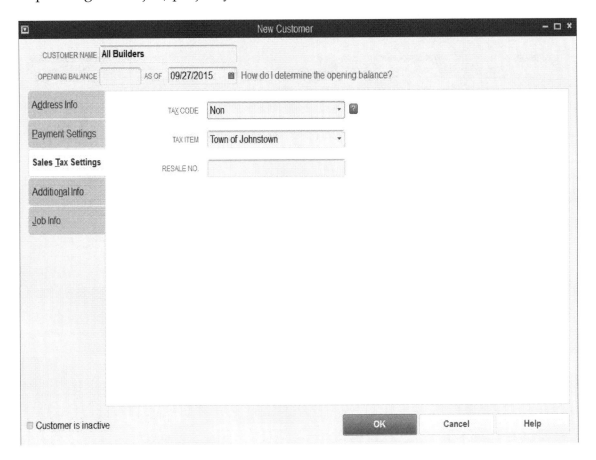

As you can see the area to type in a tax resale no. You would need to collect that resale number if they have one. If you don't have the Sales Tax feature turned on in Preferences you will need to turn that on and set up the basic account. If you are sure you won't use sales tax then skip this tab setup.

When finished click on Addition Info tab just below Sales Tax Settings tab.

Additional Info

The Additional Info tab is for additional info such as the customer type and the Rep that is in charge of this job/project for this customer. As you can see you can set up custom fields for not only customers but for vendors and employees. I just setup some custom fields for customers for this chapter and exercise. You can customize the fields for what works best for you and you don't have to use this feature either.

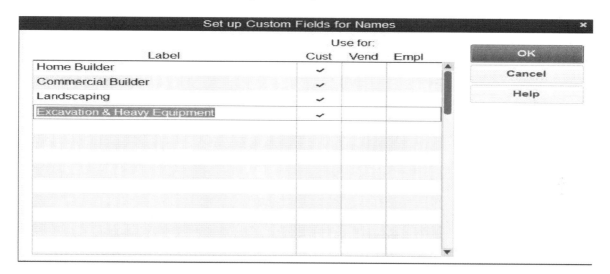

See the customized fields below. This customer is a builder that builds only homes and hires our company and others to build somethings to do the landscaping and any possible excavation work. In this fields you can type whatever info you want that fits.

When finished click on the Job Info tab next that is just below the Additional Info tab.

Job Info

I mentioned at the beginning of this chapter its better to set your customer up and skip this screen then go back and add a job. This reason for this is hopefully this customer is a repeat customer and all the jobs will be located below the customer attached to his account. If you are sure this is a onetime job then fill the job info tab in.

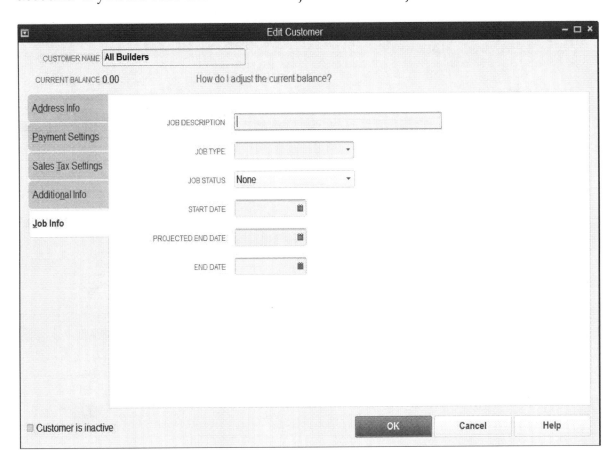

Click ok to finish setting up this Customer. On the next page we will go in and set up a couple of jobs for this customer.

Add Jobs to Customer

We are going to add jobs to the new Customer, All Builders now. To do this do the following steps:

1. Click on New Customer & Job from the drop down menu
2. Select Add Job, make sure the customer is highlighted before adding the job. This is the Add Job screen below for All Builders. I gave this job a name. Click on payment settings. You will need to add the payment settings to each job since the customer may have different ways to pay different jobs.

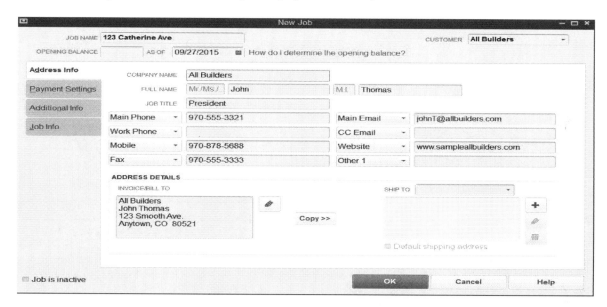

Since we already went over the Payment settings screen/entry we will go to the next tab, additional info tab. This is still set the same, so unless you need to change it click on the Job Info tab. See the screenshot below. Fill in all the information necessary except the end date and you will fill that in when you are completely done. Click ok.

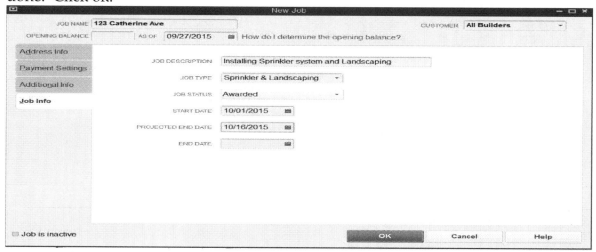

New Job and Customer. See how the new job for this customer is displayed on the screen and it's a subtitle located right under the customer.

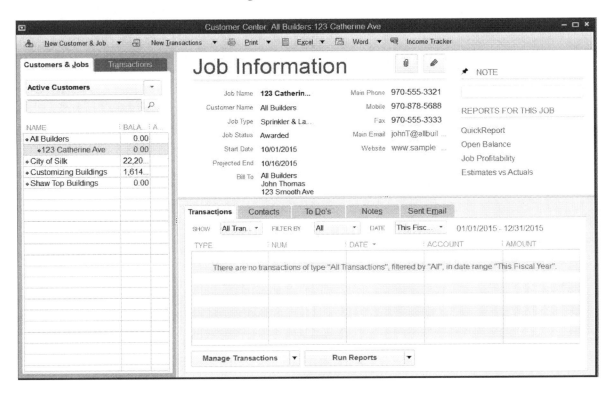

See the screenshot below now has two jobs under the new customer. We will now create an estimate that you can bill off of when the job is done.

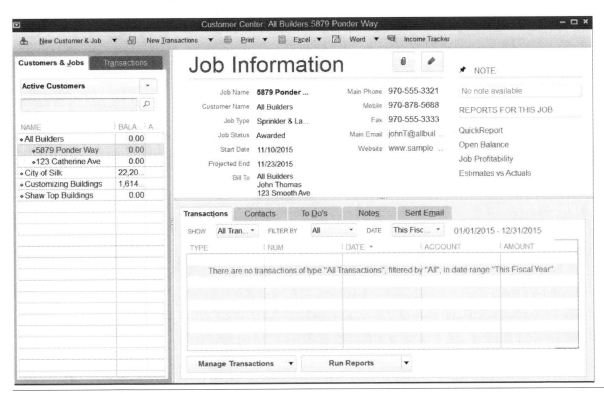

Estimates

We are going to run the estimate for 123 Catherine Ave. Be sure to highlight that job and do the following:

1. Click on New Transactions
2. Then choose Estimates and the Estimate page pops up with the current job/customer highlighted and ready to enter information. Estimate is complete and checked to email later.

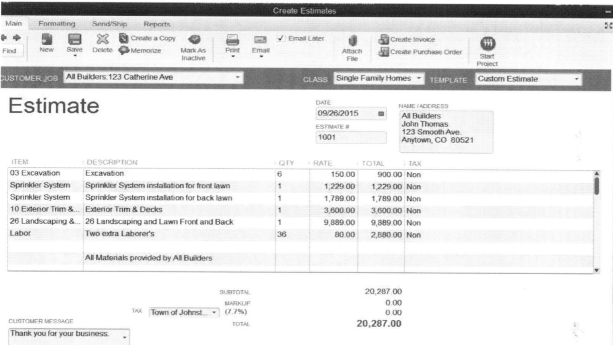

See the Estimate now shows up in the Customer information in the job it's entered for.

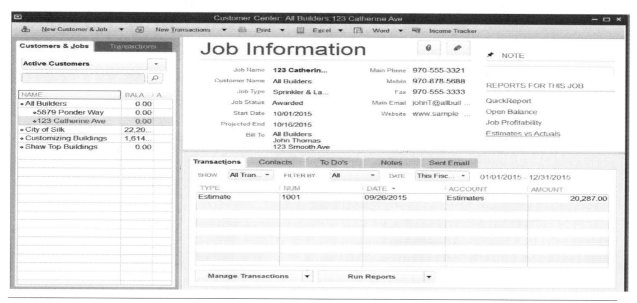

Email Estimate

Next we will send the estimate by email, the customers preferred choice. To do this do the following:

1. Click File at the top of the Main Menu Bar
2. Choose Send Forms

This form will pop up and you can see the estimate fourth one down and to the right the estimate is attached as a PDF along with the basic email/letter. You would check what you want to email right now and click send now if you are ready. You can change the letter if need and want to.

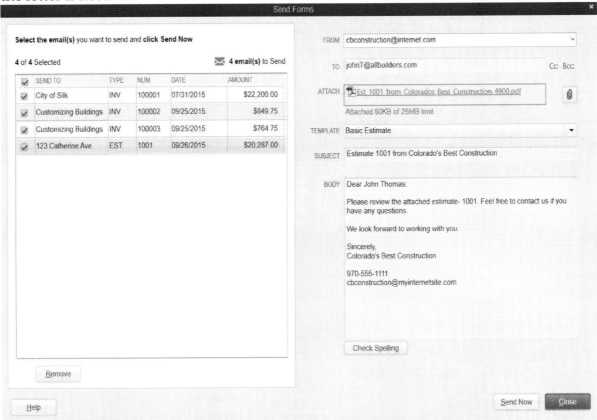

We will invoice the Customer from this estimate next as job completed.

Invoice from Estimate as Job Complete

To Invoice from the estimate do the following:

1. Highlight job with estimate
2. Click on New Transaction and choose Invoices
3. Click anywhere on the invoice screen and a screen that says Available estimates pops up.

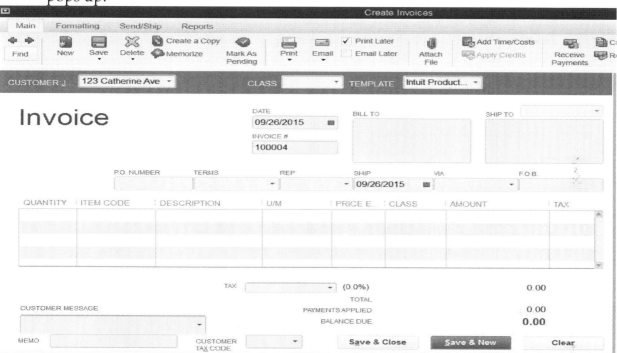

Highlight and click on the estimate in the screenshot below and click ok.

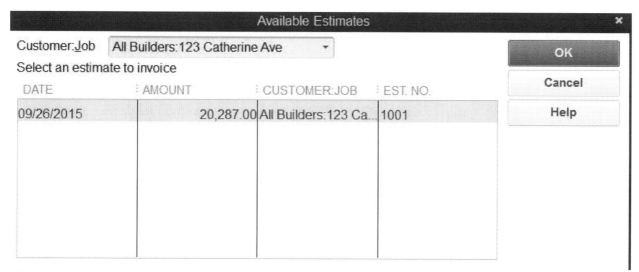

The following screen on the next page will pop up, Create Progress Invoice Based on Estimate.

Create Progress Invoice Based on Estimate screen pops up and gives you the three options. For this exercise I chose to create invoice for the entire estimate.

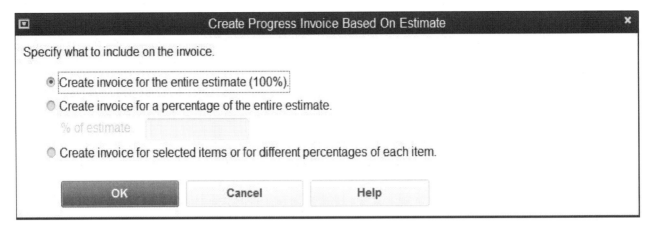

Here's the invoice created from the estimate and ready to send to the customer for payment. Click Save & Close.

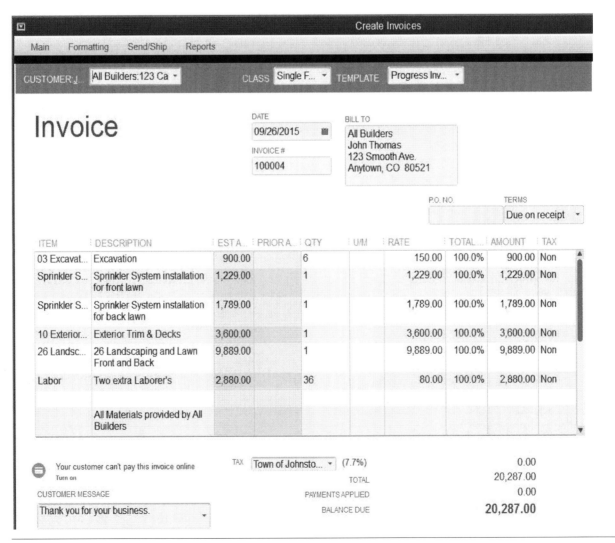

Customer Center with Invoice created from Estimate

See below the Customer's Job Information with an Estimate and the new invoice created from the Estimate.

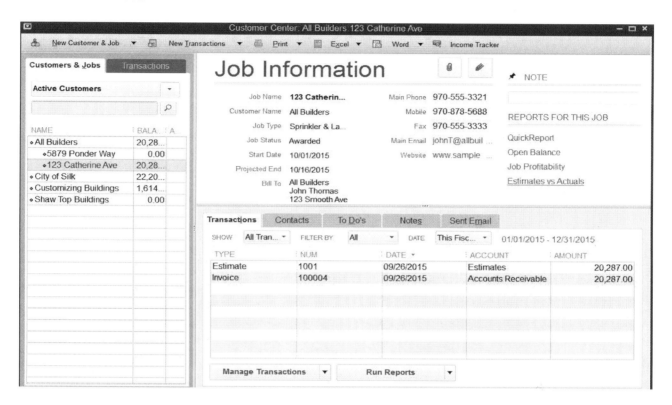

See the screenshot below the email for the invoice needs to be sent. As you can see the estimate has been sent. Click Close.

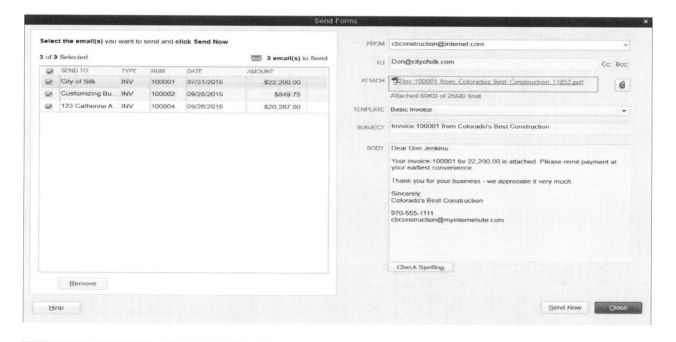

QuickBooks For Contractors

Received Payment

We will now receive payment for job performed, billed and now receiving payment for the job. We will go over deposits and receiving payment further in the Banking Chapter. You can make sure you apply the correct payment to the correct job by highlighting the correct job under active customers and then highlight the invoice under the Job Information section that you are entering the payment for.

1. Click on New Transactions and select Receive Payments

Fill in the appropriate information for your payment received and click Save & Close.

Payment Received and Entered

See the Payment entered in the correct job information below. It shows it was deposited to undeposited funds. The payment will go to undeposited funds as a holding account until you go and deposit them. It does this by default for the reason that you may have multiple deposits on one deposit for the day. You can print one deposit at a time if you want as well. We will deposit this payment in the banking chapter.

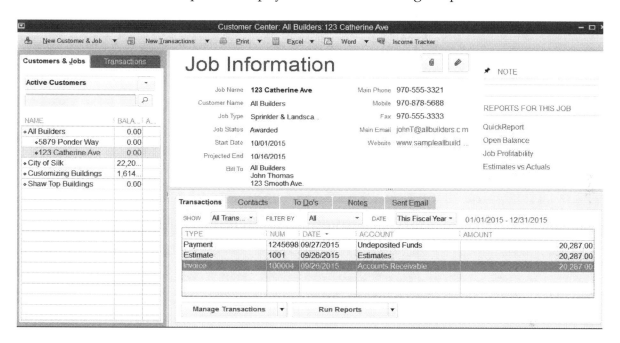

Income Tracker Screenshot. See where the payment was received from All Builders for the job we just billed and received payment for. Very handy feature to use. You can access this on the customer center menu bar to the right. See in screenshot above to the right of Word icon.

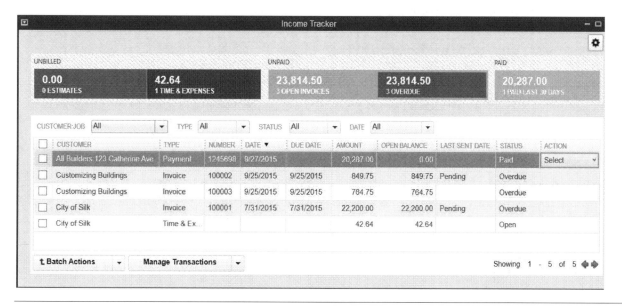

Enter Finance Statement Charges

It's time to send out Statements. We have some past due accounts we need to access statement charges on first. Click on finance charges as shown in the screenshot below with the red arrow.

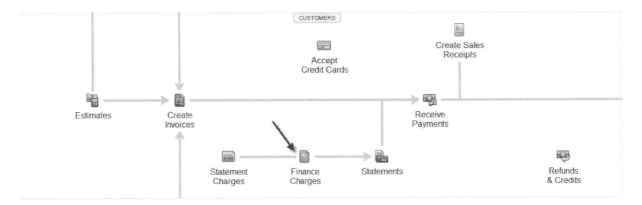

After Clicking Finance Charges icon this screen pops up. As you can see there are finance charges that need to be applied. Click Assess charges.

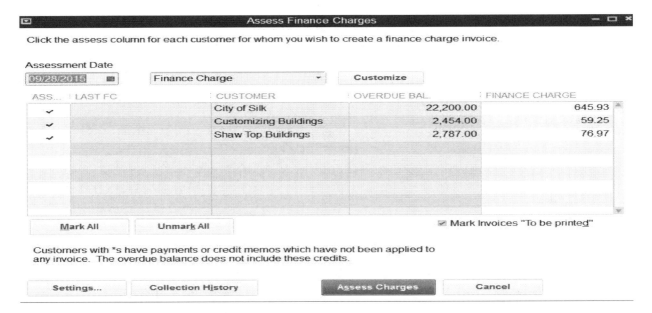

This Box pops up. Click Yes. Click on Statements icon next to the Finance Charges Icon on the customer's area on the home page.

Create Statements

After clicking on the Statements Icon the screenshot below pops up. As you can see you can assess finance charges from this screen as well, but since we already assessed the finance charges you don't need to do them again for this month. Do you want all open transactions as of Statement Date? Make sure your dates are right. Do you want to send to all customers, one customer or multiple customers?

Select Additional Options - These are the default options, but you can set the features as to your needs. Go through and click on those that apply and click Preview. By previewing you can see if anything needs correcting before printing and mailing or emailing or even faxing.

Here's a copy of the top half of one of the statements to send. See the finance charges applied?

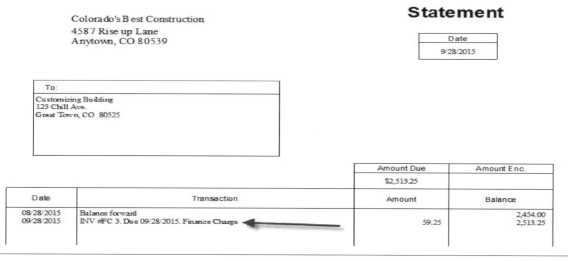

Sales Receipt

Use this procedure when you make a sale for which you receive full payment at the time of the sale. Sales receipts can include payments by cash, check, or credit card.

1. Click Customers on the top Main Menu Bar
2. Click Enter Sales Receipts

This was for a customer that came in and paid for their product and took the product with them. After entering the sales receipt go ahead and print then click Save & Close.

Note: The money received was recorded in the undeposited funds account and not in the check register. We will go through in detail how to deposit in the Banking Chapter.

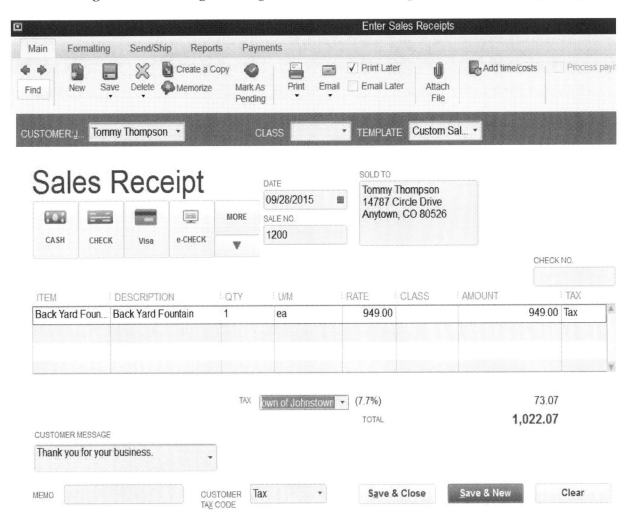

Next we will enter credit memo's/refunds. Also, I will go over how to void or delete those finance charges we just assessed.

Most companies never collect the finance charges they send out on their statements, but they send them anyway to cause their customers to pay their bills on time.

Create Credit Memos/Refund

Use the Create Credit Memos/Refunds window to issue a credit memo or refund check when a customer returns items for which you have already recorded an invoice, customer payment, or sales receipt. You can also use a credit memo as part of the process of handling a bad or bounced check from a customer.

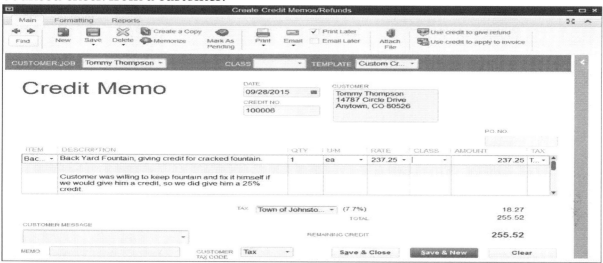

This screen popped up after Clicking Save & Close. I selected to give a refund with this transactions because he paid with a credit card.

This screen then pops up. Place check mark in box "Process credit card refund when saving" if your system is set up to do so, if not process their credit refund the way you processed their credit card charge.

Voiding/Deleting Finance Charges

As I said earlier most companies, other than loans and credit cards, don't collect the finance charges they send out at month end, but companies do this to cause their customers to get the bill paid. Instead of deleting the finance charge I recommend you voiding the charge, so you have a record of this.

To Void the Finance Charges do the following:

1. Select Customer Center
2. Select the Customer you want to void the finance charge
3. Click open the finance charge Invoice.
4. Click open Edit at the top main menu Bar
5. Select Void Invoice, see invoice below in screenshot before voiding it.

Screenshot of voided invoice. Click Save & Close.

Note: If you need to void an estimate, invoice or credit you just need to open the transaction you want to void and follow these same steps to do so.

Go to Chapter 16 on Receivables, page 254 for more in depth information Invoicing and other important aspect of customers, change orders and billing.

Chapter 8
Vendors

Vendors are who we purchase products from. Vendors are also setup to make payments on loans, credit cards, property or vehicle loans, and utility bills just to name a few. Basically if you write a check or you buy something with a credit card you will set them up as a vendor.

1. Click on Vendors at the top main Menu Bar
2. Click on Vendor Center
3. Click New Vendor from the Vendor Center Menu Bar
4. Select New Vendor from the drop down list

Vendor Center Menu Bar

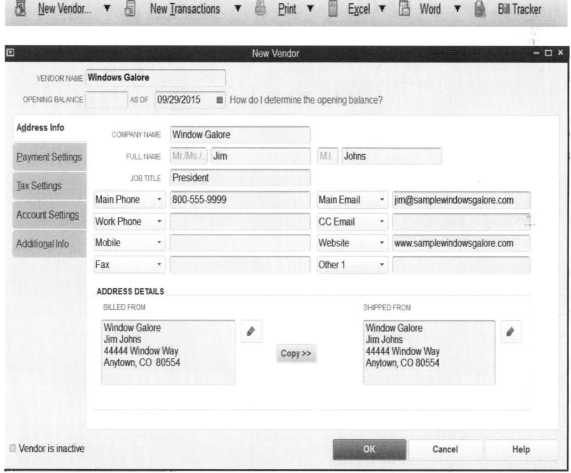

Enter the information from the screenshot above in the first New Vendor Screen under Address Info tab. I didn't enter an opening balance, but if you have an opening balance starting point you want to start from this is where you will enter the opening balance. When finished click on the Payment Settings tab located below the Address Info tab.

Payment Settings Screen

Enter the appropriate information and when finished click on Tax Settings tab located below the Payment Settings tab.

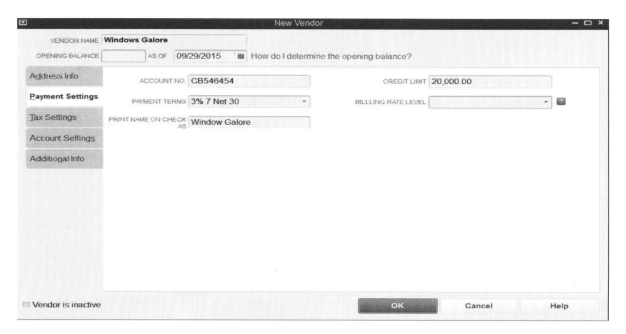

Tax Settings Screen

If you use unincorporated vendors, such as outside consultants or subcontractors, you need to send a 1099-MISC form to those who are paid more than a specific amount per year.

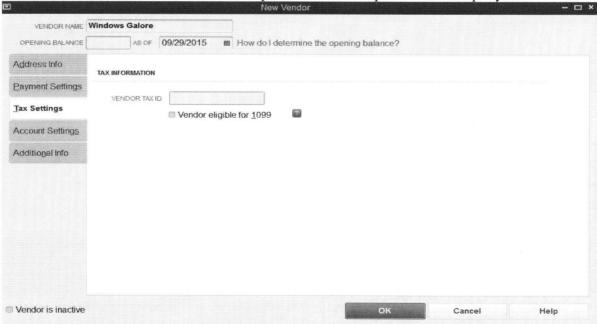

Enter the appropriate information on the Tax Settings screen and when finished click on Account Settings tab just below the Tax Settings tab.

Account Settings

The Account Settings screen is a big help when entering bills if you preset accounts. You can choose up to three accounts to set up. As you can see I entered Cost of Goods sold account for Construction Materials.

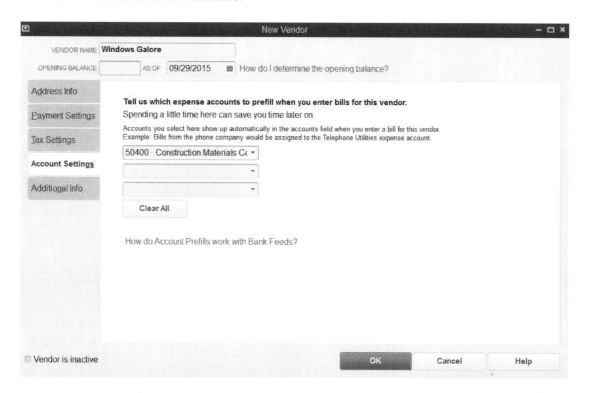

Enter the appropriate information and when done click on the Additional Info tab located below the Account Settings.

After Clicking on the Additional Tab you will see you can set up custom fields. I added the Window Materials custom field for customers and vendors. See in the screenshot on the next page where this has been added.

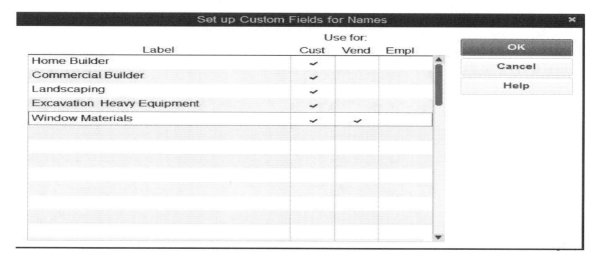

Additional Info

This tab has the vendor type and custom field's information. As you can see the custom field added along with entering the type of vendor. In the custom fields you can enter any information that fits. You could enter just a simple yes or can leave blank as to your needs. Click ok when finished.

Here is your vendor center home screen with Windows Galore now a new vendor. You have now entered your first vendor from beginning to end.

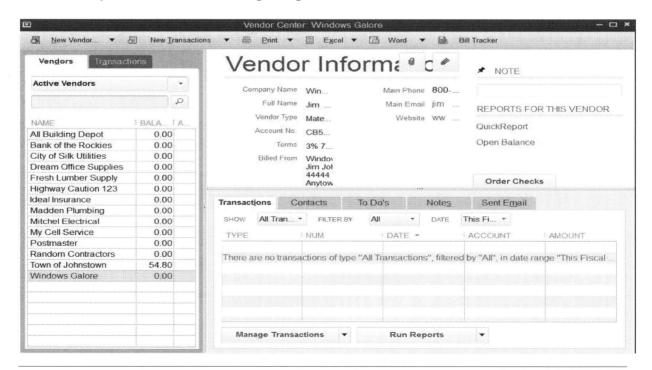

Purchase Orders

You use a purchase order to let a vendor know that you want to order goods or services. Purchase orders help you keep track of what you have ordered and what you have already received. When you have received everything on the purchase order, QuickBooks marks the purchase order "Received in full."

When you receive the goods or services, QuickBooks uses information on the purchase order to enter a bill, check, or credit card charge for the same vendor.

When you use purchase orders to order inventory items, you can see not only how many items are in stock but how many are on order and when they're due to be received.

You can also use purchase orders to order services from a contractor, office supplies, a new asset for your company, or other items that are not set up as inventory in QuickBooks.

Entering a Purchase Order

1. With Vendor Center open
2. Click New Transactions on the Vendor Center Menu Bar
3. Click Purchase Orders
4. Fill in the information
5. Click Save & Close when done.

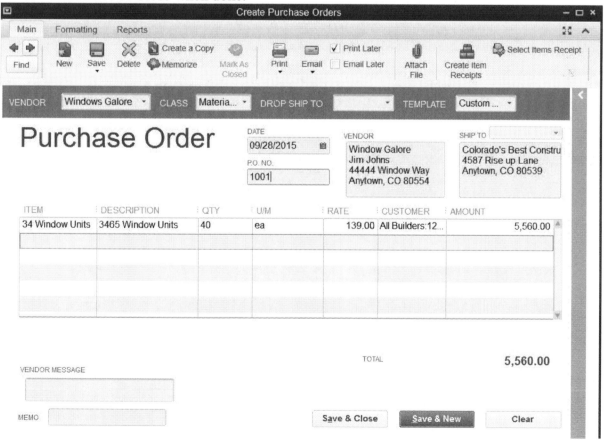

QuickBooks For Contractors

Receive Inventory with Bill

After ordering the windows from Windows Galore we received them with a bill and going to enter the inventory and bill in QuickBooks. The screenshot below is the vendor's home page area.

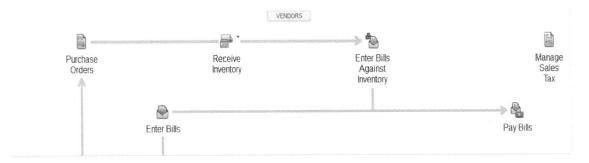

1. Click on the Receive Inventory Icon on the home page screen area.
2. On the drop down list choose Receive Inventory with Bill.
3. Enter Windows Galore in the Vendor line

This box pops up after entering a vendor with a PO. Click yes.

After entering the bill from the purchase order all the information was filled in except the Ref No. I filled in the Ref. No. and typically this would be an invoice number. Click Save & Close.

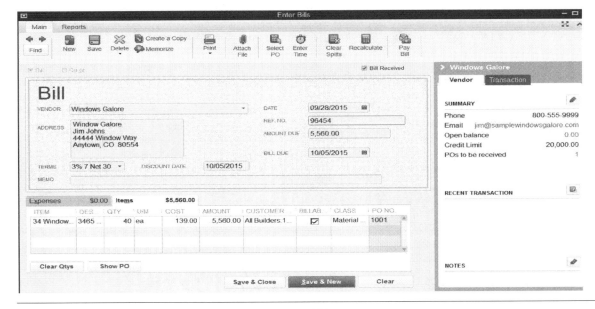

144

Enter Bills

To enter bills click on the home page the Enter Bills Icon in the Home page Vendor Area.

Enter the information in the screenshot below and when finished click save & close.

Pay Bills

We are going to pay bills next. Today we are going to go ahead and pay the Windows Galore Bill to take advantage of the Discount. Click on the Pay Bills Icon on the Vendor home page area. Click on the invoice For Windows Galore and the discount should show up. Click Pay selected bills. Click print checks later.

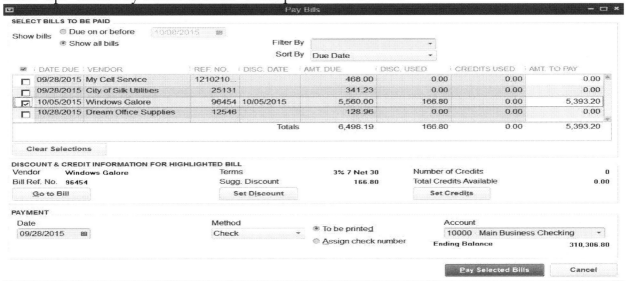

Bill Tracker

The Bill Tracker makes it easy to manage your vendor-related payables, such as bills and purchase orders.

To open the Bill Tracker, choose Vendors and select Bill Tracker. The Bill Tracker isn't available if multicurrency is turned on.

When a company file is set up, only the QuickBooks Administrator has access to the Bill Tracker. If another user needs access, the administrator must edit that user's role to include full access to the Purchases and Accounts Payable area, or full access to all areas of QuickBooks.

When you open the Bill Tracker, it shows all unbilled purchases (purchase orders), unpaid bills (open and overdue bills), and bills paid within the last 30 days.

Each colored block shows the amount for transactions in that category. Click a block to see the transactions that make up that amount. Use the drop-down arrows below the colored blocks to filter the list further. To reset the filters or see the complete list of transactions, click Clear/Show All.

This is a great feature to use.

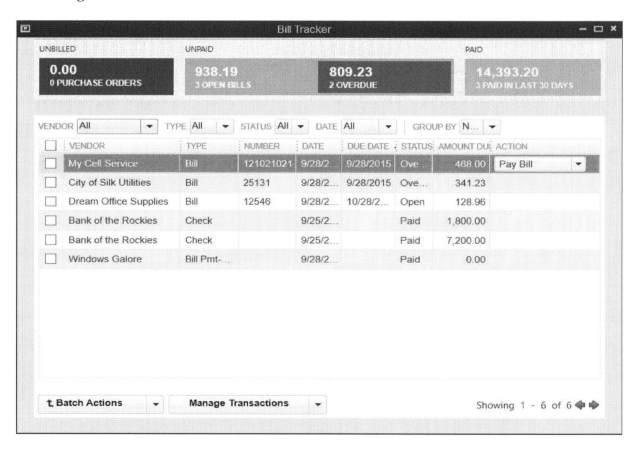

See Payables in Chapter 15, page 242 for more information on Vendors & Bills.

Chapter 9
Inventory

You can use QuickBooks to track the items for inventory and sell to your customers. If your business purchases items that are ready for resale, keeps them in inventory, and then sells them, QuickBooks can track the current number in stock and the value of your inventory after every purchase and sale. QuickBooks tracks products you assemble and resell (finished goods), adding assembled units to inventory and deducting component units from inventory when you build assembly items (QuickBooks Premier or QuickBooks Enterprise Solutions editions only).

QuickBooks makes it easier to manage your inventory with the Inventory Center. To open the Inventory Center, choose Vendors then choose Inventory Activities and click Inventory Center. If you don't see this option, you need to turn inventory tracking on.

The Inventory Center is divided into 3 screen parts:

- The left screen pane lists your inventory and inventory assembly items. To sort this list, click the top drop-down arrow and select an option.
- The top-right screen pane shows the details for the selected inventory item.
- The bottom-right screen pane has tabs that show transactions and notes related to the selected item.

Use the Inventory Center to search for inventory items, add a new inventory item, edit an inventory item, add a picture of an inventory item, add a new transaction and run inventory reports. You can access the Inventory Center by Clicking on the Inventory Activities Icon on the home page under the Company tab as shown below in the screenshot.

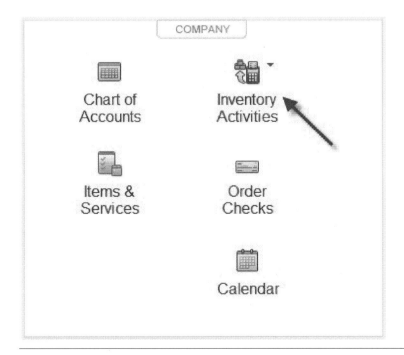

Inventory Center Screenshot

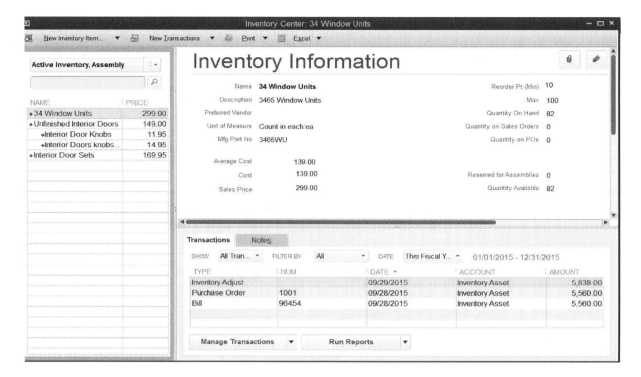

Build Assembly

You can create inventory assembly items in QuickBooks to track assembled goods that you produce, keep in inventory, and sell. To build an assembly click the Inventory Activities Icon on the home page under the company tab and select Build Assemblies. The following screen pops up. We will need to build an assembly and will go step by step how to do that next on the next page.

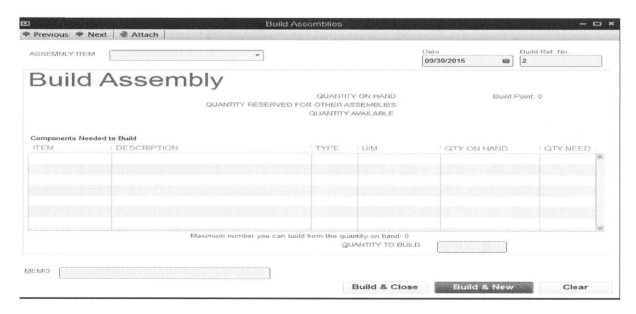

Build Assembly Continued

To build a new Assembly Item:

1. Click on the Inventory Activities Icon on the Home Page under Company Tab
2. Select Build Assemblies
3. Click on Assembly Item and Select Add New and the following Screen will appear.
4. Choose Inventory Assembly and fill in the information below and click ok.

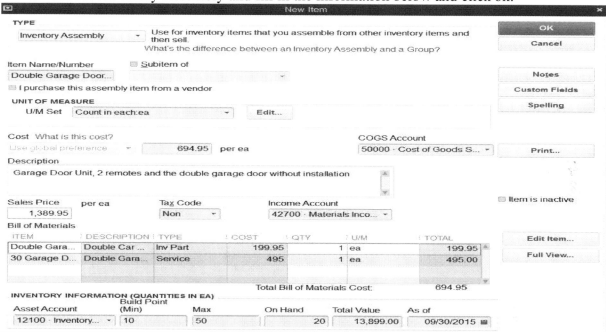

Click on Assembly Item and enter Double Garage Door Unit. The information fills in and all you enter is how many you want to build in the box that says "QUANTITY TO BUILD". Qty Needed is 10, so enter 10 in that box and click Build & Close.

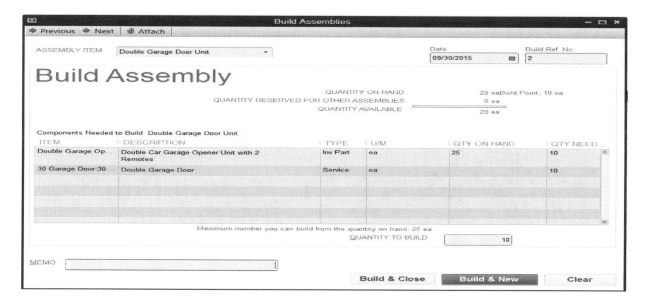

QuickBooks For Contractors

Adjust Quantity/Value on Hand

We will adjust the Interior Door Sets that have a -5 as shown in the screenshot with the red arrow pointing to On Hand. Someone forgot to enter these door sets, so we will adjust those. To run this Report:

1. Click on Reports at the Top Main Menu Bar
2. Click on Inventory
3. Select Inventory Valuation Summary Report.
4. You can customize this report, but I ran as is for this exercise.

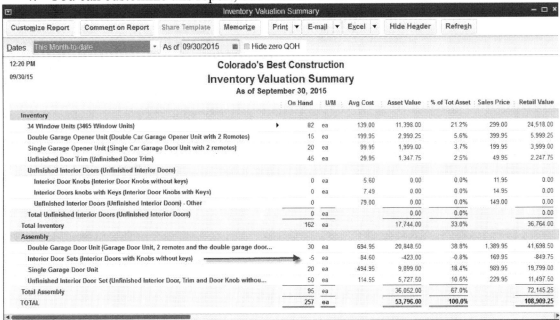

Click on the Inventory Activities Icon on the Home Page under Company Tab. Select Adjust Quantity/Value on Hand. The screen below pops up. We will fill in the appropriate information on the next screen.

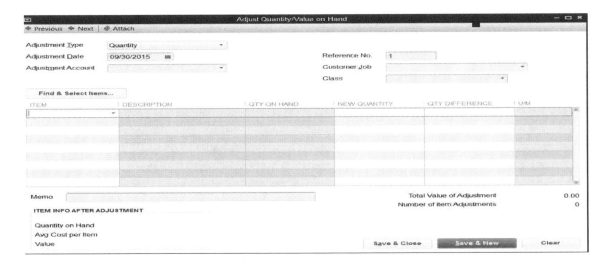

150

Adjusting Inventory on Hand

Fill in the adjustments as shown below and click save & close. We were short 5 sets, so enter new Quantity as 5 and the adjustment account to Materials Income. If it's a gain to inventory it's typically the income account. We will run a new Inventory Report to show the adjustment.

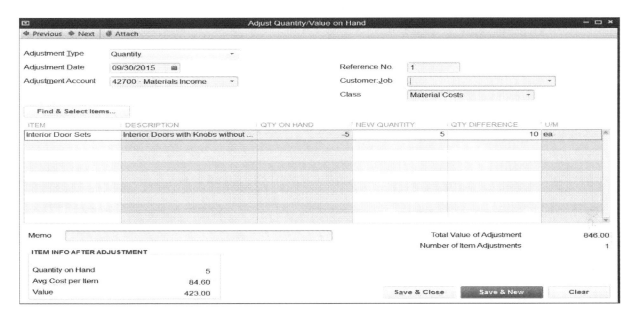

See the Inventory Valuation Summary Report below. Notice the red arrow pointing to the Interior Door sets is now 5 instead of -5. Click the x in the right hand corner of report to exit the report.

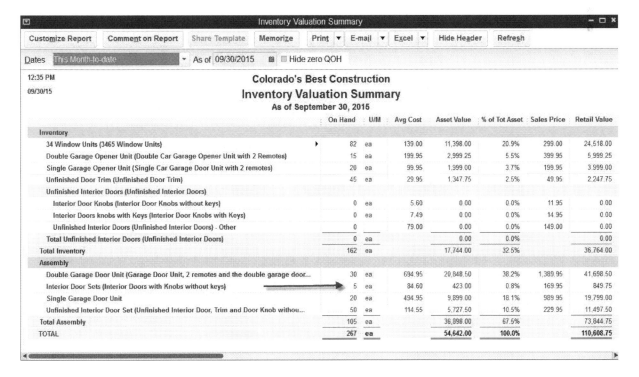

QuickBooks For Contractors

Chapter 10
Employees, Payroll Items & Payroll

The Employee Center displays information about all of your employees and their transactions in a single place. You can add an employee or edit an employee's information. Set up direct deposit for an employee, release an employee or make an employee inactive. Run reports such as a QuickReport or Payroll Summary and Send emails. Last but not least you can find, print or edit employee transactions.

To add a new Employee do the following:

1. Click on the Employees tab that is located on the Home Page. Click the tab as shown in the screenshot below with the red arrow pointing to it. This will open the Employee Center.

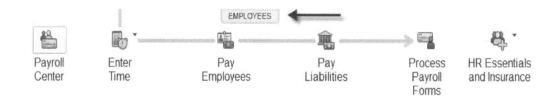

Here's the Employee Center open on the employee highlighted, Mitchell, Clark. Click on New Employee on the Employee Center main menu bar with the red arrow pointing to New Employee.

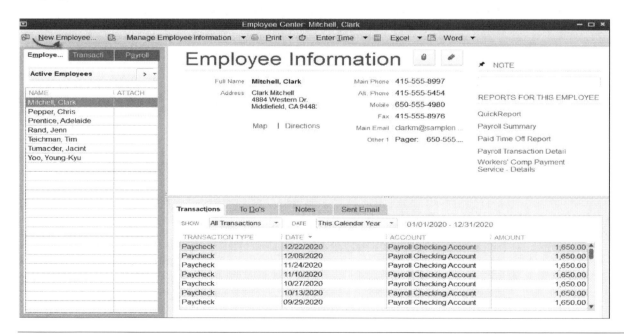

Adding New Employee

Here's the new Employee Screen. We will add all the pertinent information. See Screenshot below.

Adding New Employee Personal

Enter the information below for the new employee. When finished entering information click on Address & Contact tab just below the Personal tab.

New Employee Address & Contact

Fill in the information below. When finished filling in the information click on the Additional Info tab just below the Address & Contact tab.

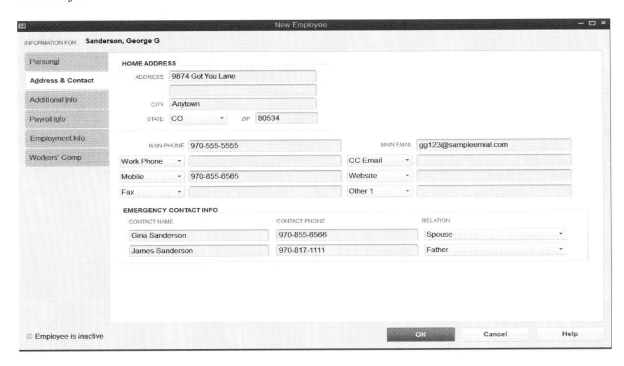

New Employee Additional Info

Fill in the information below. When finished filling in the information click on the Payroll Info tab just below the Additional Info tab.

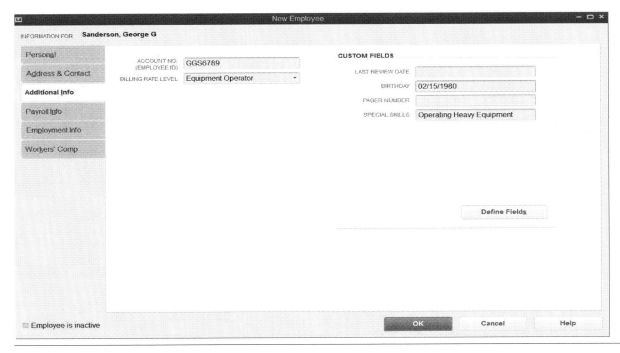

New Employee Payroll Info

Fill in the Payroll Info as shown below. When finished Click on Taxes button to the top right of the screen as shown in this screenshot. See the next three screenshots for the information. Once done with Taxes click ok then Click on the Sick/Vacation button just below the Taxes button.

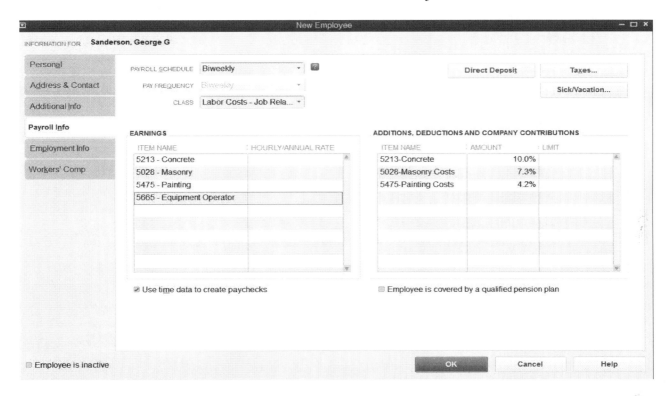

New Employee Federal Taxes

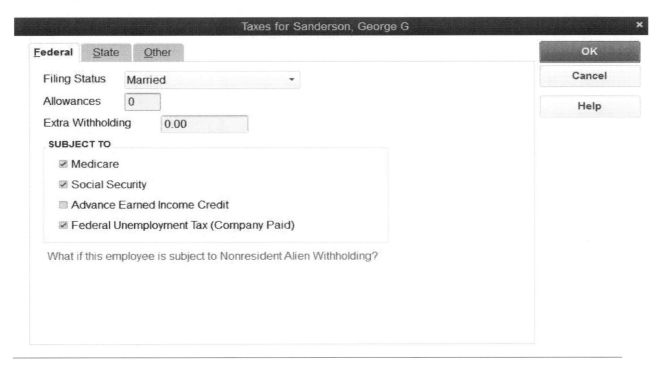

New Employee State Taxes

New Employee Other Taxes

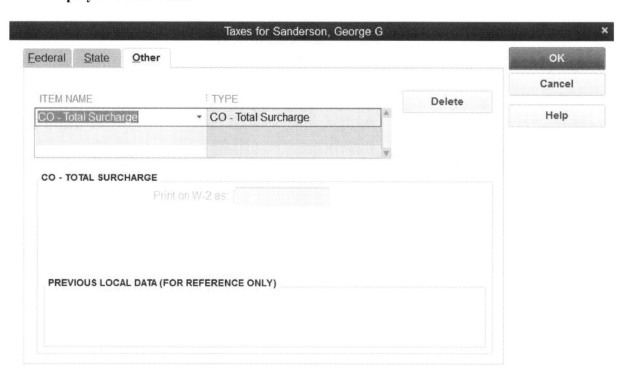

New Employee Sick/Vacation

This is the default settings and I left them at default for this exercise, however I did check the box "Reset hours each new year? Under Sick and Vacation time. We will go over these setting more in setting up payroll in this chapter. When finished click ok then click on the Employment Info tab just below the Payroll Info tab.

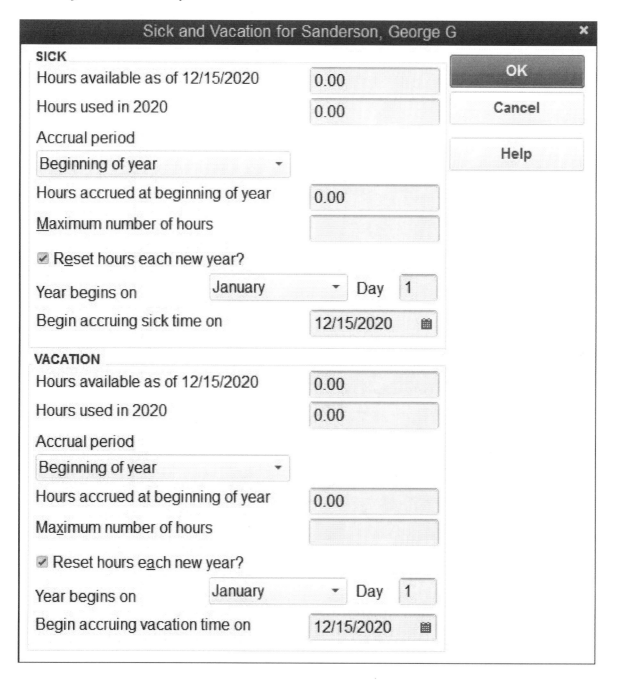

New Employee Employment Info

Enter the information as show below. When finished click the Workers' Comp tab just below the Employment Info tab.

If you haven't setup the workman's comp code you can do so here. Click ok when done.

Edit Employee Information

Here is Screenshot of the Employee Center with new employee George G Sanderson. We will go in and edit his information and to do this make sure the employee you want to edit is highlighted like George's then click on the pencil icon that has the red arrow pointing to it on the Employee Information screen.

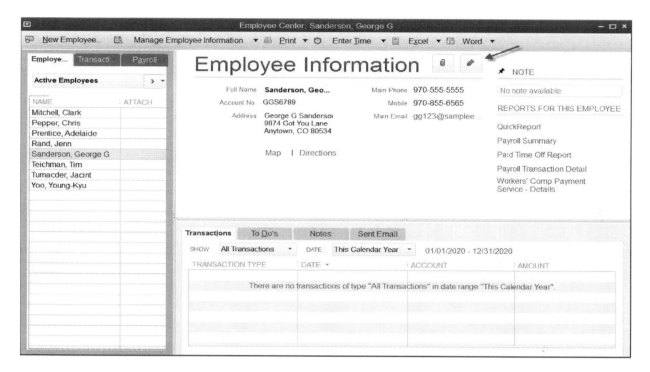

We forgot to add George's I-9 Form work Authorization Expires date. Add this and click ok.

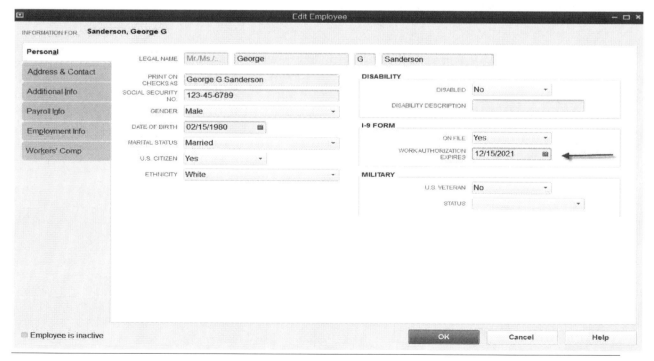

QuickBooks For Contractors

Payroll Items

The Payroll Item list holds the payroll items that are currently set up in QuickBooks. The list is initially grouped by item type, but you can resort by item name. See the Screenshot of current sample company item list below. We are going to add a payroll item.

1. Click on the Payroll Item at the bottom of the screen, see where red arrow is pointing below.
2. Select New

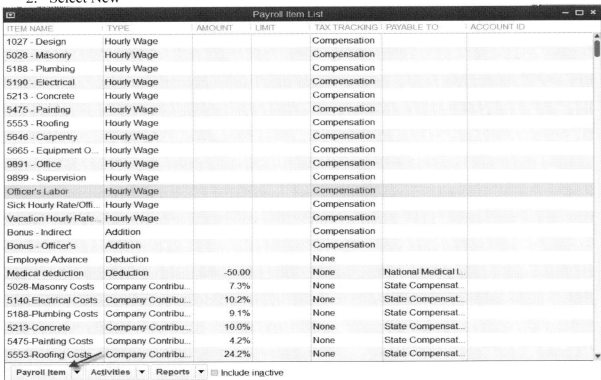

This is the first screen to setting up a new Item. The new Item will be a Labor Item. Keep the EZ Setup and click Next.

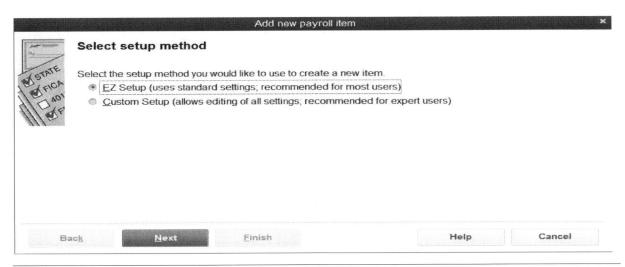

160

Payroll Item Type

Keep the Compensation selection and click Next. This will take you into Payroll setup for this item. See next screenshot.

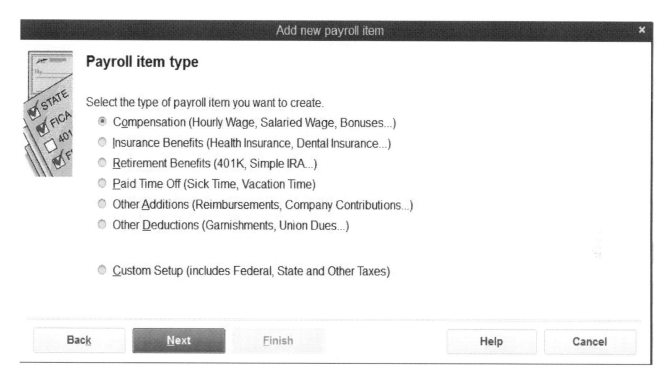

This is for Labor, so place checkmark next to the two items marked. You can mark all if you need it for your business, but I chose a typical setup for this exercise. Click Next.

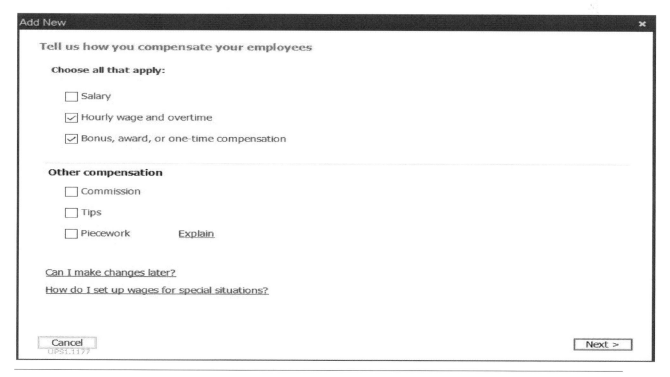

New Item Hourly Compensation

This is default setting. I added the work Labor after Hourly. Click next.

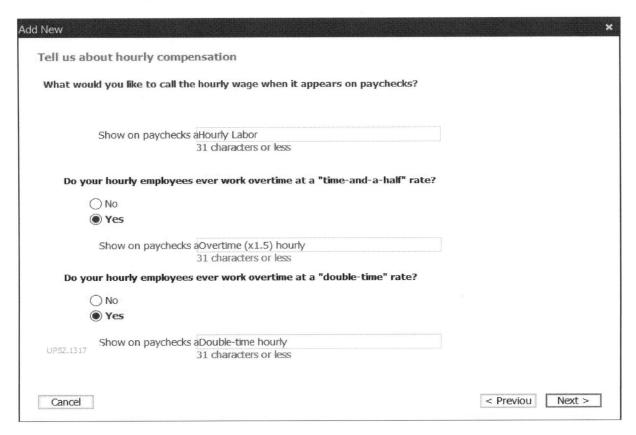

After reading click finish.

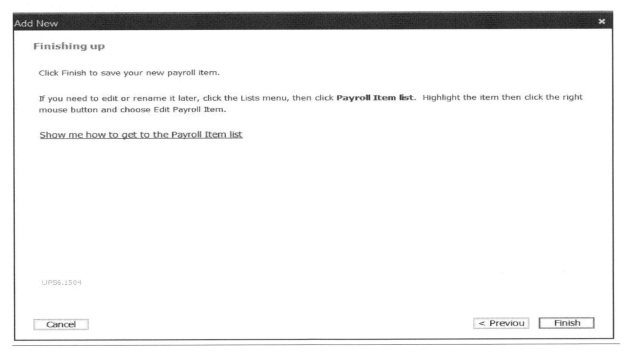

Payroll Item List

See the new Hourly Labor Item Added. I left off the number intentionally so we can go in and edit an item. Make sure Hourly Labor is highlighted as shown below. Click on Payroll Item at the bottom of the screen then select Edit Payroll Item. Change the item name from Hourly Labor to 5666 - Hourly Labor.

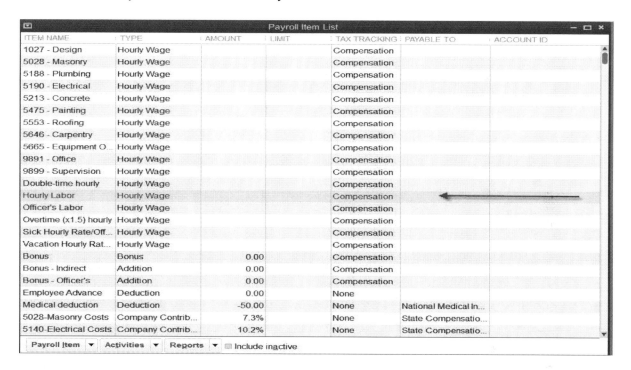

See the new name of Hourly Labor in the screenshot below. You cannot delete a Payroll Item or any item that has transactions attached to it, but you can make an item inactive. We will make this new item inactive just for the sake of the exercise and then we can reactivate it.

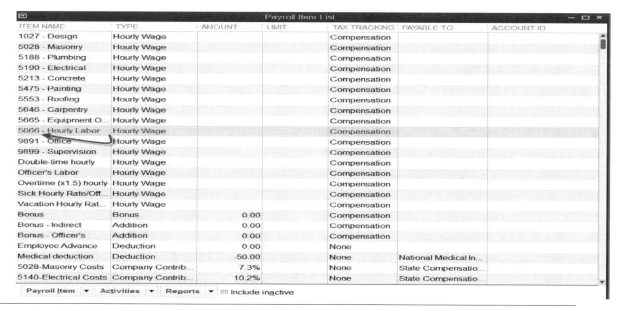

Make Payroll Item Inactive

The 5666 - Hourly Labor payroll Item is now made inactive. See the red arrow below is where the inactive item use to be. To make Inactive you need to highlight item you want to make inactive. Click on Payroll Item at the bottom of the screen and select Make Payroll Item Inactive and it will immediately be removed from the screen into inactive mode.

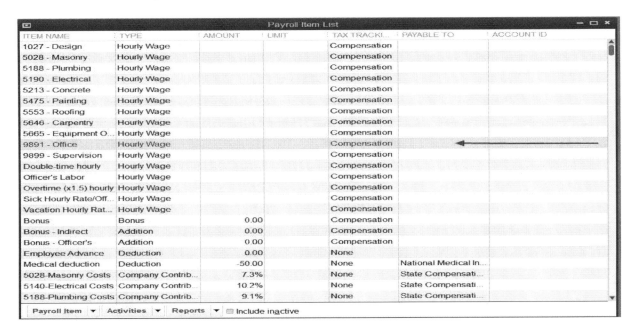

See the inactive payroll items with the x to the left of the item. To see these items click on Payroll Item at the bottom of the screen and select Show Inactive Payroll Items. To make these active again just click on the X of the item you want active. To hide the inactive payroll items just click Payroll Item at the bottom of the screen and select Hide Inactive Payroll Items.

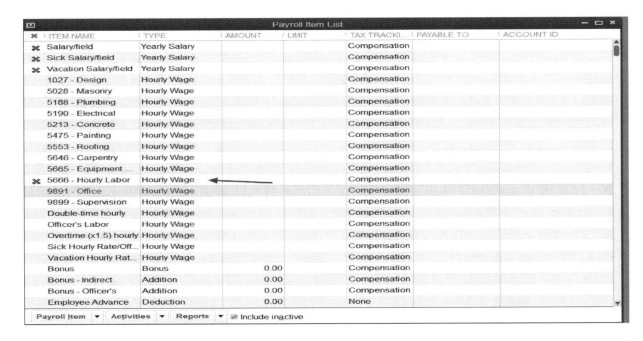

Add New Payroll Item Type

This is where we setup the Hourly Labor Compensation. You will go to this to setup Insurance Benefits along with other benefits and as you can see paid time off, other additions like reimbursement for mileage or other deductions such as a garnishment along with custom setup for taxes. So to do any of these things you would click on Payroll Item at the bottom of your screen of the Payroll Items List and select new. The EZ will be selected click next and the Payroll Item type screen pops up like the screenshot below. After making your selection then click next and continue until the item you are setting up is set up.

Note: If you are setting up Insurance Benefits, or whatever you are setting up remember to have your information at hand such as amounts, account numbers etc.

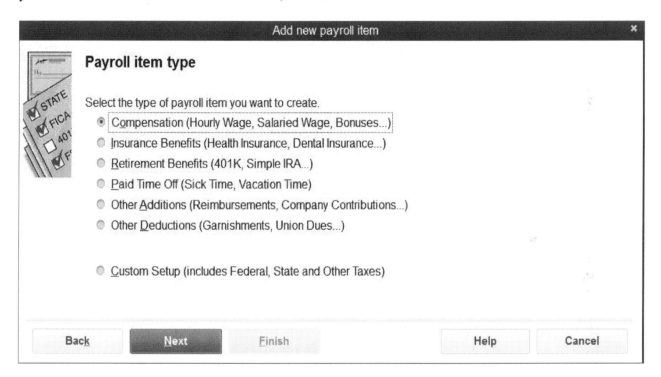

We are ready to setup payroll next. It's setup in this Sample Company, but we will go through all the necessary steps. Once we have gone through the steps of setting up payroll then we will enter employee timecards and pay employees. Last but not least we will run some reports as well pertaining to employees and payroll.

Setting up Payroll

I will take you through setting up Payroll and all the options QuickBooks has to offer for Payroll. There are several options. If you use QuickBooks for any of these options you will have to sign up and pay for QuickBooks Payroll. I will tell you it's worth it to go with any of their options. The Three options are Basic, Enhanced or Full Service and they are as follows.

- You can run all of your payroll yourself with the Desktop version or the online version
- You can run all of your payroll yourself except let QuickBooks Run your Tax Reports and pay your employment taxes.
- You can let QuickBooks Run your whole payroll including Tax Reporting and pay your employment taxes. Full Service Payroll and you enter the hours.
- You could hire someone like me, Accountant QuickBooks Pro Advisor, as well.

How to setup and run Payroll from QuickBooks

1. Click on Employees at the top of the Main Menu Bar
2. Click on Payroll Center
3. Click on the Preferences tab on the Payroll Center Icon Ribbon on top right to make sure your payroll is turned on. Seen the Screenshot on the next page for your options.

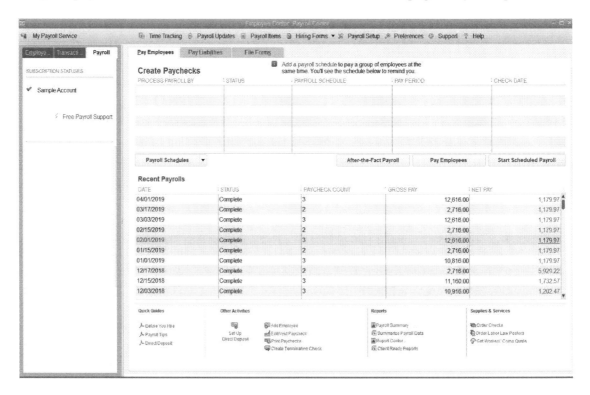

Here's the payroll preference window and as you can see you have three choices to make, Full Payroll, No Payroll or online Payroll. For this payroll exercise I chose Full Payroll. Once you have selected your options then click ok. NOTE: We went over this in Preferences, but wanted to have this in payroll as well.

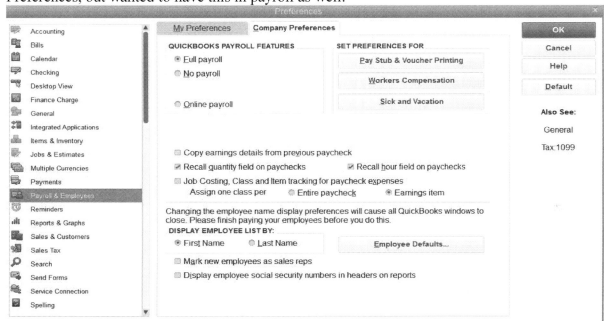

Next step is to sign up for QuickBooks Payroll. The best way to do this and to look at your options, talk with someone over the phone or chat on line is to click on the Support button on the Payroll center open screen. The Support Icon is on the upper right top in the Icon Bar on the Payroll Center screen. This will take you to Payroll signup and support. You can choose your options, talk to someone and signup.

Here's the support screen. Click on Payroll Services at the top of the menu and click on Compare Products. See on the Next Screen the products.

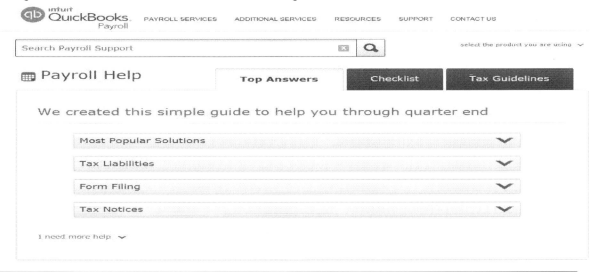

This task may look daunting, but it's not as bad as you think. There are a fair amount of steps to take, but once you are setup it is easy and fast. The hardest part is making sure your payroll/timesheets are correct after you are setup and going.

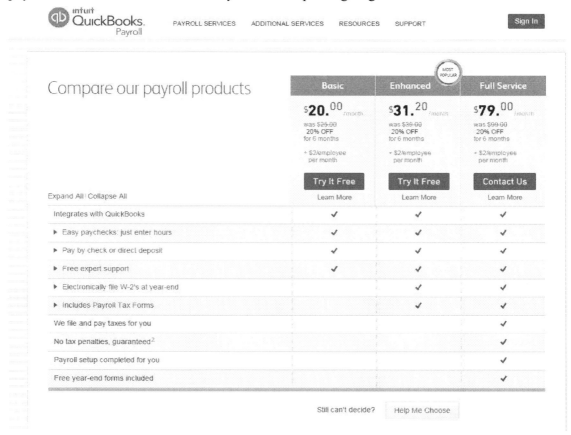

1. Once you have made you selection and paid for your payroll service you will receive a Payroll key that you will need to activate it within QuickBooks. I chose the Enhanced Service, since I am doing my full payroll.
2. Click on Employees at the top of the Main Menu Bar
3. Select My Payroll Service
4. Choose Activate Service Key
5. Click Add and enter the your Payroll Service Key Number
6. Click next and follow the prompts and finish.
7. Last step before starting the actual Payroll Setup is to make sure QuickBooks Update is turned on. See the next page.

To turn on Payroll Updates and make sure Payroll is up-to-date
1. Click on Help at the top of the Main Menu Bar
2. Select Update QuickBooks
3. Choose the Options tab as shown below
4. Click the Mark All Button to sign up for all the payroll updates
5. Click Save

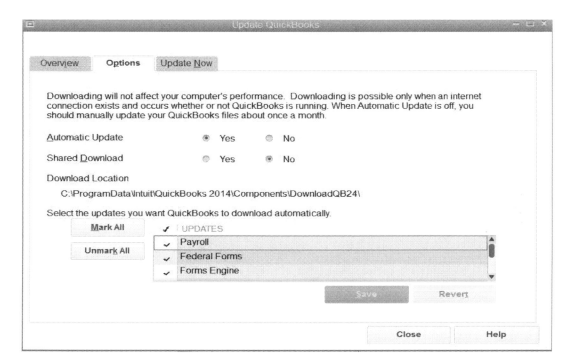

Click on the Update Now tab as shown below. Click on the Button Get Updates. You have to wait for all the updates to down load. Once the updates are done then click close and you are ready for Payroll Setup.

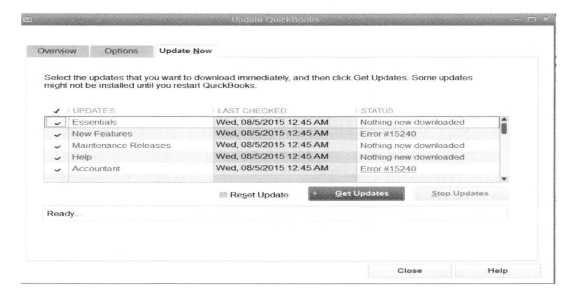

Payroll Setup

We are now ready to setup up your Company Payroll. You have turned the payroll feature on in the Preferences, you went online/called/signed up for Payroll. You activated your Payroll Service Key and you turned your payroll updates on, downloaded to latest updates. Now take the following steps.

1. Click on Employees at the top of the Main Menu Bar
2. Click on Payroll Center (this is if you closed out the window before and if you didn't then you are already ready to this point)
3. Click Payroll Setup in the Icon bar in your Payroll Center screen.
4. Click Continue and follow the prompts in the introduction.

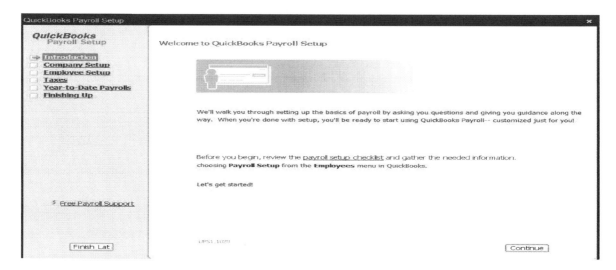

After clicking Continue on this first screen and clicked continue on the next screen the following screen came up. You need to make sure your accounts look right. You can see the buttons on the bottom left of your screen you can add, edit or delete. Once you made your changes, if any, click continue.

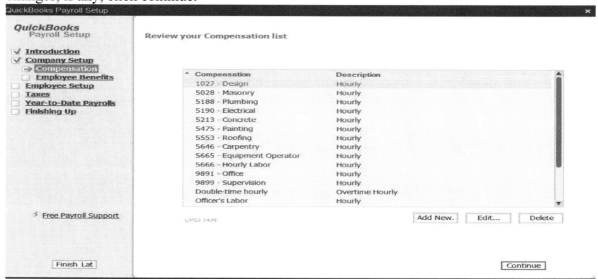

Employee Benefits

Read and follow the Employee Benefits and click on Continue. You will need to have a liability account and other accounts you will notice as you go through setup. If you go through setup and decide you need to set up accounts you can hit the finish later button in the bottom left hand of your screen. Each state has different laws and rules to abide by, so you will need to know these laws and since they are all different I can't begin to cover that plus laws change. Either talk to your CPA, or get help from QuickBooks Payroll support if you need it. For the sake of this exercise let's click continue to go through all the setup process.

As you can see the Retirement Benefits has a 401(k) set up. Here again each company has different benefits and you will need to go through the steps to set this up. Your CPA or QuickBooks Payroll support can help with this process if you need it. It's not a bad idea once you are setup to have your CPA check everything out to be sure you have it setup properly just as a precaution measure. Click Continue.

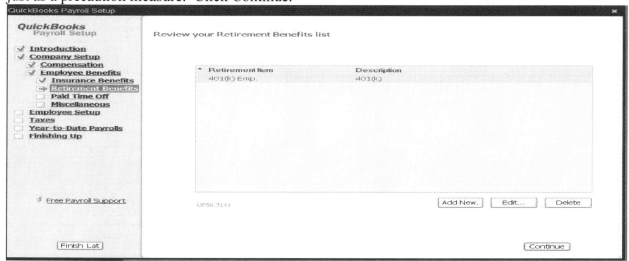

Paid Time Off in Payroll

Here again this is all different with each company and you will need to enter your company's paid time off data. Look at the accounts and even if they look right you need to click on the Edit Button to check out the information and if the Description on your screen looks right then click continue.

Here's the miscellaneous setup. Check it out and if it's right or you make changes then when done click Continue to Employee Setup.

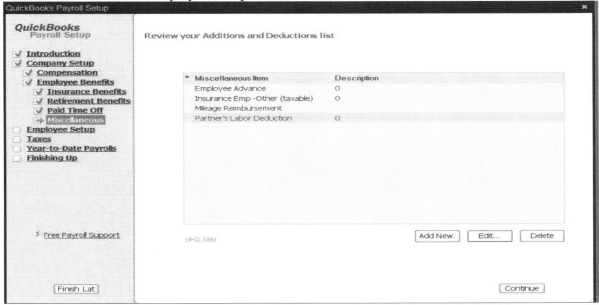

Employee Setup in Payroll

Click Continue to the Employee Setup and read the prompts then click continue. The next screen should look like this other than your employees will be different since this is a sample company.

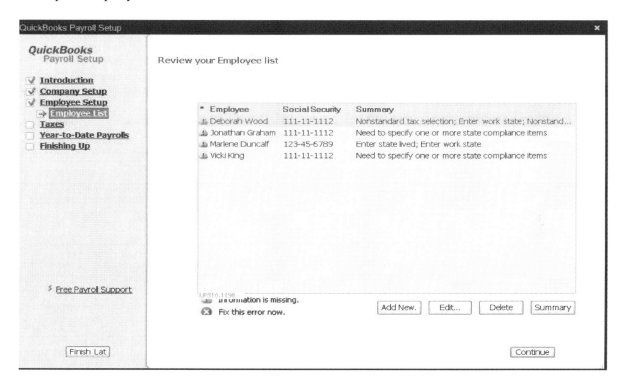

Notice at the bottom of this screen it says information missing fix this error now. Either click the Edit button or double click on the employee(s) needing updating. If you haven't entered any employees then just hit add new now. Once done click continue.

This is the Next Screen for Taxes. Read and click Continue

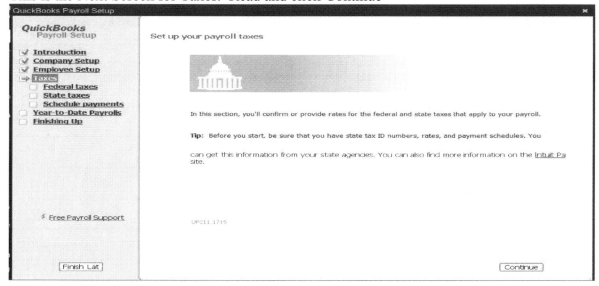

Setup Taxes in Payroll

After clicking continue this is the next screen. If everything looks right click Continue if not click on what needs editing and click the edit button. When done Click Continue.

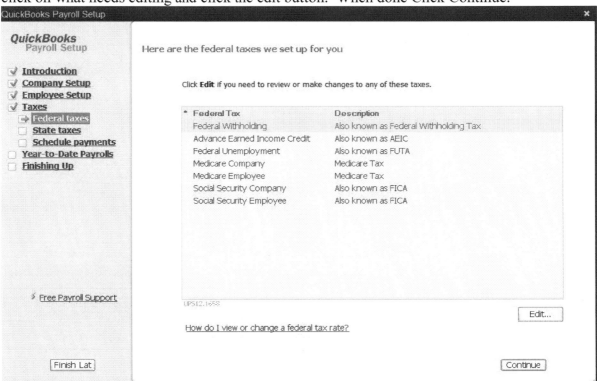

Here's the screen for your state Taxes. Here again all States are different, so check to make sure your state tax information is correct. Make any and all necessary changes, if any, and click Continue.

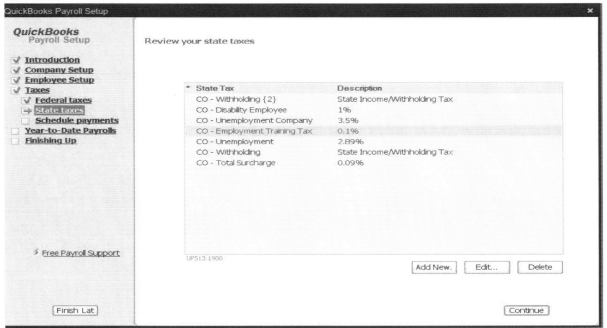

Payroll Scheduled Payments

This is where you set up the dates, and liability payments to be made monthly, quarterly and annually. If everything looks ok Click Continue and if not make the necessary changes and click Continue.

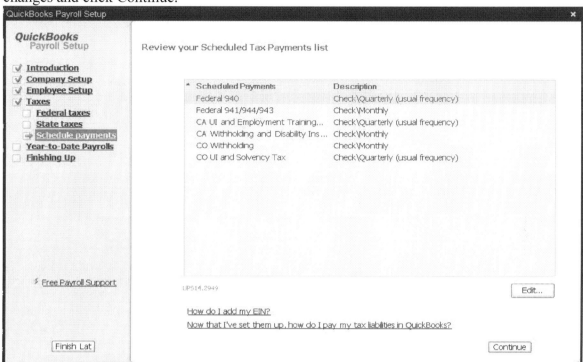

This has to do with your Year-to-date Payroll. This is where maybe you are setting up QuickBooks in the middle of the year and you need to enter months of previous payroll for the current year. Read and Click Continue.

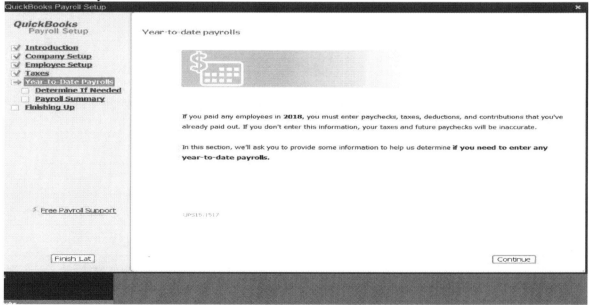

Here it asks if you have issued paychecks this year, so give the correct answer and click Continue.

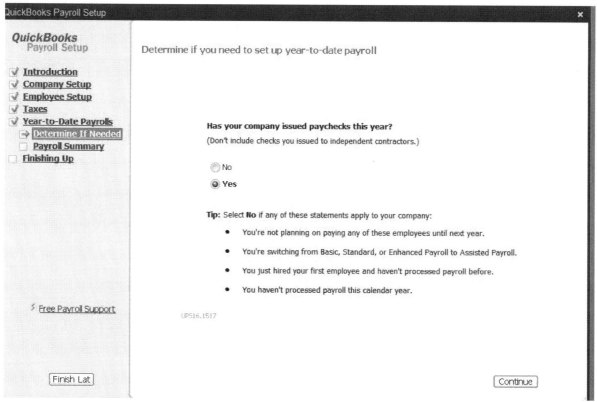

Here is where you will enter your historical payroll. It's on like a spreadsheet. Click edit and it gives you step by step instructions. You will want to enter any tax payments as well. When done click continue.

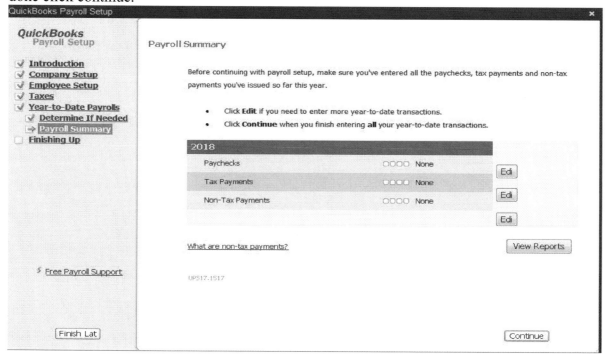

You have finished payroll setup. Click button, Go to Payroll Center.

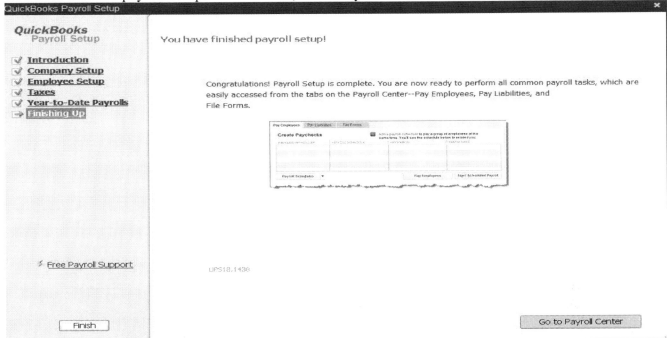

Setting up Payroll Schedule

Click on the link, add a payroll schedule in the middle of the screen to the right of the Create paychecks heading.

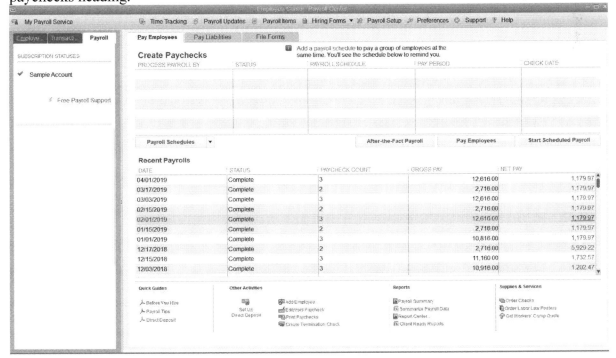

QuickBooks For Contractors

This is what it looks like after setting up a schedule. Click ok when done. If you need to set up more click on the drop down tab that says Payroll Schedules and select new. If you need to edit a schedule just highlight the schedule to Edit and click on the Payroll Schedules drop down list and click edit or delete if you need to delete a schedule.

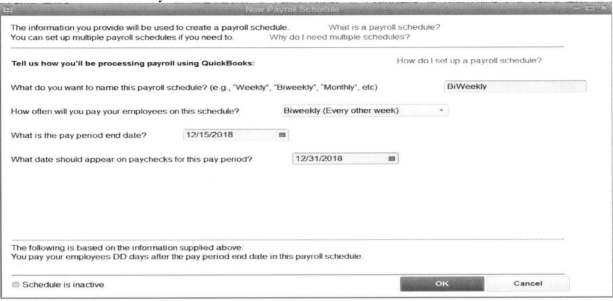

Setup Payroll schedule in Each Employee File

1. Click on Employees at the top of the Main Menu Bar
2. Select Employee Center
3. If the Employees Tab is not clicked on then click on the Employees Tab
4. Highlight the first employee and double click their file open
5. Go to the Payroll Info Tab and pull down the drop down list next to the Payroll Schedule Tab and select the schedule for the employee.
6. Enter any other pertinent information that you may still need to enter and click ok
7. Continue steps 4 through 6 until all employees are on a schedule that need to be and that all pertinent information is entered and click ok.

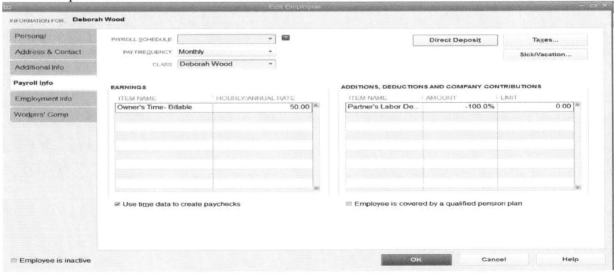

178

Entering Time

We are going to enter time in the weekly time cards. Click on the Icon shown in the screenshot with red arrow pointing to Enter Time on the Home page under the Employees tab. Select Use Weekly Timesheet from the dropdown menu.

Blank Timesheet

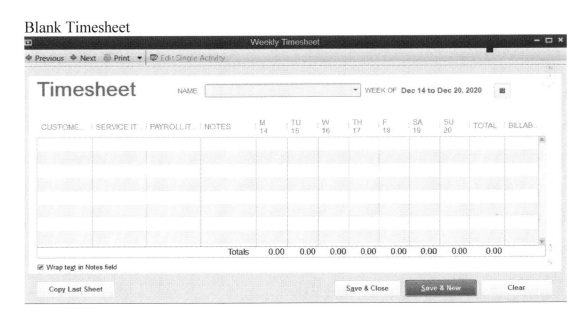

Time entered for Jenn Rand, employee. Click save & new to enter another one for payroll.

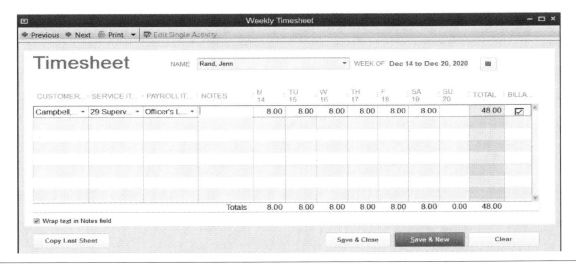

Entering Time for Payroll

Enter time and Click Save & Close to run paychecks next.

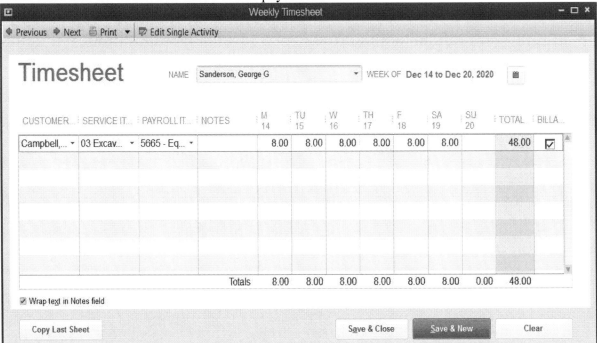

Click Pay Employees Icon on the Home Page located in the Employees section. Click on the Start Scheduled Payroll button as shown in the screenshot below with the red arrow pointing to the button.

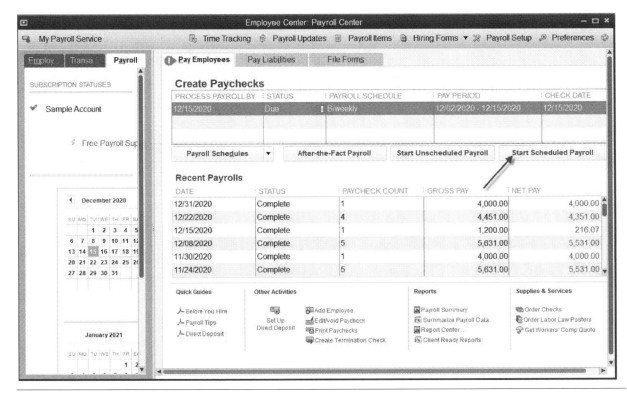

Enter Payroll Information. Make sure the check number is right. Click Open Paycheck Detail to make sure everything is right and click continue when done.

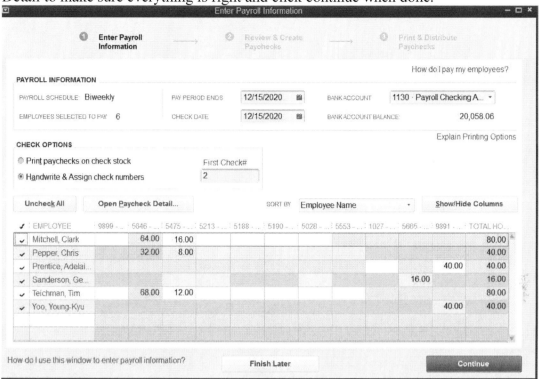

After reviewing click on print paychecks unless you want to handwrite them and when done click Create Paychecks.

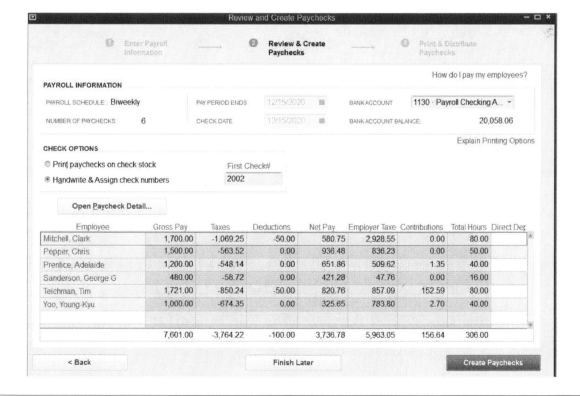

QuickBooks For Contractors

We will print later so click the close button.

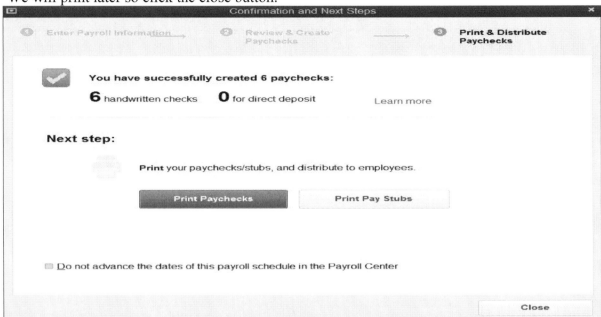

Create Paychecks schedule has now changed to the next pay period. Click the Pay Liabilities Tab next.

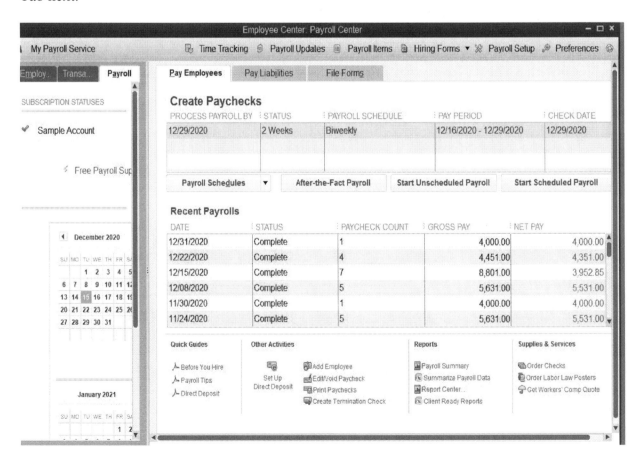

Normally when I do payroll I have liabilities due sooner than 4 weeks, but this is a sample company file. If we were paying them we would click on taxes that we are paying then click on view and pay then you would epay. Next click on File Forms tab to see what needs to be done.

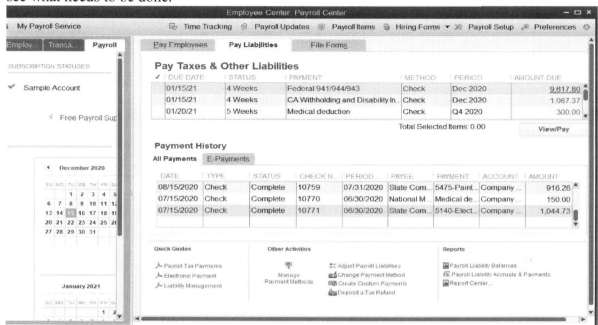

There is nothing due on the File Forms at this time. To exit the Employee Center just click the x in the upper right hand corner or you can always press the Esc button to take you out of any screen.

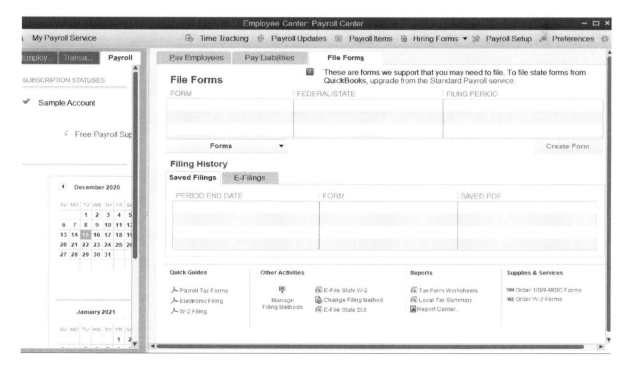

See on the next page payroll reports.

QuickBooks For Contractors

Payroll Reports

There are many reports to choose from. We will go over more of these reports in the Reports Chapter. I have ran two for you to see to put with your payroll if necessary. To run these reports do the following:

1. Click on Reports at the top of the main Menu Bar.
2. Click Employees & Payroll
3. Select Payroll Summary for this report
4. Select Payroll Liability Balances for the next report.

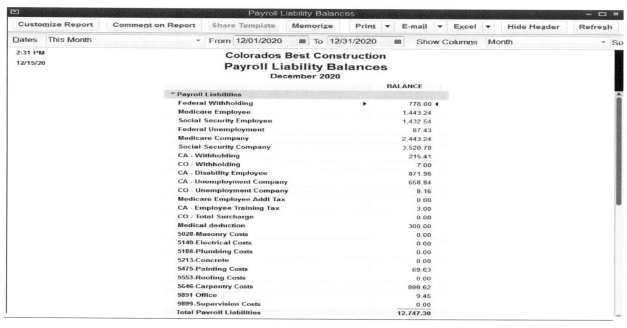

Edit Paychecks

Open the Employee Center by clicking on the Employee Center Icon on the Home Page in the Employee area. To Edit an Employee do the following:

1. Highlight the employee you want to open a paycheck to edit
2. Click on the paycheck you need to edit

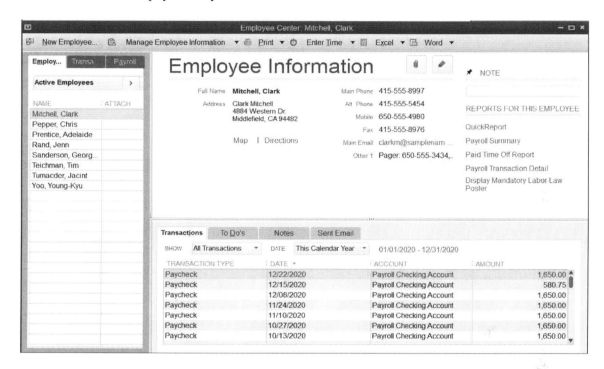

This check number was wrong, so I changed it. Then click Save & Close.

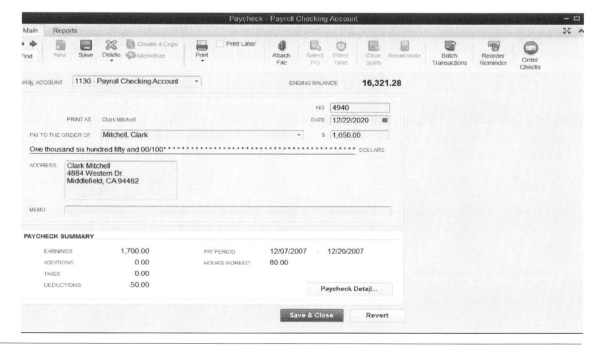

QuickBooks For Contractors

Void Paychecks

Open the Employee Center by clicking on the Employee Center Icon on the Home Page in the Employee area. To void a paycheck do the following:

1. Highlight the employee you want to open a paycheck to void
2. Click on the paycheck you need to void
3. Click on Edit at the top of the main Menu Bar
4. Click Void paycheck.

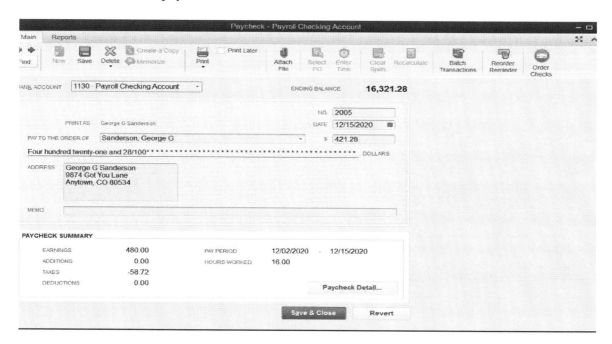

See the red arrows after voiding the check. It says VOID in the memo and the check is 0.00. Click Save & Close. You can delete a paycheck, but I would just void it to have that paper trail.

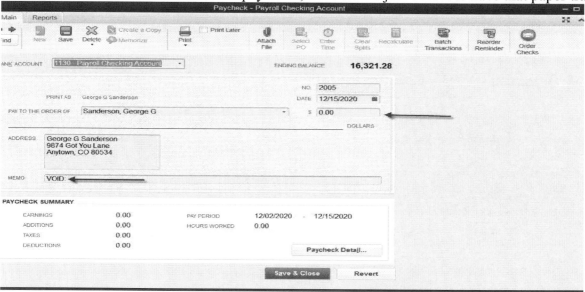

Employee Forms

QuickBooks has built in the main Employee forms you need that you can fill in and print. Now you don't have to buy or look for them online and print. Just Click on Employees at the top main menu bar, select Employee Forms and click on the form you need.

This form is one page of the I-9 form

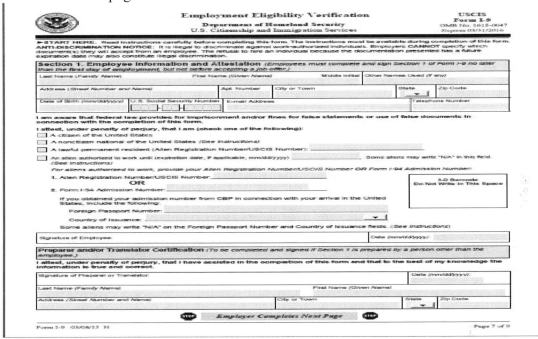

One page of the W-4 form.

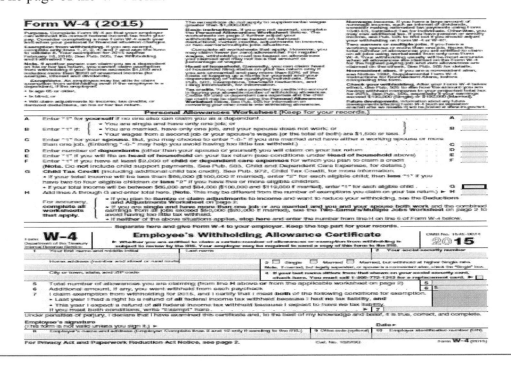

One page of the W-9 (1099) form

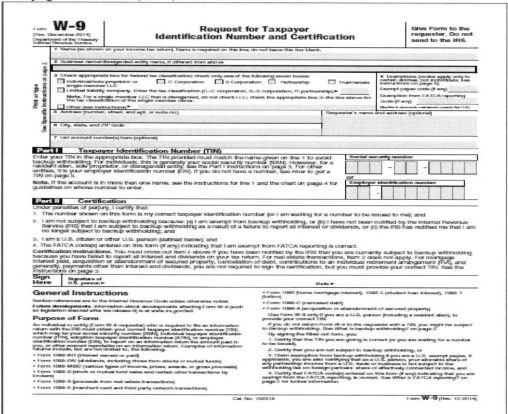

The Direct Deposit Authorization Form

After the Fact Payroll

After-the-fact payroll requires an Enhanced Payroll for Accountants subscription.

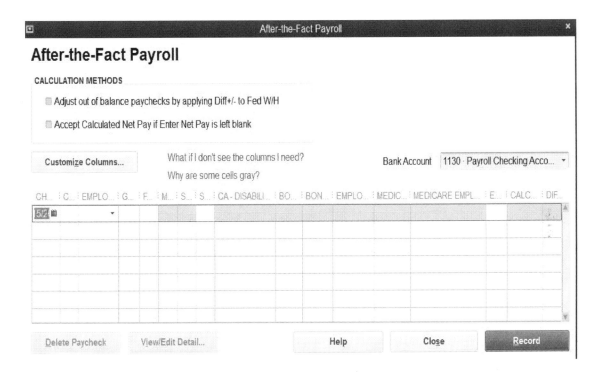

This feature is good if you are just starting QuickBooks and you want to say start entering transactions from the first of the year then you can add your payroll this way. Maybe you need your accountant to make adjustments then you can do that as well.

Worker's Compensation

Intuit offers a pay as you go Worker's Compensation. Go to the top main menu bar and click Employees and select Workers Compensation. Gives you two options. You can sign up for this service or you can manually track existing Workers Comp policy.

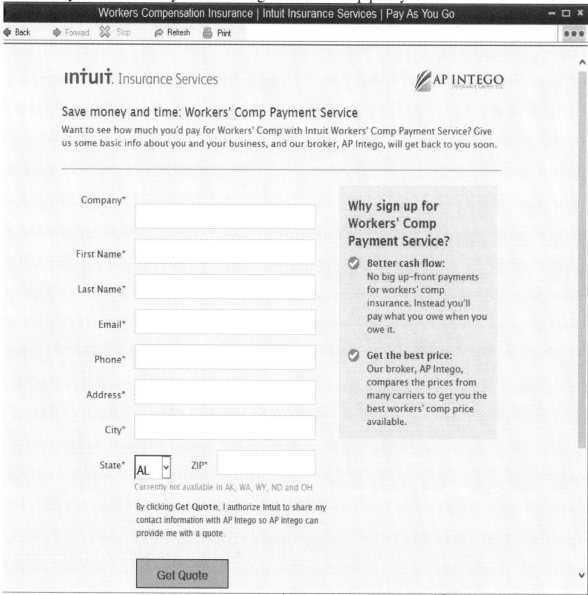

Setting up the manual Workers Compensation feature *before* you run a payroll

First, you need to set up the manual Workers Compensation feature using the Workers Compensation Setup wizard. This wizard helps you assign default workers compensation codes to employees, decide whether you want to exclude overtime premiums from workers compensation premium calculations, and enter an experience modification factor, if you have one.

Then, each time you write a paycheck, QuickBooks accrues workers compensation premiums for each earnings item that has a workers compensation code assigned to it. If you assigned a default code to an employee in the workers compensation setup, QuickBooks automatically assigns that code to the employee's earnings items on their paychecks.

To see how much workers compensation accrues on each paycheck, look for Workers Compensation in the Company Summary portion of the Preview Paycheck window.

When you want to find out how much you've accrued in workers compensation premiums, you can run a Workers Compensation Summary report.

Since your workers compensation premiums accrue as payroll liabilities, when it comes time to pay your premiums, you'll use the Pay Liabilities window to create a payroll liability check.

Manually Track Workers Compensation Setup

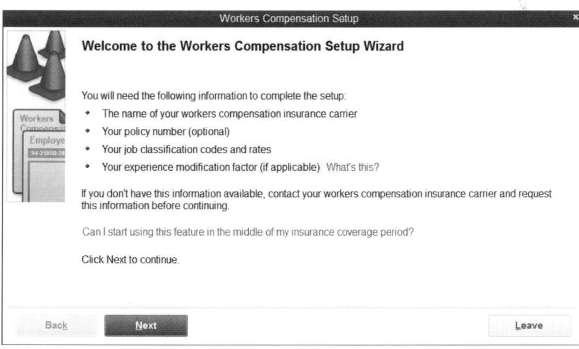

Click Next

Enter the name of your workers comp carrier. If not setup then you need to set them up as a vendor. Enter policy number and policy end date and click next.

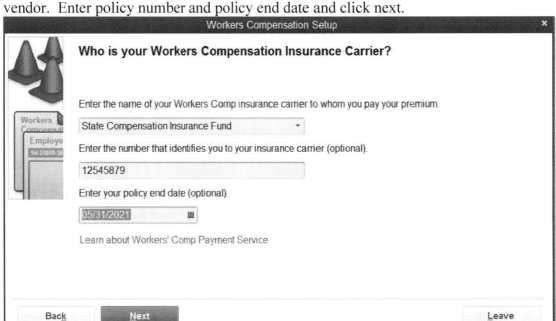

If your Workers comp codes aren't setup yet you can do so here. When done click next.

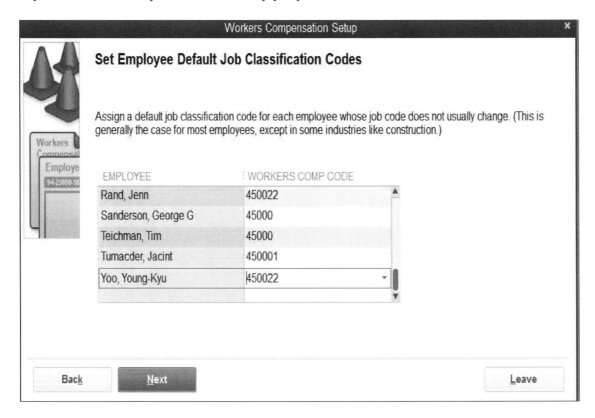

Enter your experience modification factor if you use one and the date goes into effect and click next.

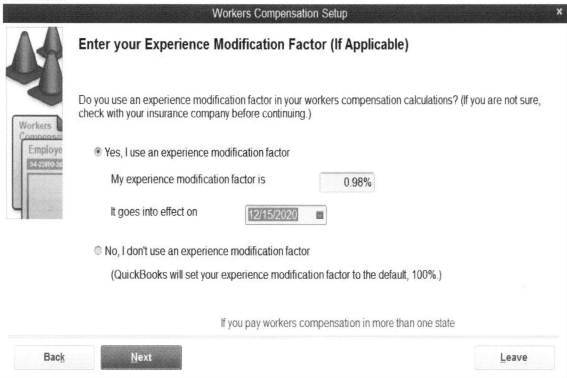

If you pay overtime wages select yes and click next.

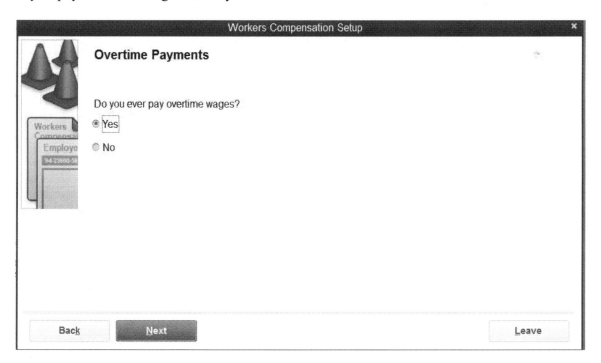

Make your selection below and click next.

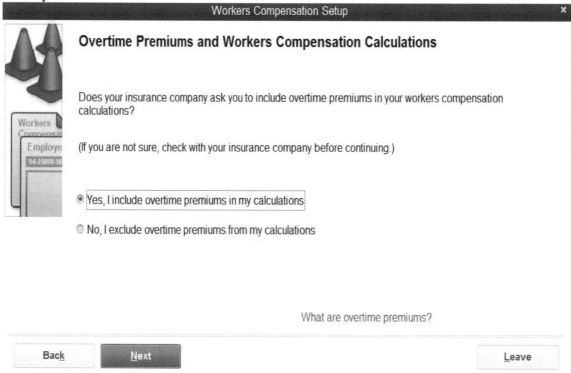

Give your Payroll Item a name and click next.

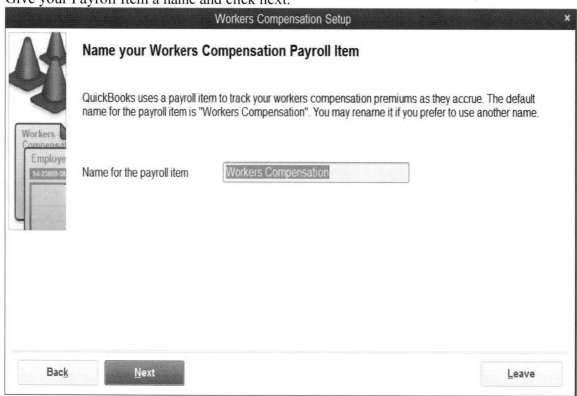

You have successfully completed the Workers Compensation setup wizard. Click Finish.

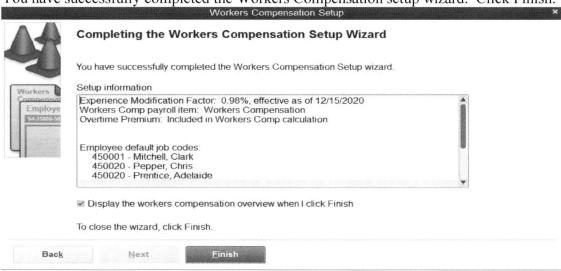

Workers Comp Code List - You can add, edit or delete and make inactive along with running reports or editing your Experience Modification. Access this from Employees from main menu bar, select Workers Compensation then choose Workers Comp Code List and Choose Workers Comp Summary report here as well.

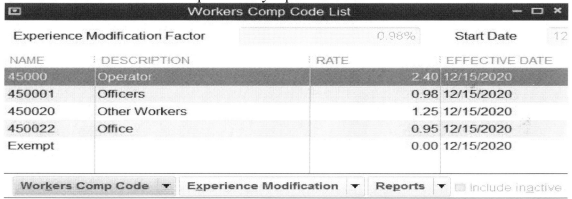

Workers Compensation Summary Report

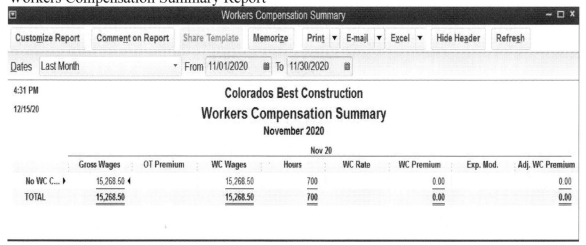

Chapter 11
Banking

This chapter covers everything with Banking from writing checks, transferring money, making deposits, credit cards, loans to reconciling bank and credit card accounts. You should have already setup your bank accounts, so we are going to go through this exercise as though you have. We will set up your credit cards in this chapter.

Writing Checks

Click on the Write Checks Icon located on the Home Page in the Banking Section as shown below in the screenshot.

Enter Vendor Name and the remaining information and click save & Close. We will print later. If you want to print now just click on print button and print. Make sure you have your check in the printer ready.

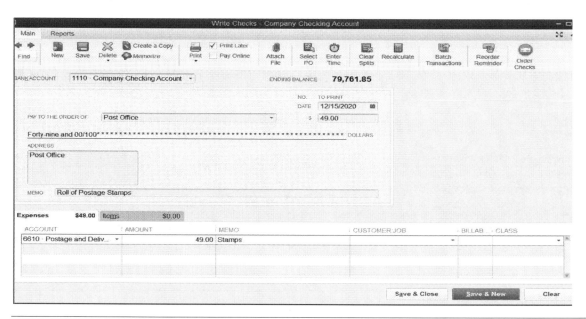

Transfer Funds

You can transfer funds between checking, savings, and money market accounts in your chart of accounts, but you cannot transfer funds between A/P and A/R accounts. For example, you might need to transfer funds from a savings account to a checking account to cover your weekly payroll, or you might want to transfer funds from your checking account to your petty cash account as shown below. **Note:** Once you make this transfer you need to go online or another way of your choice to make your banking transfer/transactions.

1. Click on Banking in the top Main Menu Bar
2. Select Transfer Funds
3. Fill in the following funds information and click Save & Close.

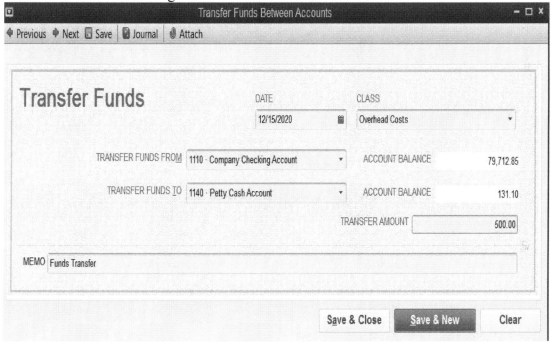

Bank Feeds

With bank feeds, you can download transactions from your financial institution or credit card provider into QuickBooks. Then you can see what transactions have cleared your account, find out your current balance, and add transactions that have been processed but aren't in QuickBooks yet.

Financial institutions provide different levels of bank feeds service. Some do not offer it at all. Others provide enhanced services, such as allowing QuickBooks to transfer money between two online accounts. Check with your financial institution to see what services it offers. See Screenshots below. I chose chase since it is a popular bank for this exercise.

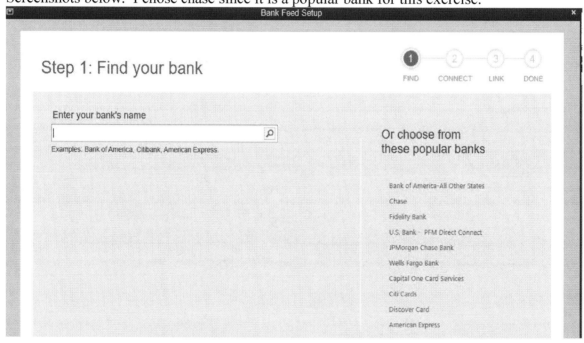

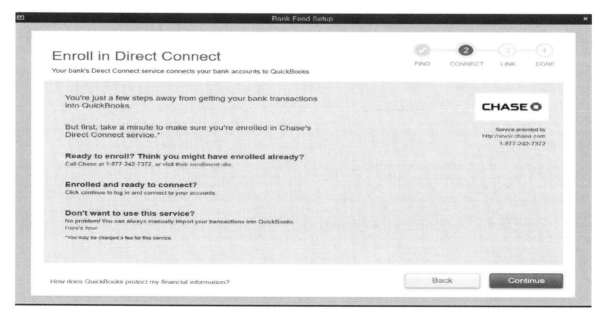

Bank Feed Setup Continued. Enter your Banking ID, click on connect and link your account.

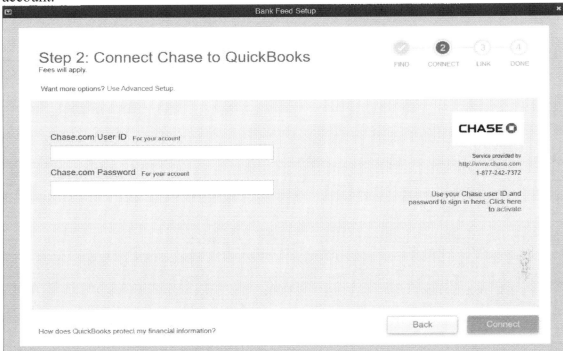

Participating financial Institution Directory/Listing

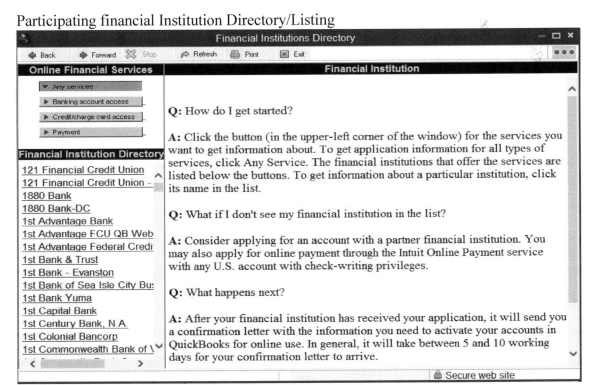

To access this listing Click on Banking at the top main menu bar, select Bank Feeds then choose Participating financial institutions.

Import Web Connect File

Sometimes, when you download an electronic statement from your banking Web site, your Web browser saves it as a file on your hard drive instead of opening it in QuickBooks.

When this happens, you can manually import the file into QuickBooks:

a. Locate the .QBO file on your hard drive and note where it is.
b. In QuickBooks, go to the File menu and click Utilities, then click Import, and then click Web Connect Files.
c. Navigate to the .QBO file and select it.
d. Click Open.

QuickBooks processes the file.

Bank Feeds Mode

You can change your bank feeds mode by going into Preferences. Click on Edit at the top of the main menu bar and choose Preferences then select the Checking Preference.

Order Checks & Envelopes

You can order your checks, envelopes, business cards and more from QuickBooks online. To do this click on Banking at the top main menu bar, select Order Checks & Envelopes and it will take you to the following screenshot below.

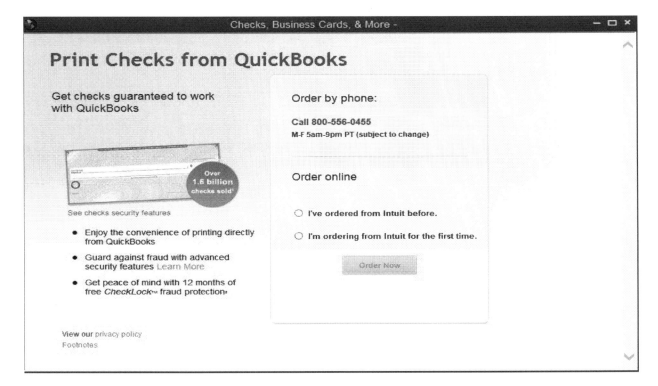

Use Checking Register

The check register is probably the most used register. It's like the old hand written check registers we used to use to record our checks and deposits. You can enter banking transactions manually as well as writing checks or entering deposits.

Click on the Check Register Icon on the Home Page under the Banking section. To enter a transaction click on the first open line. Enter date, check number or transaction number, payee/vendor, the amount, the account and memo if needed then record. To enter a deposit fill in the date, the payee/customer then deposit amount, account and memo if necessary and click record.

You can void, delete, edit or memorize a check from the register.

1. Open the Check Register and highlight check to make changes to.
2. Click on Edit on the top main menu bar.
3. Select action such as void, delete, edit or memorize the check.
4. Click Record when finished.

Record Deposits

To record a deposit click on Record Deposits on the Home Page under Banking Section.

Notice the Deposit to is set on Savings Account? Always make sure this Deposit to is set to the right banking account. This is probably the biggest error I and my clients make. Next make sure the date is the correct date. The Memo will say Deposit by default, you can change or add to that. Click on received from and enter where the payment came from, then the account it goes to, enter memo information if necessary, check number (if a check) payment method, class if you track this and the amount. You can continue to add more deposits. When finished entering deposits click Save & Close. There is a cash back entry at the bottom, but with a business account you can't get cash back from a deposit, so you will have to write a check or use a debit/check card connected to your account. This cash back works for personal accounts.

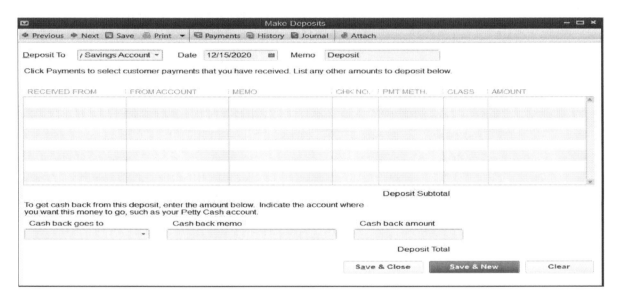

Deposit Entered - Enter the information shown in the screenshot below. Click Save & Close.

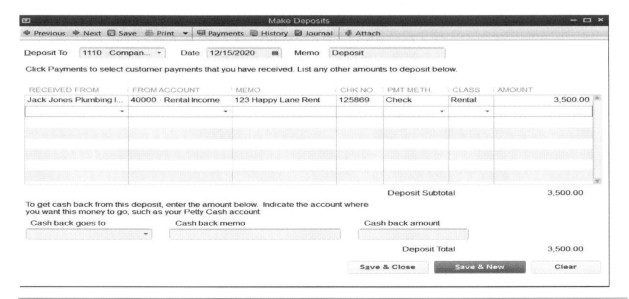

Record Deposits from Payments Received

Click on Receive Payments from the Home Page under the Customers Section. Enter the Information below in the Screenshot and Click Save & Close. Notice this is a partial payment and it states at the bottom in the underpayment section, "Leave this as an underpayment?" If the payment is a few cents or dollars then you can write that off the extra amount or you don't have to it's a choice as to your needs.

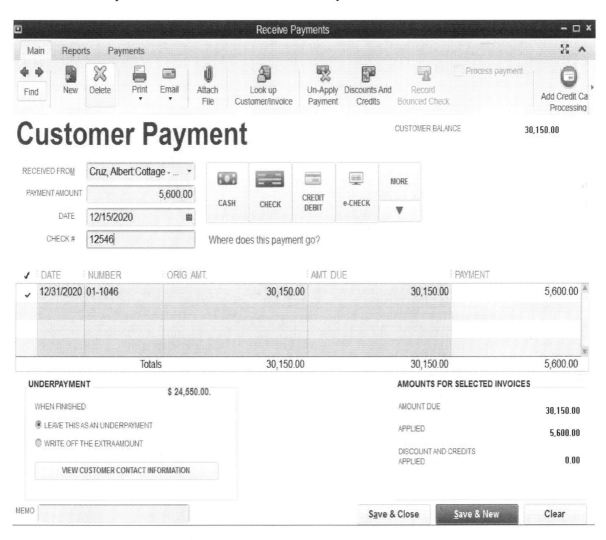

Record the Customer Payment

You need to record the customer payment when you are ready to take the deposit to the bank if it's a check or a form of payment that needs to be taken to the bank.

Click on Record Deposits from the Home Page under the Banking Section. The following Screen, Payments to Deposit, pops up. Place check mark next to the check listed and click ok or you can click on the select all button and click ok.

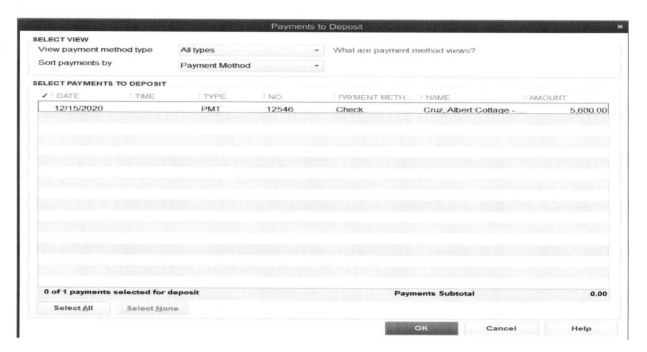

This screen pops up. Make sure being deposited to the correct banking account and date. When finished click Print if printing out deposit slip and click Save & Close.

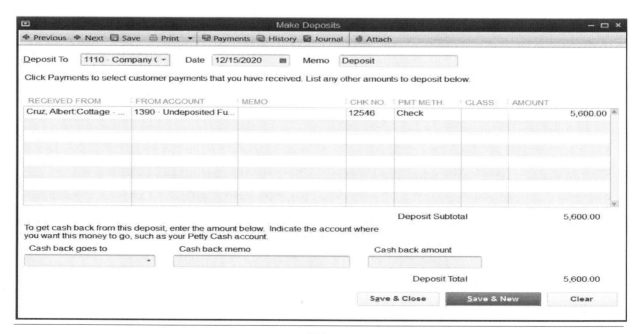

Reconciling Checking Account

Reconciling your account—matching the balances for your paper statement and QuickBooks account—is a two-step process in QuickBooks. First you'll compare the beginning balance on your bank statement to the beginning balance in QuickBooks, and make sure the information for the account you want to reconcile in QuickBooks is correct. Then you'll compare individual transactions and reconcile your account.

1. Click on the Reconcile Icon on the Home Page under the Banking Section.
2. Enter the ending balance from your bank statement that you are going to reconcile
3. Enter service and/or interest charges if any. Make sure you have correct accounts & dates.
4. Make sure you have the correct bank checking account and the dates are correct.
5. Click Continue

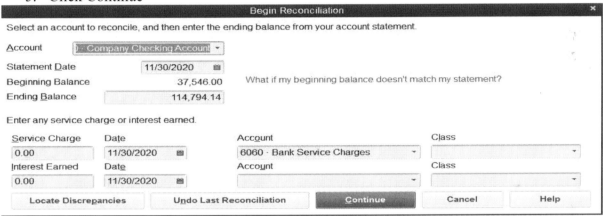

Place check mark by cleared checks and payments and deposits. When you have reconciled you should have entered all transactions and the balance at the bottom of the screen should be 0.00, then Click the Reconcile Now button.

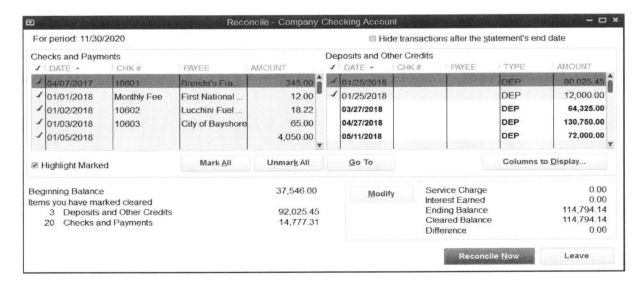

Once your reconciliation has finished the Select Reconciliation Report will pop up. Make your selection as to whether you want to display, print or both the summary and/or Detail Report. You can also just click Close if you don't want to display or print. You can always go back and print or display the report as well.

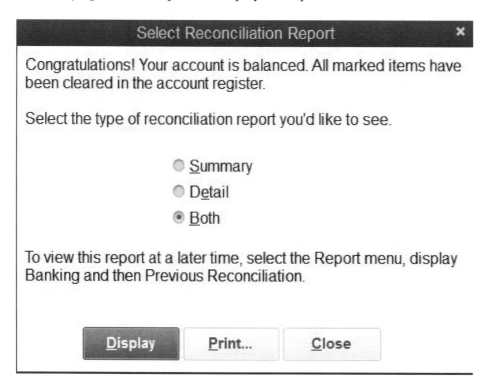

You need to reconcile all your banking accounts each month and that includes not only checking and savings accounts, but loans such as lines of credit along with Credit Cards.

We will be setting up, entering credit card charges and reconciling the statement on the next page.

Credit Cards

You can set up your credit cards as a chart of accounts account, enter credit card transactions and reconciling the credit card accounts each month.

To set up a credit card Chart of Accounts Account do the following:

1. Click on the Chart of Accounts Icon on the Home Page located in the Company section.
2. Click on the Account Tab at the bottom of the screen
3. Click on New
4. Select Credit Card as the Account Type and Click Continue
5. Type in the name of the Credit Card
6. Enter the Chart of Accounts number, if you are using numbers
7. Click Save & Close

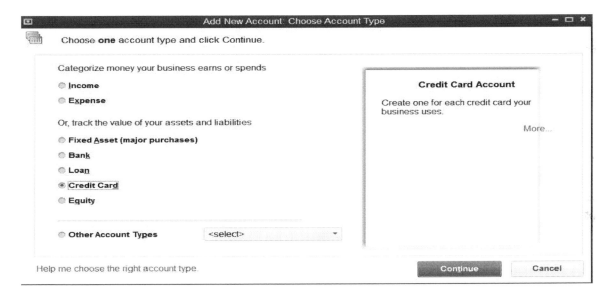

New Credit Card added.

Entering Credit Card Charges

This is a new credit card, so we are going to start entering charges and then reconcile the account. Click on the Enter Credit Card Charges Icon on the Home Page in the Banking Section.

Here's the screen to enter credit card charges. Be sure you have the correct Credit Card displayed in the Credit Card drop down box. If you are entering charges be sure the Purchase/Charge button is clicked and if you are entering a refund/credit click that button. This is steps to enter manually and you can also set up to download card charges by clicking on the Download card charges button. You will need to setup up your credit card to download the charges.

Enter these Credit Card Charges and when finished we will reconcile the account.

Reconciling Credit Cards

Click on the Reconcile Icon on the Home Page in the Banking Section. Notice the red arrow pointing to Account? Make sure you have the account on the correct one. As you can see it's the credit card we just setup in the Chart of Accounts. Make sure the date is correct and enter the Ending Balance from your credit card statement. If you have any interest you would enter that and the date along with the correct interest account and click continue.

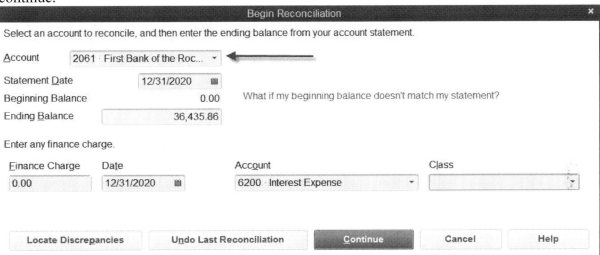

This being the first reconciliation there was no interest to enter or many charges as you can see below. Place a check mark by all the transactions and click Reconcile Now button.

This screen pops up after clicking Reconcile Now Button. Make your choice and click ok.

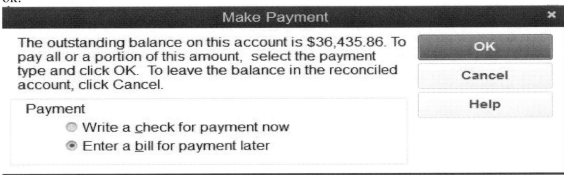

This Box appears just as it did when we reconciled the checking account. Make your selections and display, print or close. Remember you can display or print later as well.

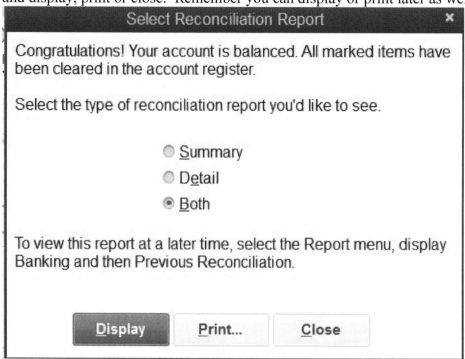

This screen popped up as well. It's the Credit Card Bill we selected to enter for payment. The Vendor is not showing up because I need to enter the Credit Card Vendor to where the payments need to be sent. Set the Vendor up and click Save & Close.

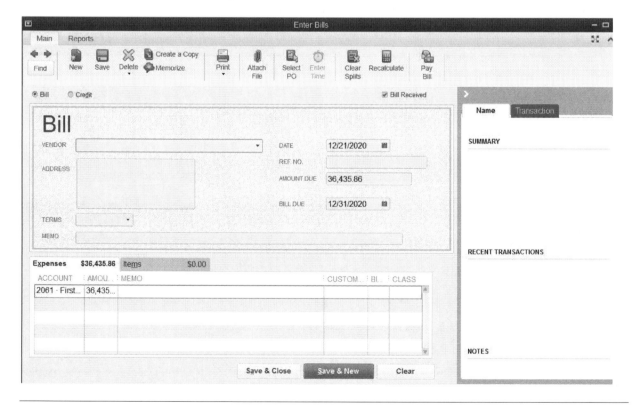

Chapter 12
Print & Send Forms

If you don't print checks or most of your other forms such as Invoices or purchase orders right away because you plan to print later is what this chapter is about and how to do that. There are eleven items/forms you can print this way. We will cover each one. You will do the following steps when you want to print any of the eleven available to print later.

1. Click on File at the top of the Main Menu Bar.
2. Select Print Forms
3. Select Bill Payment Stubs

This Select Bill Payment Stubs to Print pops up. Select the ones you want to print and click ok.

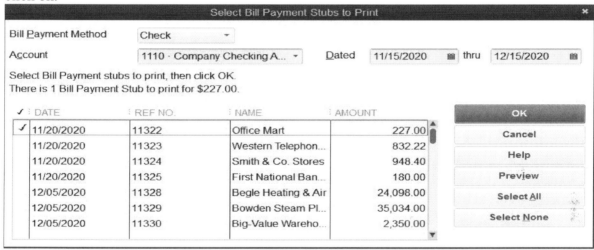

The screenshot below is a copy of the Bill Payment Stub. You may want to print out for your files and/or to send in with bill payments to vendors.

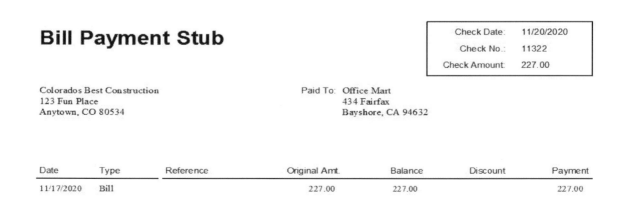

QuickBooks For Contractors

Printing Checks

1. Click on File at the top of the Main Menu Bar.
2. Select Print Forms
3. Select Checks

Click the Checks you want to print and click ok.

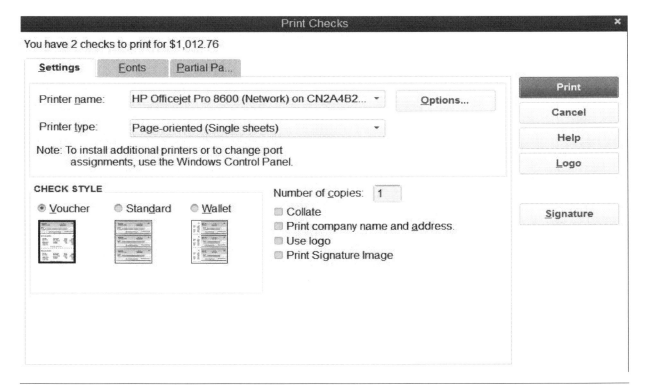

This Print Checks screen pops up next. Make sure you have the right printer and the check style is correct. You can also add logo or insert a Print Signature. When finished and ready to print click the Print button to print your checks after you have placed your checks in the printer to print.

Credit Memos

1. Click on File at the top of the Main Menu Bar.
2. Select Print Forms
3. Select Credit Memos

Select Credit memos to Print screen pops up. Place check mark next to Credit Memos you want to print and click ok.

The screenshot below is a Credit Memo that was printed.

Colorados Best Construction

123 Fun Place
Anytown, CO 80534

Credit Memo

Date	Credit No.
12/30/2019	Bad Debt

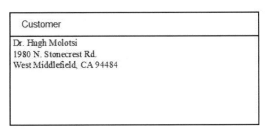

	P.O. No.	Project
		Second Story Addition

Description	Qty	Rate	Amount
Customer said carpenter broke his new bay window and refuses to pay last $2,500 on invoice.	-1	2,500.00	-2,500.00

QuickBooks For Contractors

Invoices

1. Click on File at the top of the Main Menu Bar.
2. Select Print Forms
3. Select Invoices
4. Place check mark next to the invoices you want to print or if you want to print them all click on the Select all button and click ok.

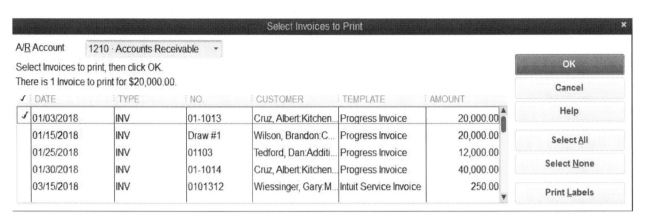

The screenshot below is a printed invoice. The paid stamp will only show up when the invoice is paid. If you ran a batch of invoices not yet paid then this paid stamp would not show up.

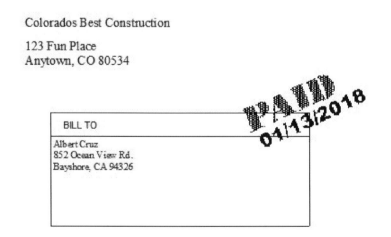

			P.O. NO.	TERMS	PROJECT	
					Kitchen Remodel	

ITEM	DESCRIPTION	Est Amt	Prior Amt	Prior %	RATE	Curr %	Total %	AMOUNT
FP Billing	10% due when materials arrive on jobsite	20,000.00			200,000.00	100.00%	100.00%	20,000.00

214

Labels

1. Click on File at the top of the Main Menu Bar.
2. Select Print Forms
3. Select Labels
4. Select All Names or Multiple Names.
5. You can choose Customer Types and Vendor Types
6. You can choose certain Zip Codes
7. Sort Labels by Name or Zip Code
8. Print labels for inactive names, print Ship to Addresses or Print Labels for jobs.
9. After making your choices then click ok

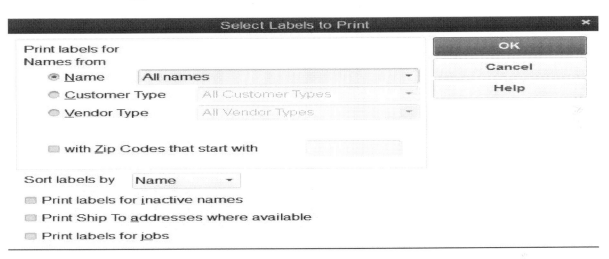

As you can see the Print Labels screen pops up and you will need to not only make sure correct printer is selected, but the Label Format as well. See the Label below Avery #5261. You need to make sure the labels are correct or you will ruin the labels and have to reprint. Also make sure the printing Direction and Label Print Range along with number of copies are right. When finished with options click Print after you place your labels in the printer.

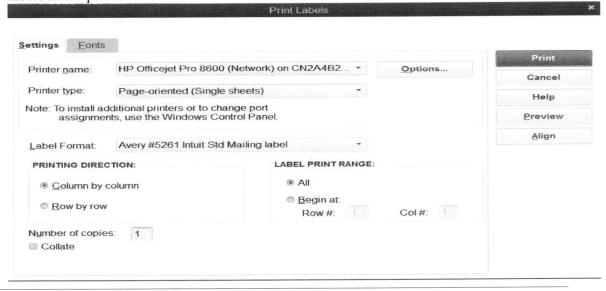

Print Paychecks

1. Click on File at the top of the Main Menu Bar.
2. Select Print Forms
3. Select Paychecks
4. For this exercise there are no paychecks needing to print, but when you do have paychecks to print you will place check mark either next to the ones you want to print or select all and click ok. Make sure you have the check number right and you have placed the right paychecks in the print to print.

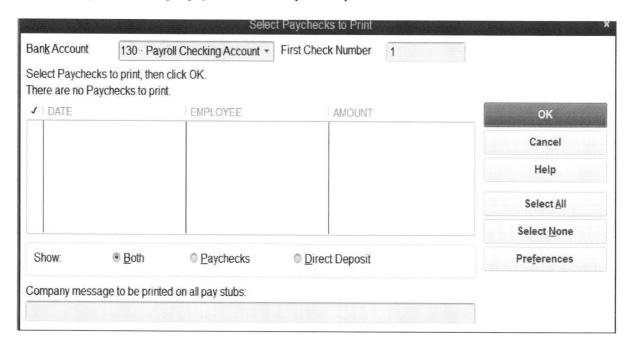

Pay Stubs

1. Click on File at the top of the Main Menu Bar.
2. Select Print Forms
3. Select Pay Stubs
4. Place check marks next to the paystubs you want to print or Select All. Click the Print button

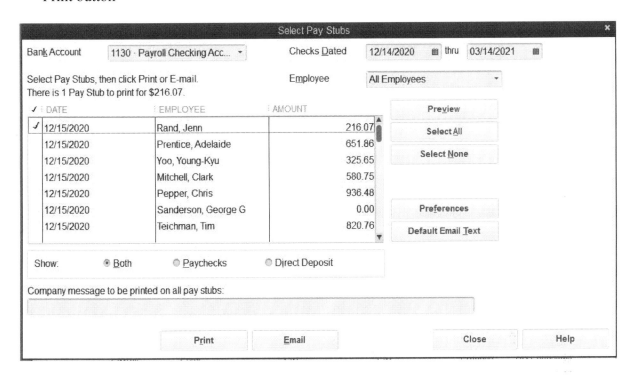

Screenshot of printed pay stub.

QuickBooks For Contractors

Purchase Orders

1. Click on File at the top of the Main Menu Bar.
2. Select Print Forms
3. Select Purchase Orders
4. Place check marks next to the purchase orders you want to print or Select All. Click the Print button

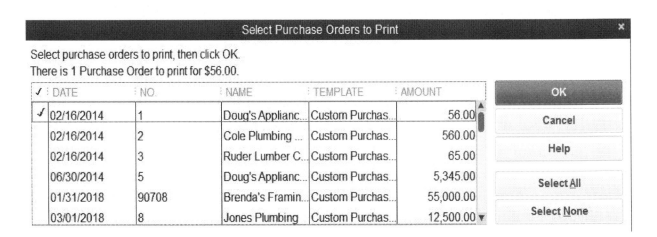

Screenshot of a printed purchase order. If you haven't received your purchase for this purchase order it will not say Received in Full.

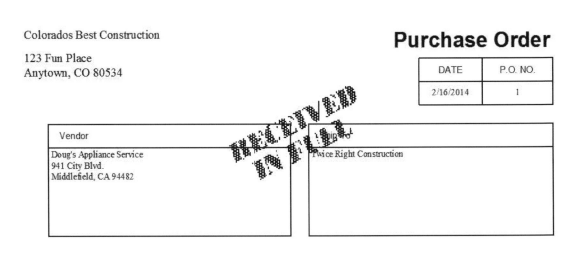

218

Sales Receipt

1. Click on File at the top of the Main Menu Bar.
2. Select Print Forms
3. Select Sales Receipt
4. Place check marks next to the Sales Receipts you want to print or Select All. Click the Print button

Select Receipts to Print

Select Sales Receipts to print, then click OK.
There are 2 Sales Receipts to print for $27,500.00.

✓	DATE	NO.	CUSTOMER	TEMPLATE	AMOUNT
✓	01/07/2018	Deposit	Campbell, Heat...	Custom Cash S...	25,000.00
✓	04/07/2018	Advance	Wiessinger, Gar...	Custom Cash S...	2,500.00

Buttons: OK, Cancel, Help, Select All, Select None

Screenshot of Printed Sales Receipt

Colorados Best Construction

123 Fun Place
Anytown, CO 80534

Sales Receipt

DATE	SALE NO.
1/7/2018	Deposit

SOLD TO
Heather Campbell
2950 Harley Ave.
Middlefield, CA 94482

CHECK NO.	PAYMENT METH...	PROJECT
4564	Check	House-New Constru...

DESCRIPTION	QTY	RATE	AMOUNT
Customer Deposit on Job	1	25,000.00	25,000.00

Timesheets

1. Click on File at the top of the Main Menu Bar.
2. Select Print Forms
3. Select Timesheets
4. Place check marks next to the Timesheets you want to print or Select All. Click ok. Then Click print.

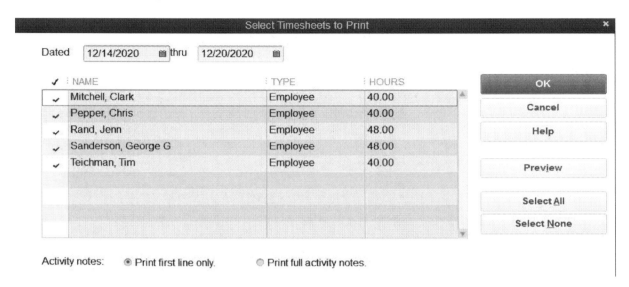

Screenshot of Printed Timesheet.

1099s/1096

1. Click on File at the top of the Main Menu Bar.
2. Select Print Forms
3. Select 1099s/1096
4. Place check marks next to the 1099 vendors you want to print or Select All. Click Continue.

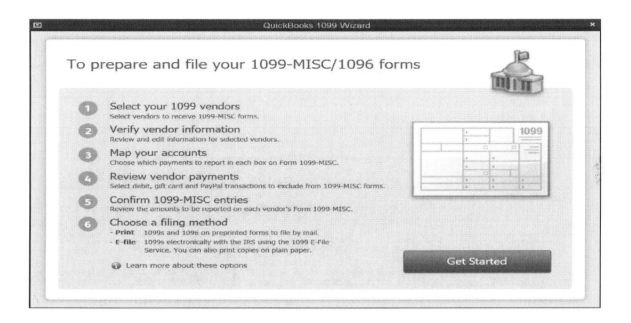

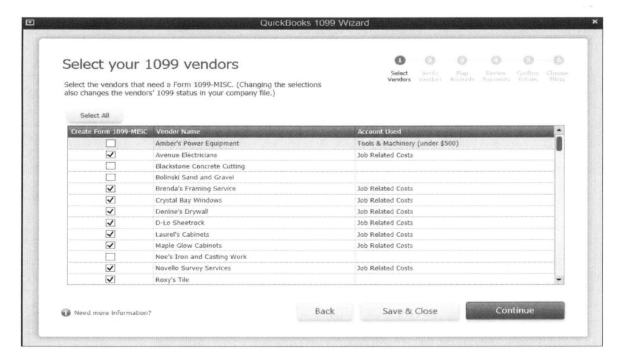

Click continue

QuickBooks For Contractors

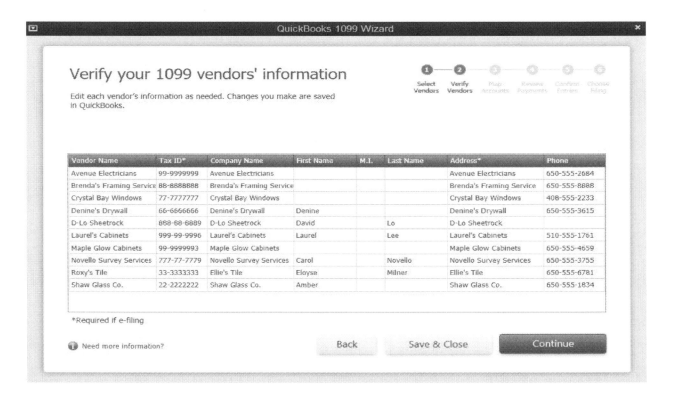

Click continue

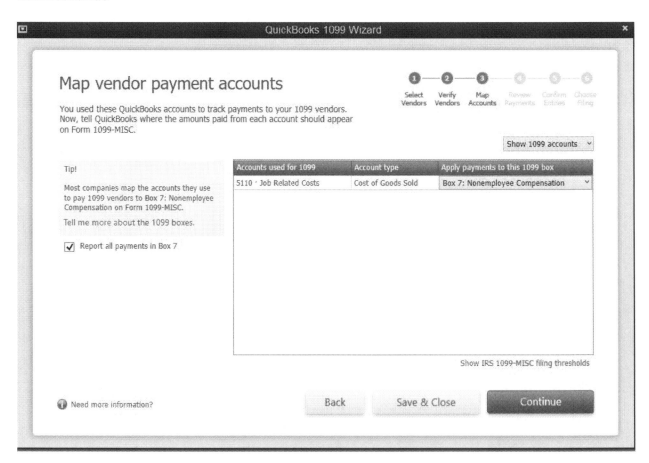

Review payments and exclusions and click continue.

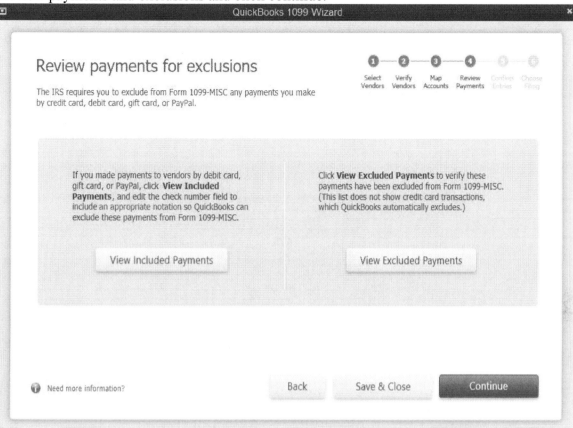

Make sure the transactions are correct and click continue.

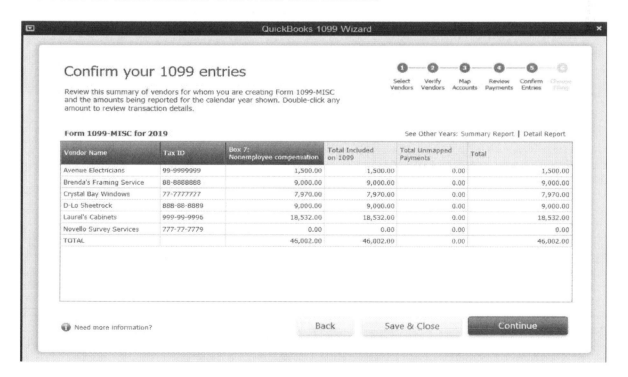

You can either Print 1099's or E-File the 1099's or you can save and close.

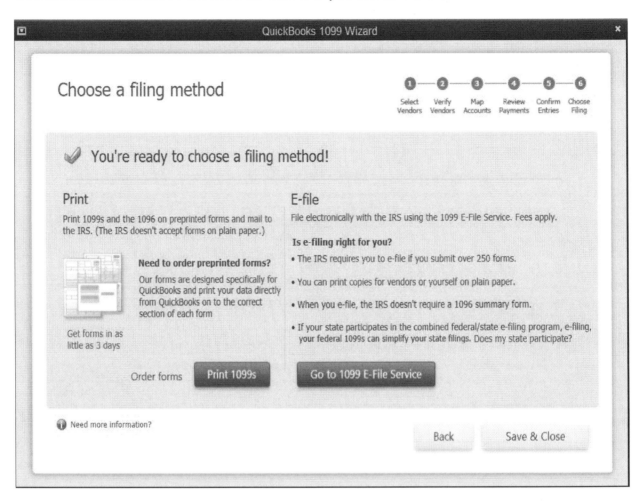

Chapter 13
Reports

QuickBooks provides many preset reports that focus on all aspects of your business finances. These reports answer many of your business questions, such as: How much do your customers owe you? How much do you owe for the business items you've purchased? Bottom line, how is your business doing?

The best way to find the report you need is to use the Report Center, where you can: Browse through report categories find what you need or close to what you need and then customize it. Learn what a report will tell you by viewing sample report images and report descriptions. Create and access a list of your favorite reports. Quickly access recently viewed reports. Search for a report based on words found in its title or description. Find more reports on the Intuit Community site. The most commonly used reports are the following:

To find out how well your company is doing

Profit & Lose Standard - Will show you how much money your company made or lost over a certain period of time. This report is also called an income statement.

Profit & Loss by Class - This report will show you how much money your company made or lost on each business segment that is tracked through QuickBooks classes.

Balance Sheet Standard - This report gives you the value of your companies, assets, liabilities and equity, showing the balances for each account.

Balance Sheet by Class - This gives you the balance sheet for each aspect of your business that you are tracking by class.

Statement of Cash Flows - This report gives you the cash inflow from profit and additional cash received and cash outflow, cash spent, during a certain time frame.

To find out how much your customers owe and when it is due

Open Invoices - This report shows which customer invoices and statement charges haven't been paid and when they are due.

Customer Balance Detail - This report displays the payments and invoices that have each customer's current balance.

Accounts Receivable Aging Summary - This report will show you how much each customer owes and how much of each customer's balance is overdue.

Most Commonly Used Reports Continued

To find out how much money your company owes & how much of it is overdue

Vendor Balance Detail - This report gives you your company's total purchases, broken down by transaction from each vendor.

Purchases by Vendor Summary - This report will display all your company's purchases from each vendor.

Unpaid Bills Detail - This report will lay out how much your company owes each vendor and whether any payments are overdue.

To find out about account activity

Transaction Detail by Account - This report display's recent transactions and their subtotals for each account in your Chart of Accounts.

To find information about your employees, payroll, and payroll-related expenses

Payroll Summary - This report gives you the accumulated totals for the payroll items, taxes withheld, and so on for each employee's recent paychecks.

Payroll Item Detail - This report gives you the line-by-line breakdown of each current payroll transactions by item.

Payroll Transaction Detail - This report gives the line-by-line breakdown of each recent payroll transaction, by employee.

Access the Report Center - Click on Reports and the top Main Menu Bar and select Report Center.

Snapshot of Report Center in Carousel View

Report Center in List View

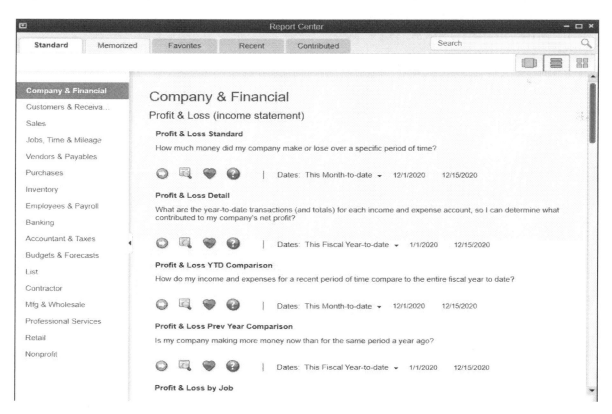

QuickBooks For Contractors

Report Center in Grid View

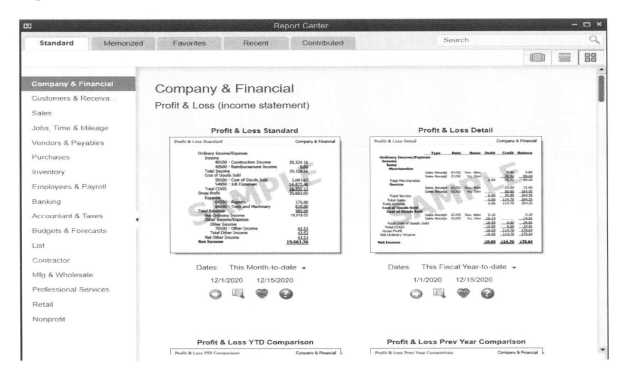

Report Center Contractor Tab

Notice the red arrow in the left column? This column displays all your report categories. This being the accountant edition it gives industry specific reports such as Contactor, Mfg & Wholesale, Professional Services, Retail and Nonprofit.

The Tabbed bar on top of the screen gives you Memorized reports, favorites, recent and contributed reports.

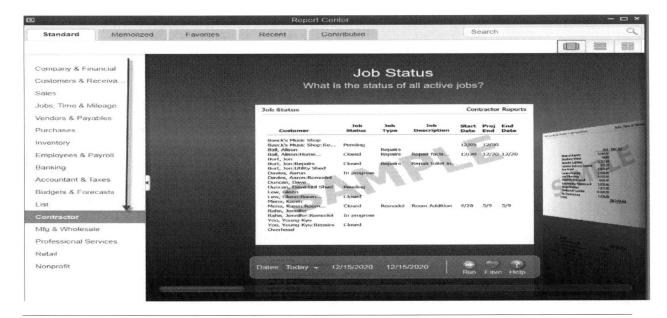

Manage your memorized reports

Click the Memorized Report drop-down arrow to edit or delete a memorized report. You can create a memorized report group, print the list, and more. When you edit a report, you can rename it or move it to another group.

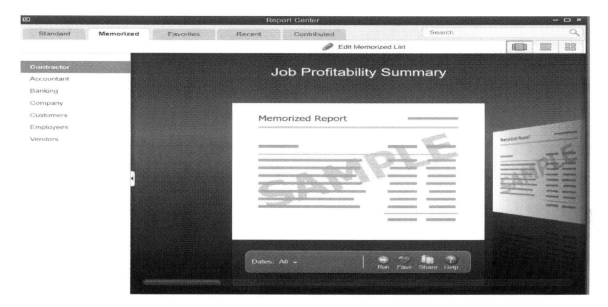

Favorites, Recent and Contributed

You can store you most favorites and go to reports under the Favorites tab. To save report in favorites. Click on the Fave Heart in the screenshot below that is located in Carousel View.

The Recent Tab are Reports that you have ran/viewed recently. You will have this same bar in the Recent Tab as the Favorites tab, so you can Run the report and save as a favorite as well from the Recent tab.

The Contributed Tab gives additional reports submitted by individuals and Intuit for your use and can save you lots of time. As you can see in the screenshot below you can run, Fave and Rate reports.

Customizing Reports

Maybe you are not getting exactly what you need from a report and need to just tweak it a little bit, this is where Customizing Reports comes in to play. To customize a report just pull up the report you want and click on the Customize Report button as shown in the screenshot below with the red arrow pointing to the button.

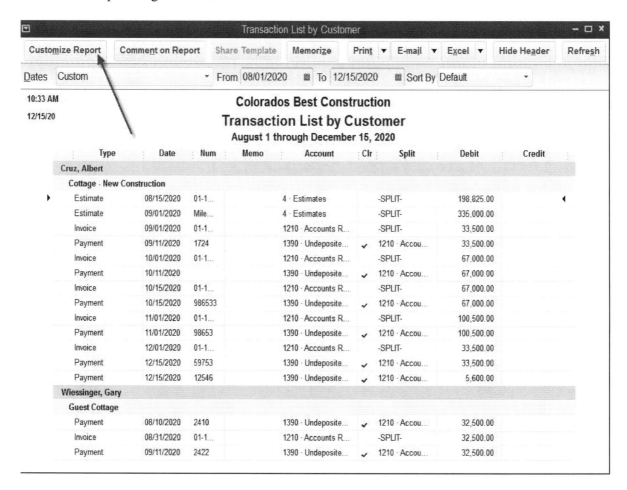

Modify Report Screen

Use the Display options to modify a report

Use the options on the Display tab to modify the appearance of the report data. (**Note:** Not all of these fields are available for every report.) You can:

- Change the date range of the data
- Change the report basis to cash or accrual
- Add or remove columns
- Sort columns
- Group and subtotal the data
- Group data on time reports
- Set advanced options

Click Revert at any time to return to the default settings. (You can do this even after changing the options, then closing and reopening this window.)

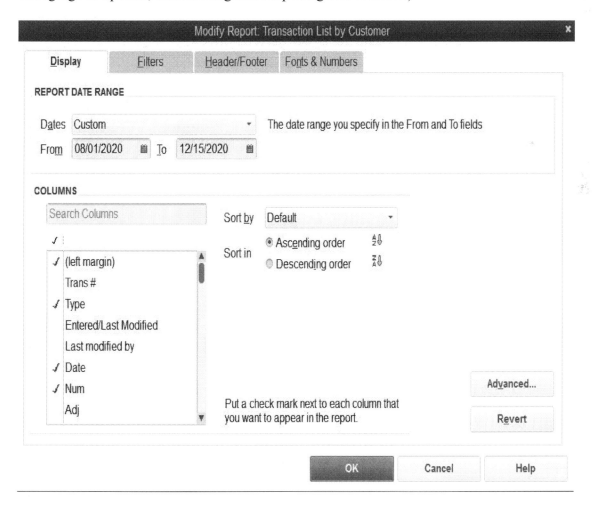

Filters Tab Customizing Reports

When you create a report, it may show more information than you need. For example, a sales by customer report initially shows your sales to all customers for the current month. This would be too much information if all you wanted was to see this month's sales to one of your customers.

Filters let you change the scope of a report. When you apply a filter to a report, you choose how you want QuickBooks to restrict the report; for example, to certain customers. QuickBooks then excludes from the report any transactions that don't meet your criteria. You can apply filters either one at a time or in combination with each other. Each additional filter you apply further restricts the content of the report.

QuickBooks provides many different types of filters for reports. The ones you'll probably want to use most often are: Account, Amount, Date, Item (for the goods or services you sell), Memo (for your memo notes on transactions), Name (for customer, job, vendor, or employee names), Number (for transaction numbers like check numbers), and Type (for specific types of transactions like bills or invoices).

You can also use the Centers to get a filtered list of transactions. For example, another way to find last year's sales to a particular customer is to select that customer in the Customer Center, choose All Sales Transactions from the Show drop-down list above the transactions, and then choose Last Fiscal Year from the Date drop-down list.

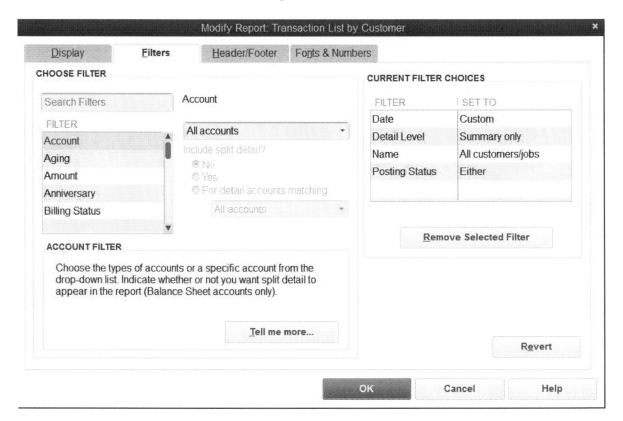

Header/Footer Customizing Reports

To do this task

1. In the Report window, click Customize Report at the top of the report.
2. Select the Header/Footer tab.
3. Change, as needed, the header information.
4. Change, as needed, the footer information.
5. (Optional) Choose a different layout (Left, Right, Centered, or Standard) from the Layout list.
6. Click OK.

Note: You must memorize the report to save your changes.

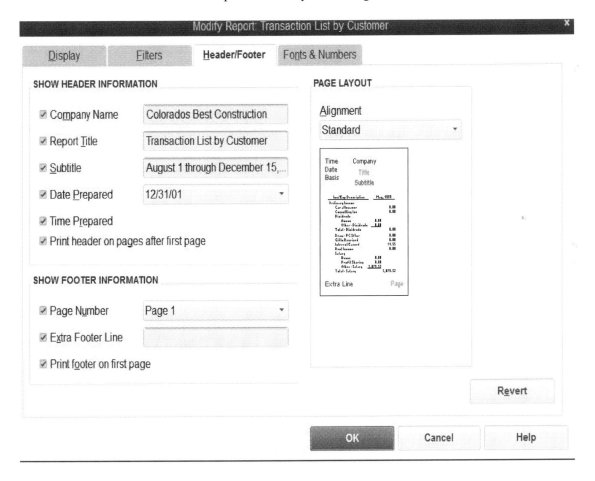

Fonts/Numbers Customizing Reports

Change Fonts

1. Open the report.
2. With the mouse, point to the element whose font you want to change. Click the right mouse button.
3. Select the font, font style, and size you want.
4. Click OK.
5. Click yes if you want your new font selection to apply to all the other elements in the report.

Note: You must memorize the report to save these changes.

Change Numbers

1. In the Report window, click Customize Report, and then click the Fonts & Numbers tab.
2. Select the options you want in the Show Negative Numbers area.
3. Select the options you want in the Show All Numbers area.
4. Click OK.

Note: You must memorize the report to save these changes.

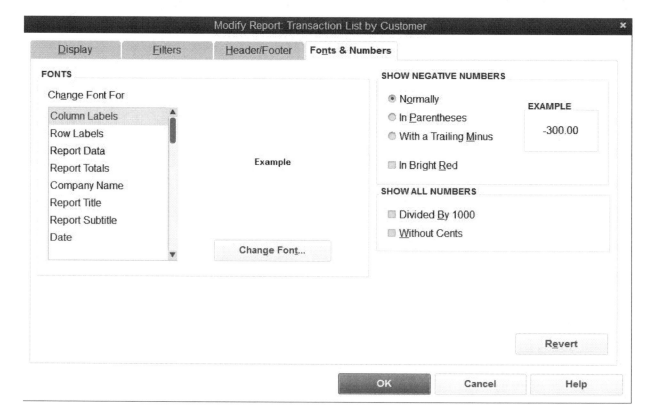

Commented Reports

You can add comments to any report, which you can then save, print, or share.

You can: Add comments to a report, View, edit, or delete comments in a report, Delete a commented report, Rename a commented report and Print or email a commented report.

Add comments by click on the little clear comment box next to each line/column as shown where the red arrow is pointing in the screenshot below. Remember to save when you add comments.

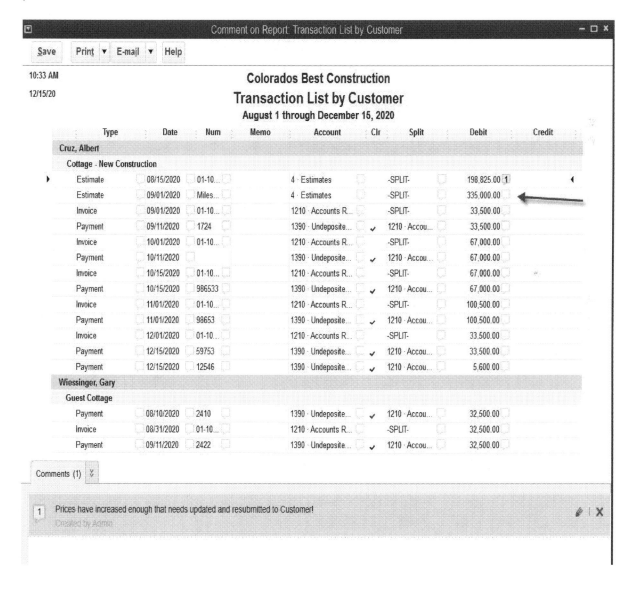

QuickBooks For Contractors

Process Multiple Reports

1. Choose Reports from the top of the main Menu Bar then select Process Multiple Reports.
2. Select the reports you want to print, display, or email. You can process memorized and commented reports at the same time.

To select memorized reports:

At the top of the window, select Memorized Reports.

   a. Click the Select Memorized Reports From drop-down arrow and choose All Reports, Ungrouped Reports, or a specific memorized report group.
   b. Click the column to the left of each report you want to process.

To select commented reports:

   c. At the top of the window, select Commented Reports.
   d. Click the column to the left of each report you want to process.

236

Company Snapshot Report

Use the Company Snapshot to get real-time company information and perform tasks from a single place. This is a great place to start each day along with your reminders.

Depending on your access permissions, you can add any of the following content.

- Income and Expense Trend
- Prev Year Income Comparison
- Account Balances
- Top Customers by Sales
- Customers Who Owe Money

Double-click any reminder, account, customer, or vendor to view details and perform tasks.

- Add content and customize this page
- Set this as your opening page
- Print the entire snapshot, or a single panel
- Choose which accounts and reminders you want to see
- Receive payments
- Pay bills

Chapter 14
Opening Balances

Getting everything going is quite a task, but so worth it. If you are using another Accounting/Bookkeeping Program, just make sure everything balances and is correct before transferring. You don't have to start using and setting up QuickBooks with opening balances. You can always go back and change your beginning balances, but it does save time and make your setting up easier.

You will need to enter beginning balances entering a journal entry if you did not enter balances when setting up your company file. I will show you how to enter balances when setting up a new account now that you have set up your company file and beginning accounts.

To Enter a Journal Entry take the following steps:Click on Company at the top Menu Bar

1. Select Make General Journal Entries
2. Enter Asset, Liability and Capital account balances. Assets usually have debit balances (except accumulated depreciation). Liabilities and Capital have credit balances. See the example Journal Entry Below.

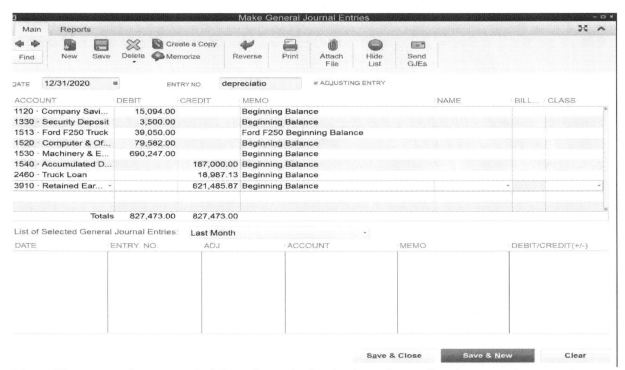

Note: If your starting to use QuickBooks at the beginning of your fiscal year, only enter Asset, Liability, and Capital account balances. Do not enter beginning income, cost of goods sold, or expense account balances.

Once you have finished entering opening balances, print a Balance Sheet to make sure everything is in order and balances.

1. Click on Reports at the top of the Main Menu Bar
2. Select Company & Financial
3. Click Balance Sheet Standard
4. Click Esc button to close the open windows once you have finished or click the X in the top right hand side of the window/report. Be sure it's the X in the report and not the very top of the screen because this will close QuickBooks.

Note: Do not enter Accounts Receivable or Accounts Payable balances. These account balances come in automatically when you enter the outstanding invoices from your Invoices/Receivables and bills owed/Payables.

Entering Invoices for Accounts Receivable

Remember Accounts Receivable is money your customers/clients owe you. If you are using another accounting program, you should be able to print a report with each customer and the balance they owe you.

Click on the Create Invoices Icon and enter an invoice for each customer/client outstanding balances as shown in the screen shot below.

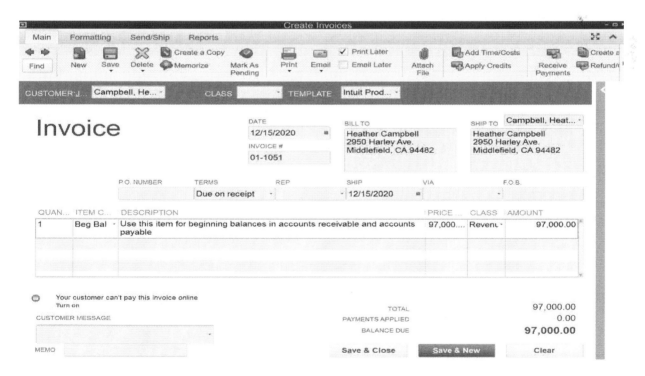

Note: if you have not set up Beg Bal in the items you will need to do so before entering invoices.

QuickBooks For Contractors

Entering Bills for Accounts Payable

Accounts payable is money you owe to vendors, subcontractors and other things. If you are currently using another accounting program, you should be able to just run a quick report with vendor name, date of each outstanding invoice/bill, invoice/bill number along with amount due to enter into QuickBooks.

Click on Enter Bills Icon on the Home Page Under Vendors Section and start entering your outstanding bills. See example below. Make sure you are entering under the Items tab in the bottom of the screen.

Click Save and New until you have entered all outstanding bills and when finished Click Save and Close.

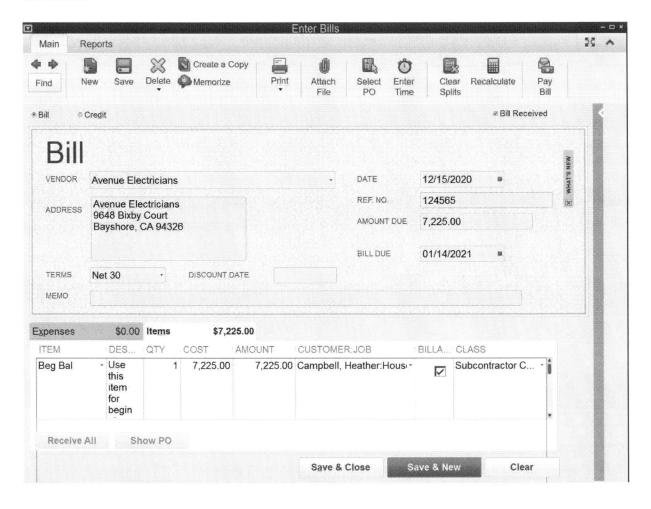

Beginning Job Balances

Entering Beginning job balances by item and or job phases for jobs still in process/progress. You will want to do this or your job reports will not be right because you need to enter the costs prior to using QuickBooks.

1. Click on the Enter Bills Icon on the Home Page under the Vendors section.
2. In the vendor field enter beginning job balances, press tab, at the prompt to enter new vendor click Quick Add.
3. At the Date enter the date one day prior to starting to use QuickBooks. Like if you started using QuickBooks 1/01/16 then you would use the date 12/31/15.
4. In Ref No enter Beg Bal Job and the job name or number
5. In the memo area enter something along the lines like my example.
6. Click the Items tab.
7. Enter the balances by item for this job, including customer job, class information.
8. Make sure Billable field is NOT checked.
9. Enter balances by item again, like above, but with a negative amount. Leave customer job and class blank. This will clear out accounting and leave the job information intact. You want to make sure the amount on the bill is 0 then Click Save & Close.
10. Do this for all your jobs that had balances prior to the date you started using QuickBooks.

Note: Entering each item twice is essential to have all the costs to each job, once to bring in the job and enter second time with a negative quantity to clear the balances from your accounting.

Chapter 15
Payables

In this chapter I will go over entering and using purchase orders to track multiple draws and costs. Entering bills for job-related and overhead expense without purchase orders, selecting bills for payments and printing checks. Payables and vendor workers' comp reports.

I have based everything using the accrual method because of the advantages such as job cost reports will include unpaid vendor bills, accounts payable reports will help track the vendors you owe money to and profitability reports will be more accurate as well.

As always enter as much detail as possible to help make sure you place your expense into job related or non-job related expenses. You want to keep this accurate so you can rest assured you are making a profit, but not over estimating at the same time.

We will be creating and using Purchase orders next. Use purchase orders to track items that you've ordered and check against what you have received. This will help keep track of things too.

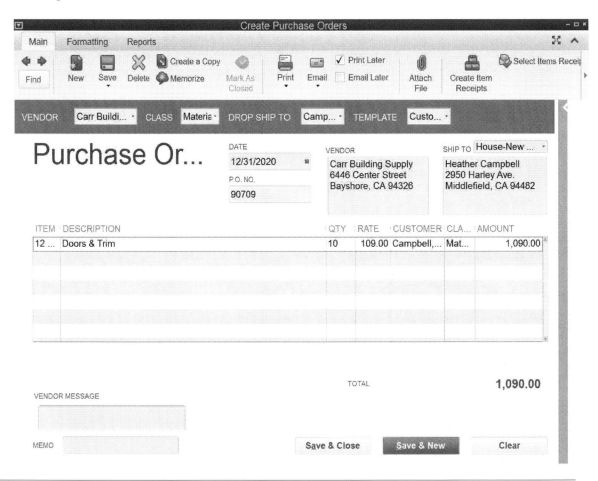

Creating Purchase Orders

1. Click on the Purchase Order Icon on the Home Page Under Vendors
2. Click on Vendor top of Form and enter vendor
3. Click on Class and enter the class and click on drop ship to job
4. Make sure the Date, Vendor and Ship to is correct
5. PO No. should automatically assign a number
6. Start Entering your items, qty, rate and finish information.
7. When done Click Save & Close or Save & New to enter another purchase order.

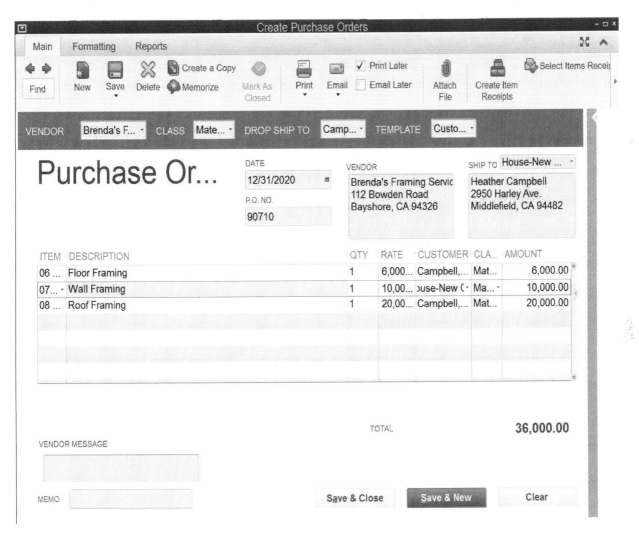

QuickBooks For Contractors

Purchase Orders to Track Draws and Costs

QuickBooks allows you to assign each line item in a purchase order to a job. This great feature allows you to use the purchase order to track multiple payment draws and committed costs to subcontractors.

Draw Scheduling

Let's take the Purchase Order on page 243 and pay it out in multiple draws. If you make an agreement to pay this out in multiple draws you should enter the draw schedule as a purchase order. We will set up the first draw as the Floor Framing, send draw as the Wall framing and the third draw as the room framing.

When we received bill for Brenda's Framing Service for the first Draw, floor framing, they used the same purchase order to record the payment of the first draw.

1. Click on Receive Inventory Icon on the home page under Vendors
2. Select Receive Inventory with Bill.
3. Select Vendor, in this exercise I am using Brenda's Framing Service.
4. A screen will pop up with open a warning that open purchase exists and Click Yes.
5. Click in the column to choose the correct PO and click ok.

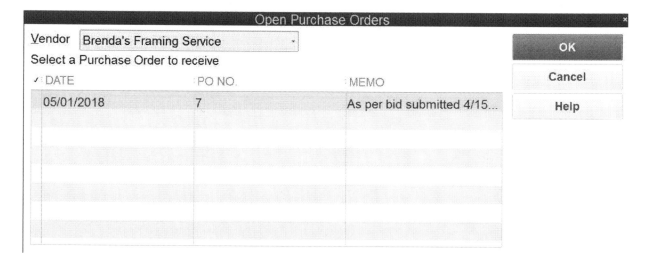

In the enter bills window as shown on the following page.
Enter the date on the vendor's bill
Enter the Invoice Number in the Ref. No.
In the amount due enter the amount you plan to pay, see example on following page.
In Qty, enter 1 for any draw you plan to pay now. If you only want to pay half, then enter 0.5 in the Qty and if you don't want to pay any of the draw now enter 0.
The Amount column calculates automatically. The amount on the Items tab should be the same as the amount you are paying. The amounts for the other Items will and should be 0.00.
Click Save & Close.

First Draw to Brenda's Framing Service

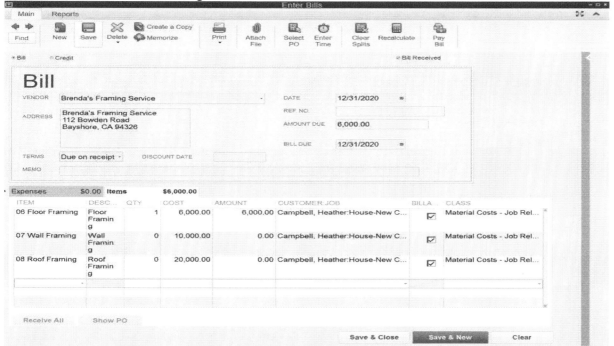

Committed Costs

Purchase Orders can be used to track your costs that you have bid on or committed to pay a subcontractor using the same method. Enter a purchase order at the beginning of the job/project and compare it to the final bill you receive. In my example below we used this PO from our bid contracted price. Now when we receive our bill we will compare.

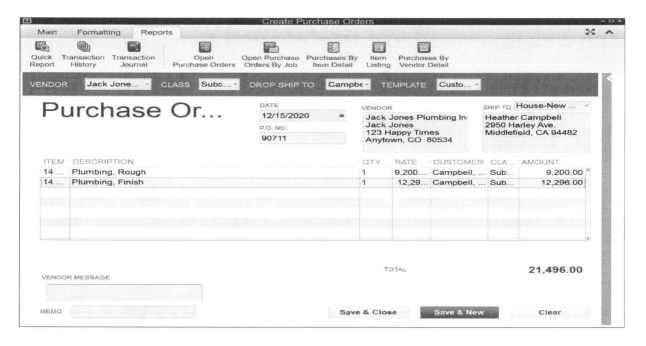

Tracking Open Unfilled Purchase Orders

To stay on top of outstanding purchase order you can run a report in a matter of seconds.
1. Click on Reports at the top of the Main Menu Bar
2. Select Purchases
3. Click Open Purchase Orders

This is a standard Open Purchase Orders Report. Remember you can always modify this if there's information missing or you want to change the report for other reasons.

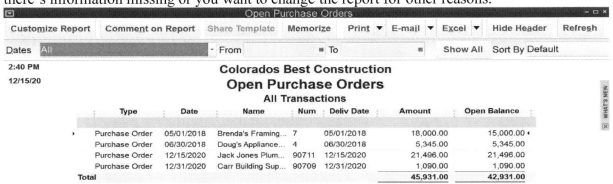

Entering Bills without Purchase Orders

I will cover entering bills for job-related Expenses and overhead expenses as well. First I am going to go over entering bills for job-related expenses.

1. Click on the Enter Bills Icon under Vendors on the Home Page
2. Fill in the top half of the bill and enter a description in the Memo what bill is for. Be sure to do this because it will show up in reports
3. Click the Items tab and always enter the job-related expenses in the Items Tab. Fill in the appropriate information. Make sure its correct sometimes you might need to edit information because it may pull up the last bills information.
4. Remember to fill in the customer job and class.

Entering Bills for Overhead Expenses without Purchase Order

1. Click on the Enter Bills Icon under Vendors on the Home Page
2. Fill in the top half of the bill and enter a description in the memo field describing what the bill is for.
3. Click the Expenses tab and always use the Expenses tab of the enter bills window for non-job related expenses.
4. Make sure every bill entered is assigned to the correct account.
5. When finished Click Save and Close or Save and New if you have more to enter.

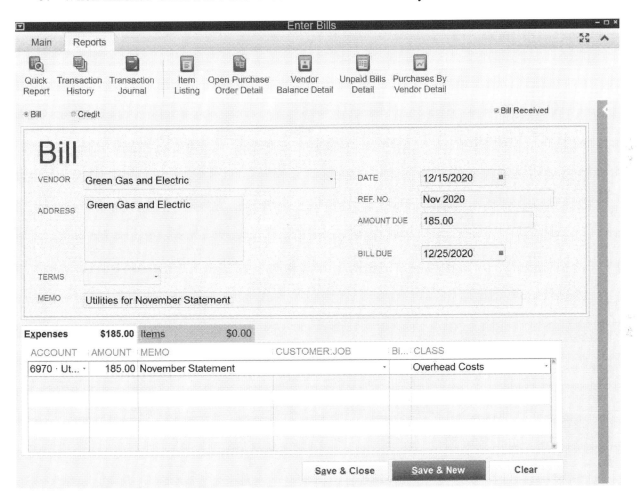

Selecting Bills for Payment

We are going to take and select bills to pay. Sometimes people call this bill run or check run.

1. Click on the Pay Bills Icon on the Home Page under Vendors.
2. Place a check mark in the left column next to the bills you want to pay.
3. When finishing selecting bills to pay click on Pay Selected Bills Button.
4. Notice at the top of the screen you can choose show all bills or bills due on or before a certain date. You can sort by due date.

Here's the Payment Summary Screen.

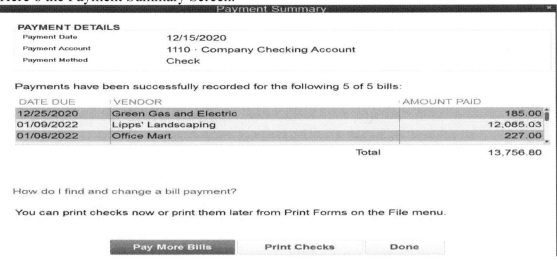

Click on the Print Checks button. You can always click done or pay more bills and print the checks later.

You can either print all the checks from the bills we just paid or you can print certain ones. Place a check mark as shown below to print the checks you desire. Make sure the check number is correct and the bank account number you are pulling the money out of to pay the bills.

Click ok when finished with selections.

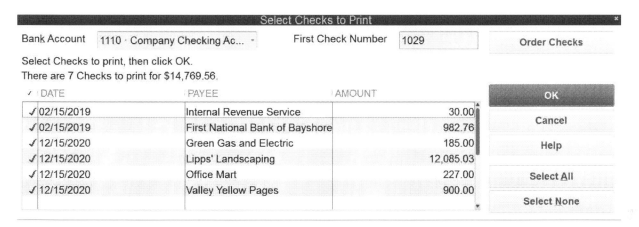

Here's the Print Checks Screen. Make sure your check style along with making sure the rest of the settings are correct then click Print when you are ready to print your checks.

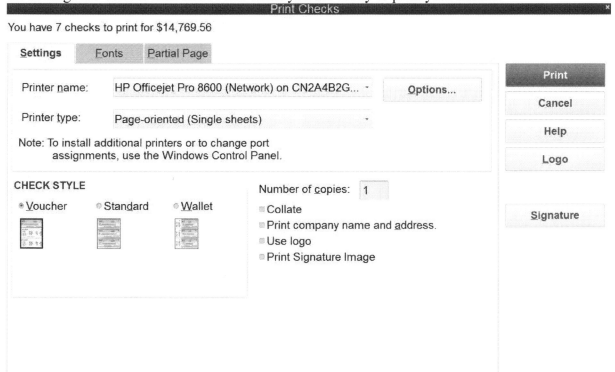

If you chose to print your checks later then do the following to print later:
1. Click on File at the top of the main menu bar.
2. Choose Print Forms
3. Select Checks and the select checks to print screen will pop up.
4. Select the Checks to print. Make sure your checks are loaded in printer and click ok when you are ready and all information is correct.

QuickBooks For Contractors

Worker's Comp Reports

Keeping up with making sure your Subcontractors are up to date on their Workman Comp Insurance is a headache, but is important and necessary. To help you track this we need to set up a custom field, so you can track in reports.

1. Click on Vendors at the top main menu bar
2. Select Vendor Center
3. Double Click on any Vender in your vendor center
4. Click the Additional Tab Info tab.
5. In the lower right of the Custom Fields section Click on Define Fields
6. In the setup for your custom fields name give the name you choose under Label and place check mark in the vendor area
7. Click ok and click ok again on the vendor. See Below Screen Shot

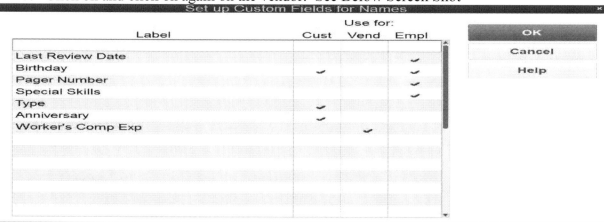

In the new custom field, you would enter the subcontractors Workers Comp expiration date.

Adding Custom Fields to Purchase Orders or Forms

In order to customize a form, go to the templates list.
1. Click on Lists at the top of the main menu bar
2. Select Templates
3. Double Click on Purchase Order.
4. Click on Additional Customization button.

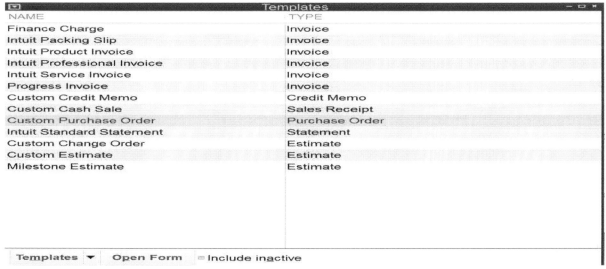

This screen pops up after click on Additional Customization button clicked.

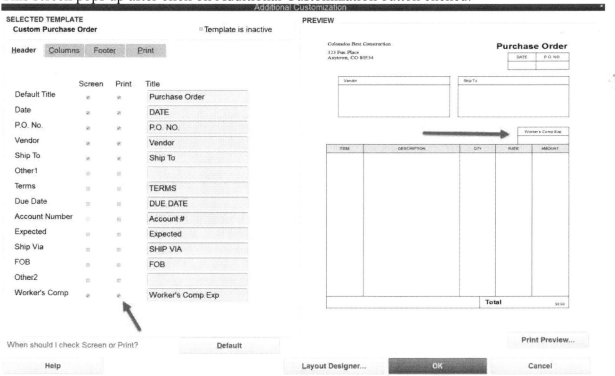

Place check marks in the screen and print buttons next to the Worker's Comp Exp. See in the screen shot above now the box on the purchase order forms shows Workers comp box where the subcontractors work comp expiration date will appear. Next I will go over steps to run a report.

Custom Field Reports

To Customize a report for the Workers Comp Exp field we just set up do the following:

1. Click on Reports at the top of the main menu bar
2. Select Vendors & Payables
3. Choose Vendor Contact List
4. Click on Customize Report
5. Click on the Workers Comp Exp under Columns as shown below. Click Ok.

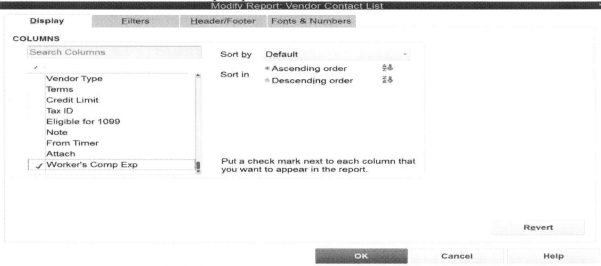

See the modified report below. Notice the arrow points to an expiration date for a vendor.

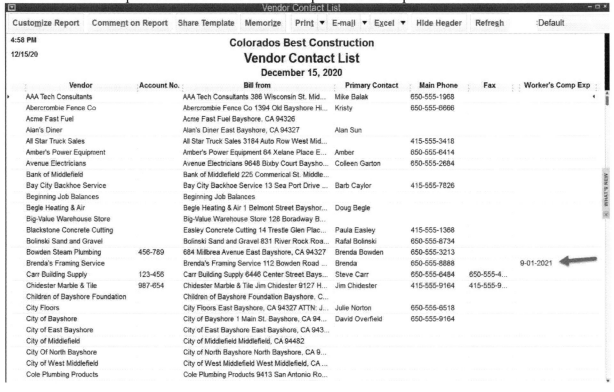

Saving the New Customized Worker's Comp Report

When you exit the report the following screen will appear asking if you want to save these settings click yes.

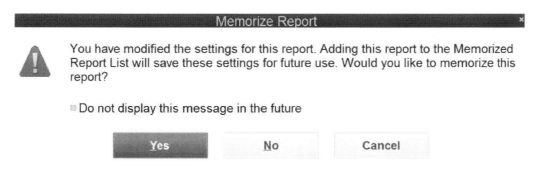

After Click yes this screen pops up, I renamed it as the following name in the screen shot. Place a checkmark in the Save in Memorized Report Group. Click on down arrow and choose Vendors. You don't have to choose a group if you don't want to. If you decide not to choose a group just don't place check mark in the Save in Memorized Report Group. Click ok.

To access this new report, do the following:

1. Click on Reports at the top of the main menu bar
2. Choose Memorized Reports
3. Select Vendors (for this report)

Chapter 16
Receivables

I will go over and show you how to use QuickBooks to track money owed to you, Accounts Receivables. I am working on the accrual method. I will go over invoicing customers/clients, handling change orders, retainage, customer payments and deposits.

You may or may not have set prices for items/jobs or tasks. I am going to go over setting prices next. The great thing about a set price is the invoice is quick and out the door to the customer and that means getting paid faster. We will set up Item with a set price first then create a quick set price invoice.

Set Price Invoice

1. Click on Lists at the top main menu bar.
2. Select Items
3. Click on Item button at the bottom of Items Screen
4. Select New

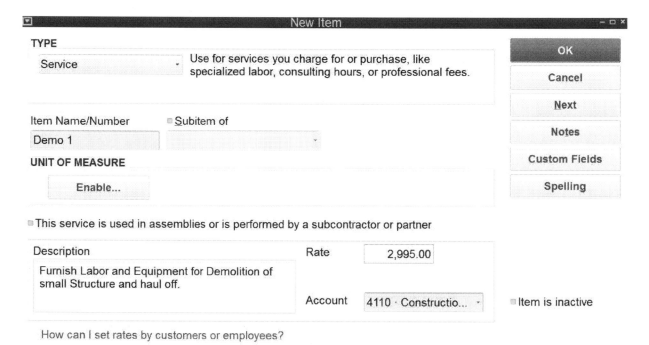

Here's the new set price Item. Notice I set this up as demolition of small structure including labor, equipment and haul off. Let's say this is something you do and you also do the same thing for medium and large structures, so you will want to charge more. You can just set up as many one set price on what you need by setting up multiple different ones.

Creating a Set Price Invoice

1. Click on the Create Invoices Icon on the Home Page under Customers Section.
2. Click on Customer in the box as shown below. If you have not added the customer just click add new and fill in their information.
3. Click on Class and add the correct class.
4. If you used a PO then add that, click on the terms.
5. Enter 1 for the quantity, enter the Item and the rest is filled in as shown below.
6. Click Save & Close if you are finished or if you have more to invoice then click on Save & New.

Note: You may want to change the ship to as to where the project is or you can add the description of the job location in the description area. You are ready to Print and or email your client the bill. Also, if this client had more than one small structure to demolish, then just add to the quantity, like if you demolished 3 small structures then add 3. You could also have 3 separate line items. As you can see a multitude of ways to bill this out.

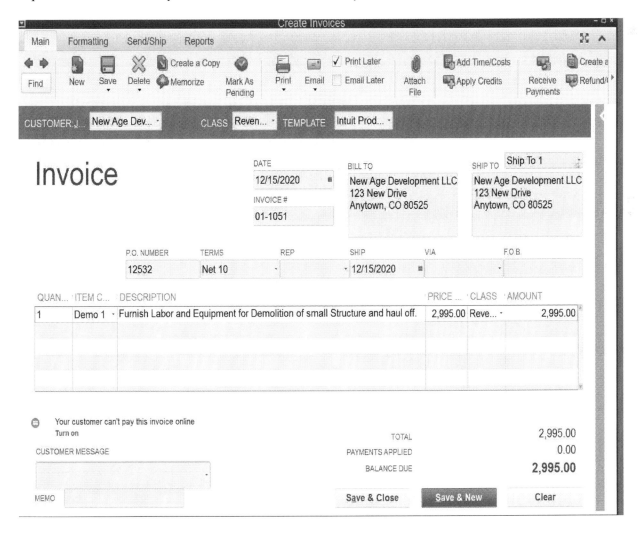

Time and Materials Invoice

Creating a time and materials invoice:

1. Click on the Create Invoices Icon on the home page under Customers.
2. Select a customer from the drop down menu. Choose one with an estimate for this example. See the screen that pops up once you choose the customer with estimate
3. Click Ok.

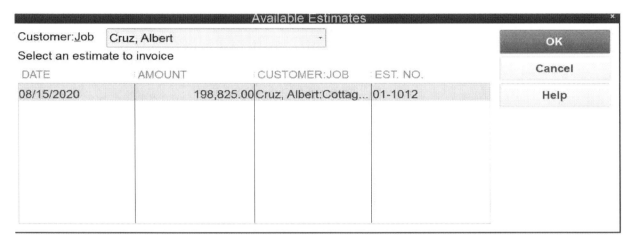

The screen pops up next. If you want to bill out the whole estimate, then choose top choice of create invoice for the entire estimate. If you have a customer that you bill on percentage basis, then choose the second one or choose the third option when you pick and choose what to bill. Click ok once you have made your choice. I chose the last option create invoice for selected items or for different percentages of each item.

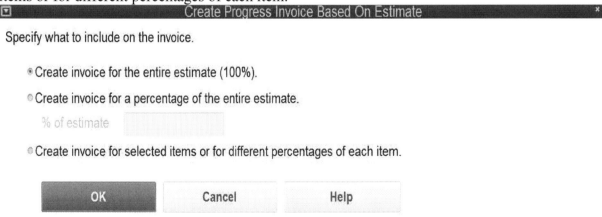

Time and Materials Invoice continued

After click ok this screen pops up. As you can see in this screenshot I entered 1 under Qty on the items I am billing for. You can also enter a percentage on any and all items if this is how you need to bill your customer. Click ok once you are ready to create your invoice.

Specify Invoice Amounts for Items on Estimate

Progress Invoice for: Cruz, Albert:Cottage - New Construction

For each item below, specify the quantity, rate, amount or % of the estimate amount to have on the invoice.

☑ Show Quantity and Rate   ☑ Show Percentage

ITEM	EST QTY	EST RATE	EST AMT	PRIOR...	PRIOR AMT	PRIOR %	QTY	RATE	AMOUNT	CURR %	TOT %
01 Plans &...		100.00	100.00		0	0.0%	1	100.00	100.00	100.0%	100.0%
01 Plans &...		125.00	125.00		0	0.0%	1	125.00	125.00	100.0%	100.0%
02 Site Wo...		100.00	100.00		0	0.0%	1	100.00	100.00	100.0%	100.0%
03 Excavat...		3,000.00	3,000.00		0	0.0%	1	3,000.00	3,000.00	100.0%	100.0%
04 Concrete		1,000.00	1,000.00		0	0.0%	1	1,000.00	1,000.00	100.0%	100.0%
05 Masonry		1,500.00	1,500.00		0	0.0%	1	1,500.00	1,500.00	100.0%	100.0%
06 Floor Fr...		6,000.00	6,000.00		0	0.0%	1	6,000.00	6,000.00	100.0%	100.0%
07 Wall Fr...		7,000.00	7,000.00		0	0.0%	0	7,000.00	0.00	0.0%	0.0%
08 Roof Fr...		9,000.00	9,000.00		0	0.0%	0	9,000.00	0.00	0.0%	0.0%
09 Roof Fl...		3,000.00	3,000.00		0	0.0%	0	3,000.00	0.00	0.0%	0.0%
								Total	11,825.00		

Note: All items will transfer to the invoice. The quantities and amount will be as you indicated. Although items with a zero amount display on screen, they can be set not to print from the Jobs and Estimates Preferences.

After clicking ok this screen pops up. If you are billing for time/labor, then you would select the outstanding billable time and costs to add to this invoice. If you are only billing for materials, then click on Exclude outstanding billable time and costs at this time. I chose the second option.

Billable Time/Costs

 The customer or job you've selected has outstanding billable time and/or costs.

Do you want to:

⦿ Select the outstanding billable time and costs to add to this invoice?

○ Exclude outstanding billable time and costs at this time? (You may add these later by clicking the Add Time/Costs button at the top of the invoice.)

☐ Save this as a preference.   Help

Click ok when done. See the Invoice for time and materials on the next page.

Invoice for some materials billed out. See next screen show where I added the time for both options.

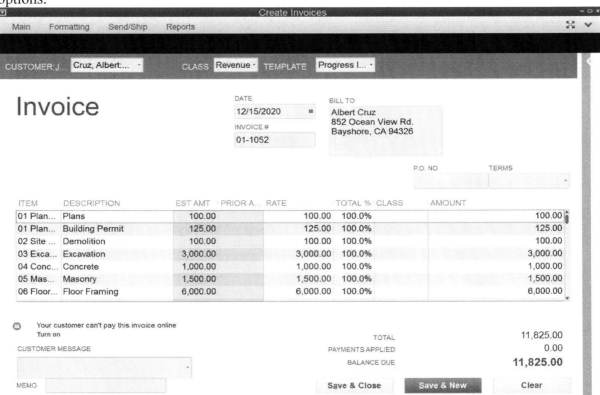

I went back to add time and costs. The screen shot below is the screen that pops up you choose the select outstanding billable time and costs.

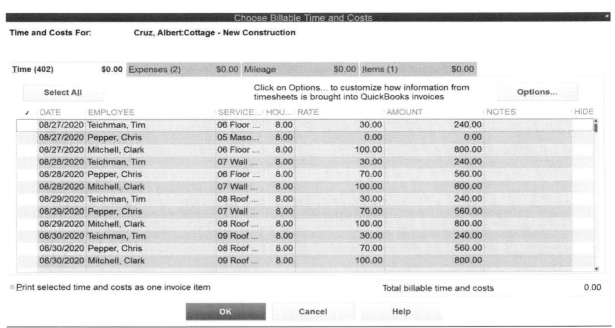

On the next page is the invoice reflecting the outstanding billable time and costs. I chose the time for a few days and then the two outstanding expenses. You will see a much larger invoice.

The first invoice was for $11,825.00. This invoice is for $54,752.00. This screen shot doesn't show the extended items that were for time and expenses.

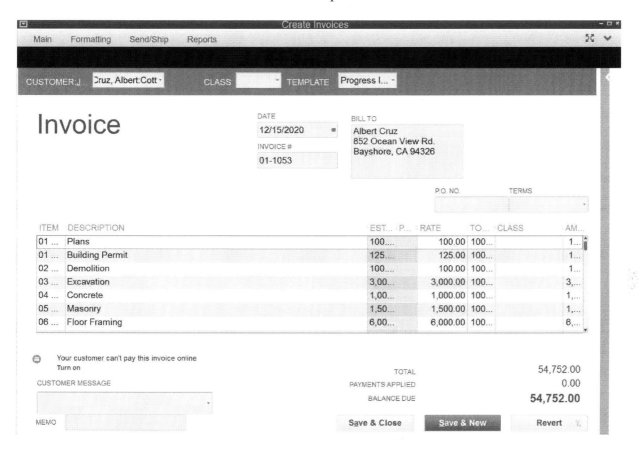

How to bill out a Set Priced Contract

This is typically a contract that you have a contract saying you will do the compete job for a certain price and assume all risks other than maybe certain things agreed upon for change orders. This can be good and bad. The good is if you get the job done sooner than thought without complications then your profit is probably and should be larger. The bad is if it takes you much longer than you anticipated and if you run into complications that you are responsible then you could break even or lose money

Going with this type of contract its usually set up to be billed out in phases such as a certain date you would invoice 25% and then next time another 25 percent and so on until the job is complete and billed out. More often than not there is usually 5 to 10% retainage held for a certain time frame after work is finished to allow for anything that goes wrong or that was overlooked etc.

First we will create an Item for Set Priced Contract Invoicing. See the following page for setting up the item and creating an invoice for Set Priced Contract billing/invoicing.

QuickBooks For Contractors

Setting up new Item for Contract Set Price Billing

1. Go to Lists at the top of the main menu bar
2. Click on Item List
3. Click on Items button at the bottom of the screen
4. Select New and choose Service.
5. Fill in the necessary information like you see in the screen shot. The account is your construction Income account/ or what you named your income account that you use.
6. Click OK when finished.

Here is the Item set up for Contract Set Price Billing. You can name this item what fits for you and fill in the description that works for you as well. You can Change the Description each and every time.

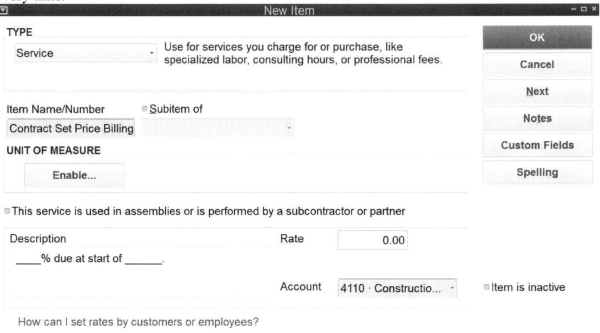

To Create the Contract Set Pricing Invoice:

1. Click on the Create Invoices Icon on the Home Page under Customers.
2. Click on the Customer:job drop down list and choose a customer. If the customer has an estimate click cancel this time because this is set price and don't need a estimate.
3. Select Revenue – Job Related on the Class pull down list.
4. Click in the Item from the pull down menu the Contract Set Price Billing or what you named this item.
5. In the Quantity enter as a decimal the percentage of the contract your are billing for. Such as .3 for 30% of the contract.
6. In the Rate enter the full amount of the contract.
7. Make sure everything is right then click print or email or you can do both.
8. Click Save and Close unless you have more invoicing then you click Save and New.

See the Contract Invoice on the next page.

Notice in the Quantity 0.3 is 30 percent of 389,000.00. This is an example, so I didn't fill out a lot in the description, but you can and may need to put more information in the description.

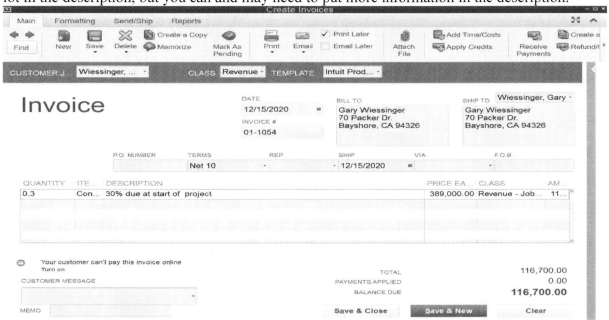

Progress Invoicing/Billing

First to use progress billing you need to make sure your preferences are setup correctly. You will want Estimates and Progress Invoicing turned on. To turn these features on do the following.

1. Click on Edit at the top Main Menu Bar.
2. Select Preferences
3. Choose Jobs & Estimates and Click Yes for create estimates and Progress Invoicing.
4. Click Ok when finished.

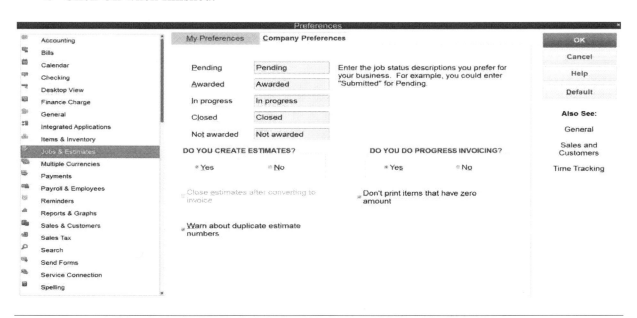

Creating a Progress Invoice

1. Click the Create Invoices Icon on the Home Page under Customers.
2. Click the drop down Customer:job list and choose a customer.
3. The screen shots below are what follows. Click ok for the estimate, check mark third option to create invoice for selected items and click ok

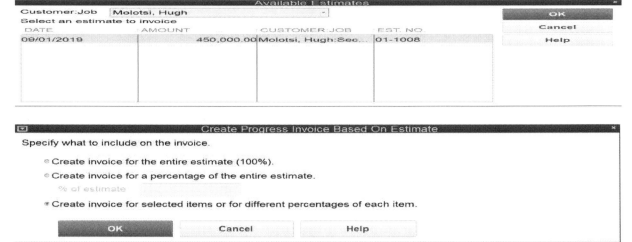

This is the specify amounts you want to bill for. I selected 100% on first 3 items.

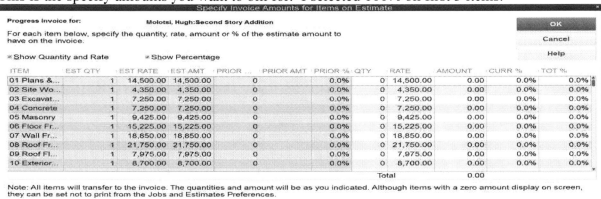

This is the last screen before Invoice is finished for billing. I chose time billable for the period. Click Ok.

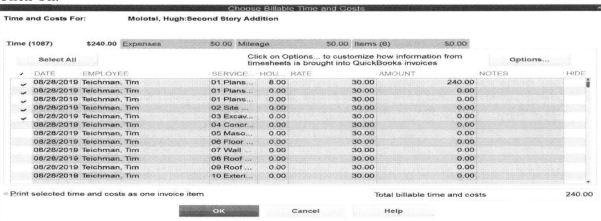

The Screen Shot below shows the finished Progress Invoice. This is first Invoice for this job. See Prior Amount has no amounts. For this exercise I will bill out a second time and you will see these figures billed for in the Prior Amount Column.

Screen Shot of 2nd Progress Invoicing for the Same Customer and Job. Notice now there is a prior amount billed and that prior amount was the amounts form the Invoice on the previous page. Also on the excavation we only finished 50 percent as you can see below.

Change Orders and Estimates

With the QuickBooks Contractors Edition, you can track change orders. When you change or modify items in an existing estimate you have the option to save the changes as a change order in the description field at the bottom of the estimate form. Let's make a change order now.

1. Click on the Estimates Icon on the Home Page under Customers.
2. Either choose the Customer you need to make the change order or you can click on Reports Tab then click Estimates by Job at the top of the blank Estimate and this will list all the estimates by job. Click on the Estimate for the Job you need to modify.

This screen shot is of the Estimate I entered changes at the bottom.

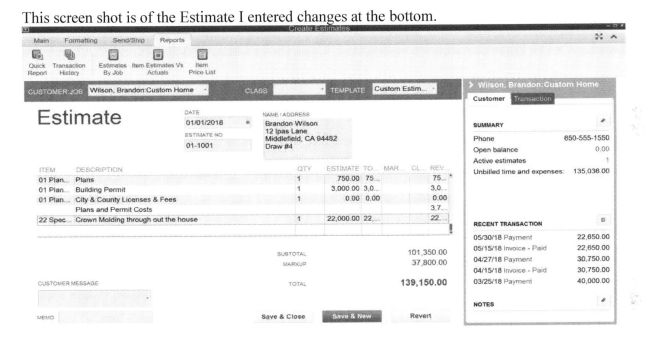

This is the Add Change Order Screen, Click the Add button. See the additions to the estimate on the next page.

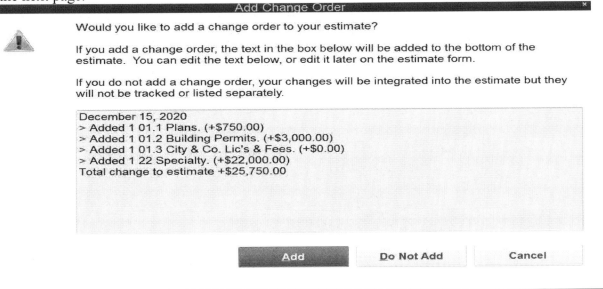

QuickBooks For Contractors

Estimate modified with new change order. See bottom of estimate with change order description of changes.

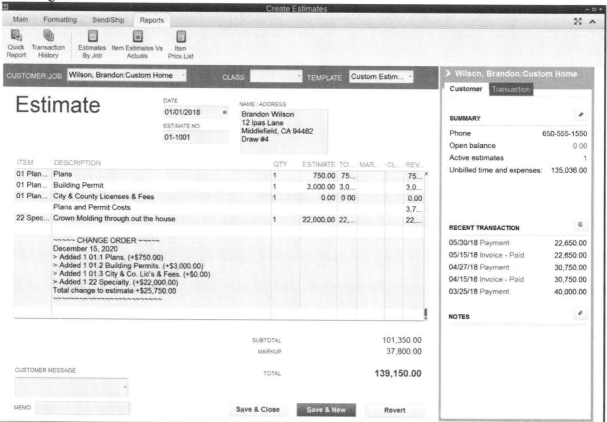

Retainage/ Retention

Companies and Contracts will vary. Some contracts will require 10% retainage, some 5% and some none. To setup retainage take the following steps.

1. Click on the Chart of Accounts Icon on the Home page under the Company tab.
2. Click the Account button at the bottom and of the page.
3. Select New
4. Choose Other Account type
5. Select Other Current Asset from the pull down menu
6. Click Continue
7. Name is Retainage or Retention Receivables or whatever you choose
8. Give the account number
9. You can give a description if you want.
10. Click OK when finished

See Screen Shots of the Retainage Account on the next page.

Add the new account Screen, choosing the type of account.

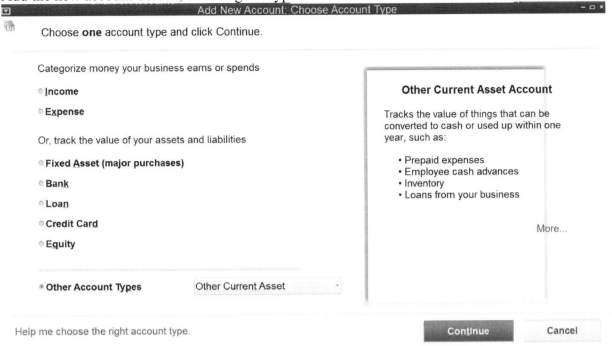

Add the New Account screen entering the name and number of the new account.

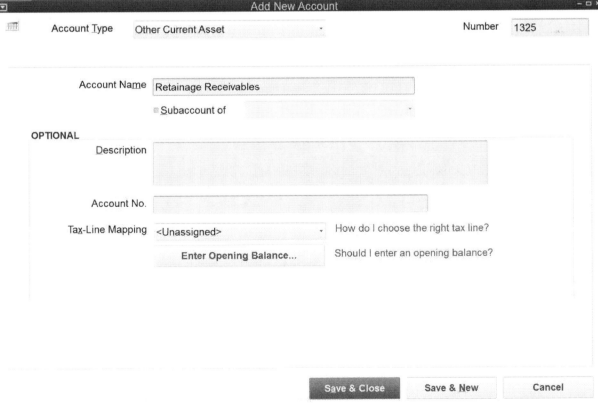

Next we will set up an Item for Retainage/Retentions Receivable.

QuickBooks For Contractors

Item for Retainage/Retentions Receivables

You need this Item for Billing/Invoicing.

1. Click on Lists at the Top of the Main Menu Bar.
2. Choose Item List
3. Select the Item button at the bottom of the Item List Screen
4. Choose New and select other charge from the drop down list.
5. Type in Item Name
6. Type in Description
7. Enter the amount to -10%
8. Enter the new Retainage account you just set up.
9. Click OK.

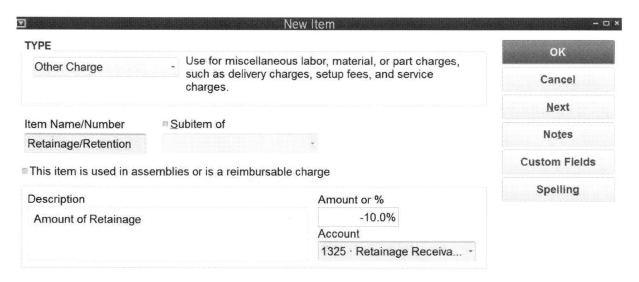

You now have your Retainage account in your Chart of Accounts and your new Item for Retainage setup, so we are going to create a quick Invoice and add the retention to it.

1. Click on the Create Invoices Icon on the Home Page under the Customers Tab.
2. Click on Customer drop down list and choose your customer. If an outstanding estimate screen pops up just exit out of that screen and exit any other screens until you reach the Invoice Screen.
3. Click on the drop down class list and enter Revenue job related
4. Fill in any other pertinent information in the top half of invoice
5. Click on Quantity enter the information like in the invoice on the following page.
6. Note: Once you enter the items for the if you have more than one item you need to enter the subtotal Item.
7. Enter the Retainage Item and the -10% is automatically calculated from the subtotal as shown on the next page.

New Invoice with Retainage withheld

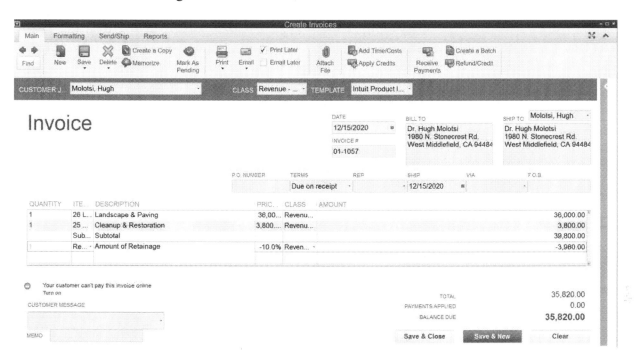

Let's take a look at the Retainage account in your Chart of Accounts to view the transactions. This ledger view will show who currently owes you for Retainage.

1. Click on the Chart of Accounts Icon on the Home Page under the Company tab.
2. Go to your Retainage account and double click open.

This is the ledger in your Chart of Accounts showing who owes you retainage.

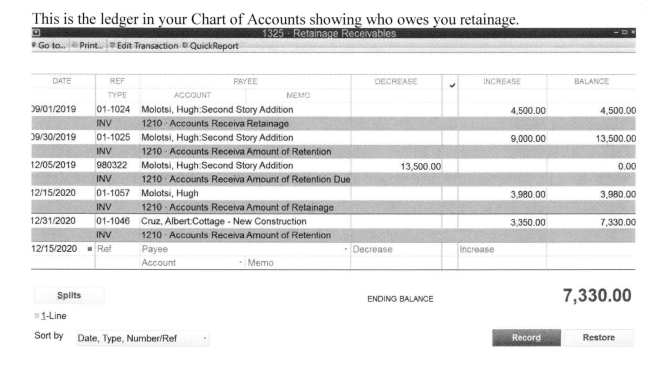

QuickBooks For Contractors

Invoicing for Retainage/Retention

1. Click on the Create Invoices Icon on the Home Page under the Customers tab.
2. Click on the drop down Customer: job list and choose the customer that we just created an invoice with retainage for. If the customer has more than one job be sure it's the right job.
3. Fill in the top half of the invoice.
4. Click the Item and select the Retainage item, enter 1 on Quantity
5. Enter the amount of the retainage withheld from the invoice as a positive number.
6. Print or email and save & Close.

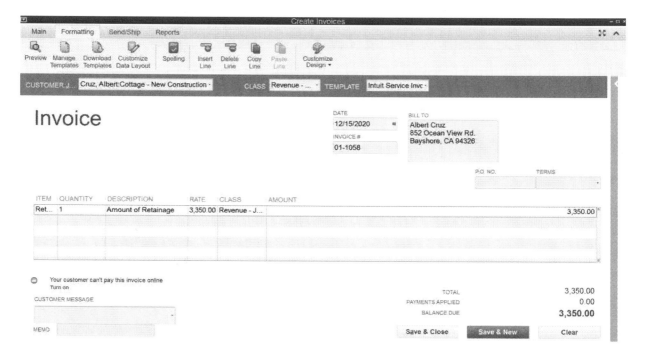

Notice in the Retainage Account where you invoiced for the Retainage in the screen shot below.

Entering Payments Received on Account

1. Click on the Receive Payments Icon on the Home Page under the Customers tab.
2. Place a check mark next to the invoice received and QuickBooks will enter the amount in the payment amount received. Click on the check button and enter the check number.
3. Click on Save & Close. The payment will be recorded in the Undeposited Funds Account. We will need to record the deposit next.

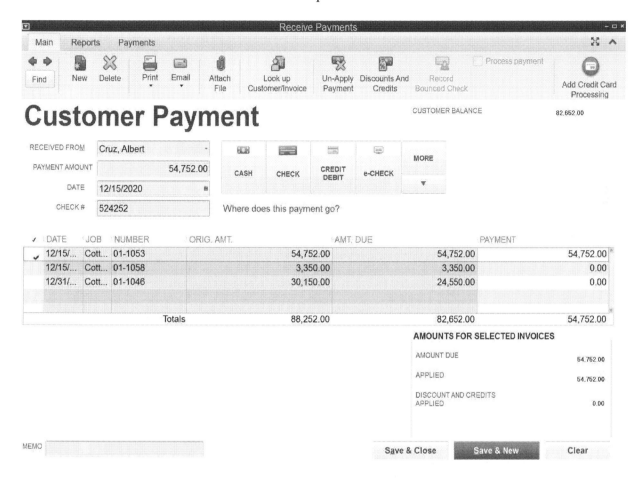

Depositing the Payments Received

1. Click on the Record Deposits Icon on the Home Page under the Banking tab.
2. Place a check mark on the Payment to deposit as shown in the screen that pops up. See on the following page.
3. Click ok when finished selecting the payment to deposit. There is only one payment to deposit this time, but often times you may have more than one. You can deposit one at a time or multiple payments at a time.

Select Payment for Deposit.

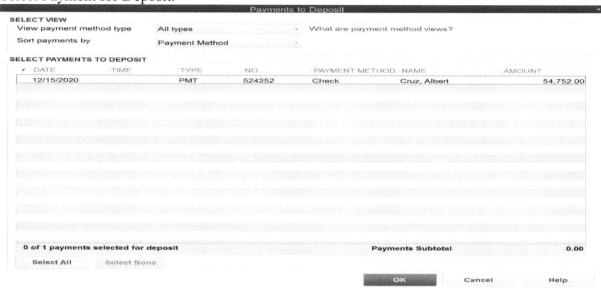

Deposit Screen where payment is recorded. When finished Click Save & Close.

Job Deposits

A job deposit is money that a customer gave you to be held for work to be done and fulfilled. You will not have earned this money until job satisfactorily complete. You would record this as a liability until job is complete even though you have recorded this as a deposit. Once your customer agrees the job is finished then you will apply the job deposit to job costs.

1. Click on the Create Sales Receipts Icon on the Home Page under the Customers tab.
2. Select customer from the Customer:Job drop down list.
3. Enter Class as Revenue – Job Related.
4. Click the Check button and enter the check number.
5. Type in deposit under the item tab and enter the description
6. Qty is 1 and enter the Rate and Class as Revenue – Job Related.
7. Print or email now or later
8. Click Save & Close to record the Payment in the undeposited funds account.
9. We will record the deposit next.

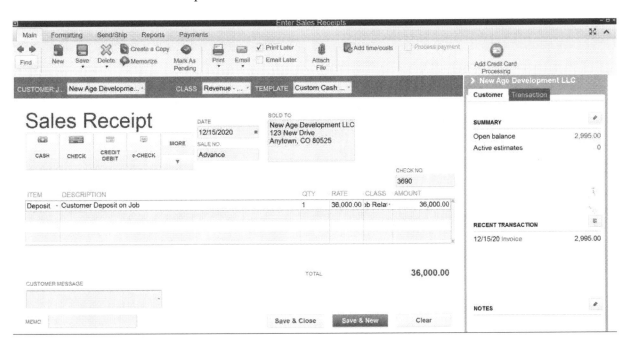

To record this payment as a deposit, do the following:
1. Click on the Record Deposits Icon on the Home Page under the Banking tab.
2. The Payments to Deposit Screen pops up.
3. Place a check mark next to the deposit to record.
4. Click OK
5. Enter any information missing on the Record Deposit Screen
6. When finished then Click Save & Close

See Screen shots of deposit on the following page.

QuickBooks For Contractors

Select Payment Screen

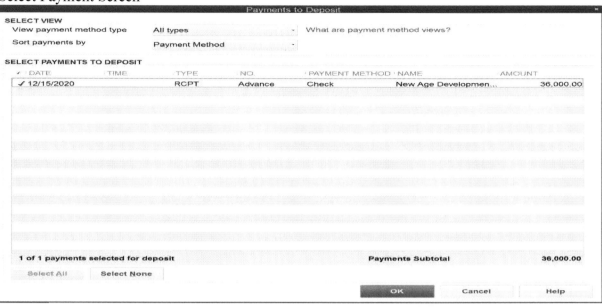

Record Deposit Screen

Create Invoice for Job with Job Deposit

1. Click on the Create Invoices Icon on the Home Page under the Customers tab.
2. Fill in the invoice as follows. See the deposit applied as a negative to the invoice to subtract it from the total due.
3. When finished click save & close unless you are entering more invoices then you would click Save & New.

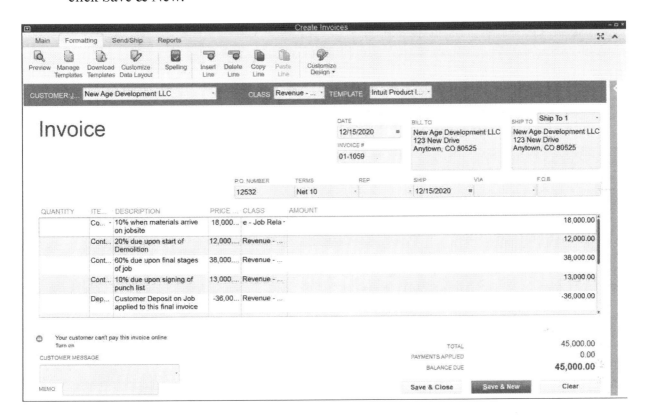

QuickBooks For Contractors

Chapter 17
Estimating

Using the estimating program is a great way to go and to get a more accurate job cost and accounting. Once you have created an estimate you can then turn that into an invoice. The progress billing is great for sending out detailed billing for work done and work to be completed. By using the estimating feature is an accounting road map so to speak.

Setting Preferences for estimating

First to use estimating you need to make sure your preferences are setup correctly. You will want Estimates and Progress Invoicing turned on. To turn these features on do the following.

1. Click on Edit at the top Main Menu Bar.
2. Select Preferences
3. Choose Jobs & Estimates and Click Yes for create estimates and Progress Invoicing.
4. Click Ok when finished.

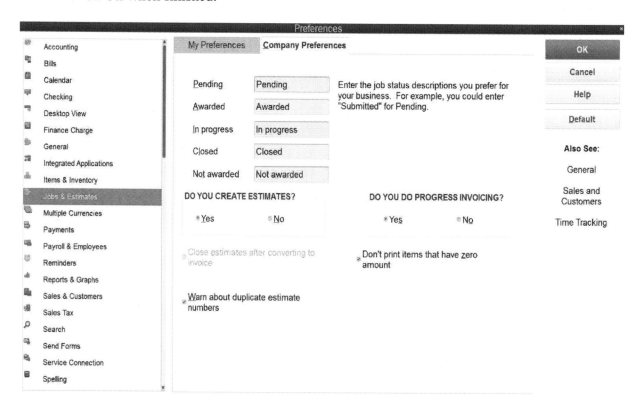

You will need to set up Sales Tax Item next. If you do not need or pay sales tax then you can skip this step on the next page.

276

Setting Sales Tax Preferences

1. Click on Edit at the top Main Menu Bar.
2. Select Preferences
3. Choose Sales Tax in the column to the left.
4. Name your Sales Tax Name and the description automatically fills in
5. Fill in the tax rate and the vendor (tax agency) If you haven't set this up you can just click down arrow key and add new.
6. Click OK when finished.

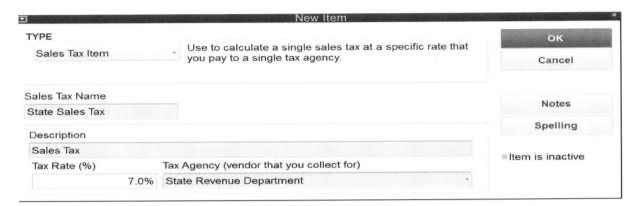

The box is checked automatically that says Identify taxable amounts as T for Taxable when printing, you need to uncheck that box. Click OK.

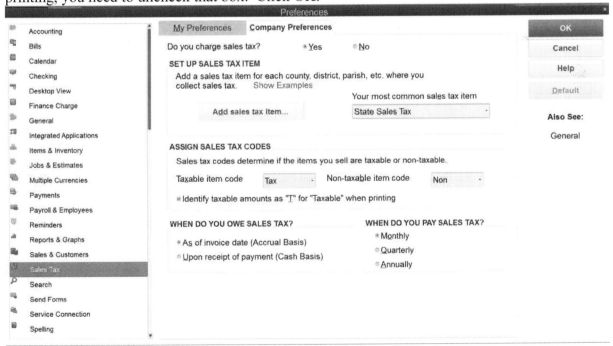

Note: Check with your Accountant about your sales tax laws. Many states the materials you install are taxable to your customer, so if this is the law and you are not charging them the sales tax you would/could be liable to pay and that is money lost.

Building your Item List

It's important to think out your item list and to build it in the beginning of setting up your QuickBooks. If you set your list up right your accounting will be better and not as many missing pieces that you may have to go back and fill in.

If you find you need to charge your customers sales tax on materials you install, I recommend that you separate your items on the estimate/invoices tax and non-tax items just for more clarity for you and your customers.

Even if you don't have to charge your customers sales tax it's a good idea to separate your labor and material costs on your item list and on your estimates/invoices.

You need this Item for Billing/Invoicing.

1. Click on Lists at the Top of the Main Menu Bar.
2. Choose Item List
3. Select the Item button at the bottom of the Item List Screen
4. Choose New and select None-inventory Part from the drop down list.
5. Type in Item Name
6. Type in Description
7. Place check mark in box This Item is used in assemblies
8. Enter the expense and income account.
9. Enter the cost of the Item even though I didn't.
10. If you charge sales tax, then the code is Tax if you don't its Non Tax.
11. Click OK if done or if you are adding more items click next.

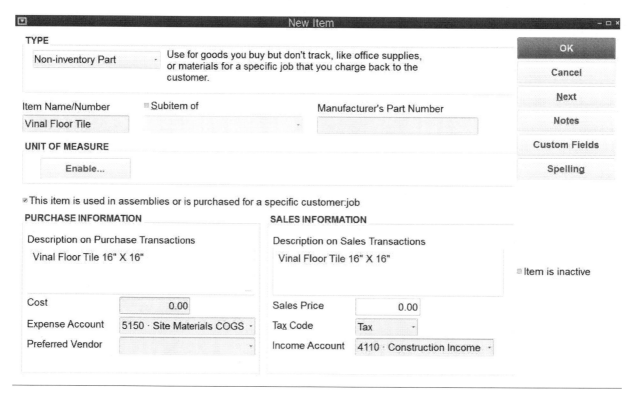

Creating Estimates

1. Click on the Estimates Icon on the Home Page under the Customers tab.
2. Click on the Customer:Job drop down list and choose your customer or you can Quick Add the customer here as well.
3. Enter the items, Qty and amount. Make sure the class is filled in as well.
4. Print or Email or both. You can print or email later as well.
5. Click Save & Close

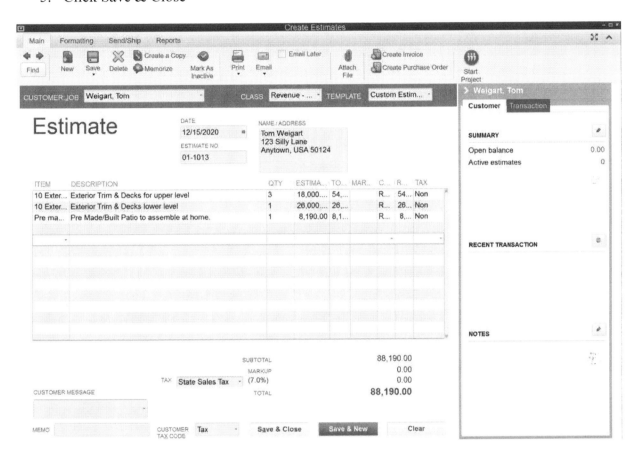

Grouping Items

Once you have your items list put together you might want to do some grouping of materials and labor costs for quicker estimating. Group like Tile and Labor together. See Group in screen shot on next page.

You need this Item for Billing/Invoicing.

1. Click on Lists at the Top of the Main Menu Bar, select Item List.
2. Select the Item button at the bottom of the Item List Screen
3. Choose New and select Group from the drop down list.
4. Type in Item Name and Description
5. Enter the Items and click on Print Items in group.
6. Click OK.

QuickBooks For Contractors

Creating Group Item Screen Shot.

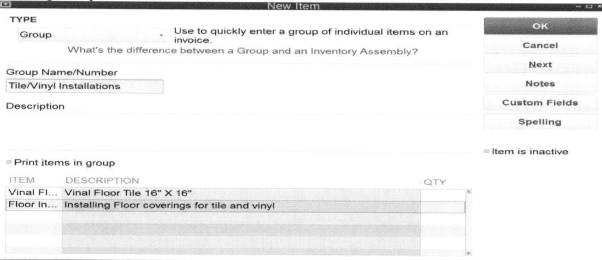

Creating Invoice from Estimate

1. Click on the Estimates Icon button on the Home Page under the Customers tab.
2. Click on the drop down menu and choose the customer you want to create invoice for.
3. Once you bring up the estimate for the customer then click on the Create Invoice in the ribbon above the estimate to the right with the arrow pointing to it below.

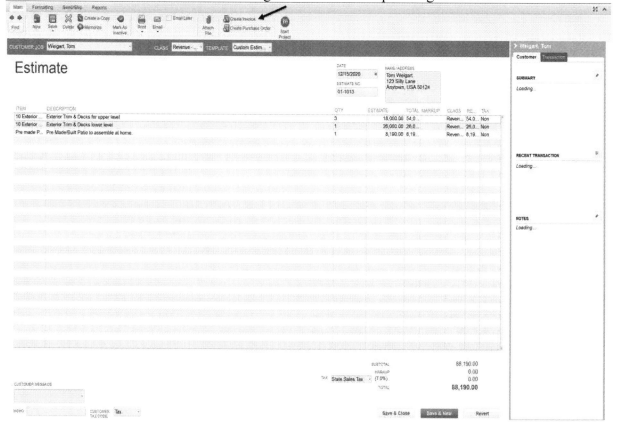

When you click on the Create Invoice button this screen pops up. Make your selection and click ok. I chose create invoice for the entire estimate for this example.

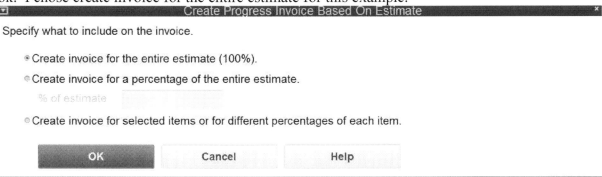

Here is the invoice created from the estimate. Everything you see was added and I just clicked on the save and close button. If you need to add or change anything you can.

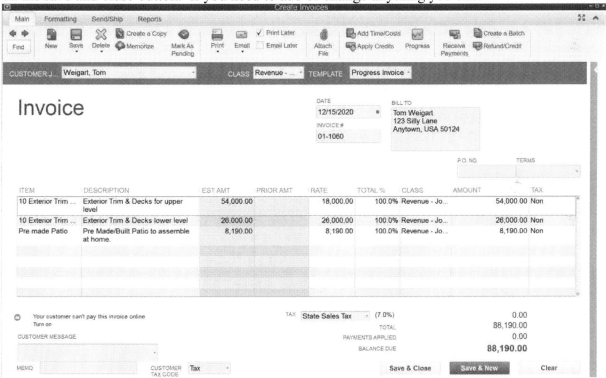

Chapter 18
End of Month and Year Procedures

I want to go over ideas on closing the end of the month out and the end of the year procedures. As always check with your Accountant on things he or she recommends.

End of Month

1. Reconcile all checking accounts, savings, credit cards and loans with the statements from your bank and or financial institution.
2. Run reports to make sure all transactions are accurate.
3. Print Monthly Reports.
4. Back Up Data (QuickBooks company file) and close the month.

See Chapter 11, Banking Page 196 for reconciliations.

Run Reports to insure accuracy

Transaction Detail by Account, Accounts Receivable Aging Detail, and Accounts Payable Aging Detail. These are just a few that I would run along with Balance Sheet plus the Profit and Loss Statement.

Make a file for the end of each month filing all the reports and noting any changes.

End of Year

1. Follow the procedures for month end for December or the last month of your fiscal year end.
2. Write off Bad Debts, (discuss with your accountant)
3. Print Financial Reports and file them along with giving a copy to your accountant.
4. Back up your QuickBooks file, close and lock the year.

If you have a bad debt, but don't have the bad debt expense set up in your Chart of Accounts you will need to set that up. It would be an expense.

Also, you need to set up an Item as a bad debt and that would be a service type. The account would be the bad debt account you set up in your Chart of Accounts called Bad Debt.

There are a vast number of reports made and you can create your own and modify the ones made. For more about reports check out chapter 13, page 225.

Quick Tips

Now that you just finished setting up your new Company File back it up. This is number one always is to back up regularly. Depending on how many transactions/how big your company is you may want to back up daily. I would say at least back up once a week.

If you do not back up consistently and something happened to your QuickBooks file it could be very costly to have to reenter everything.

All these accounts can be edited and renamed. If there is an account, you don't think you need or will ever use then delete it now. You can always delete an account as long as there are no transactions linked to that account.

If you have two accounts say that are similar and want to put them under just one account, then you can merge them.

To merge most accounts whether it's a chart of accounts account, customer, or vendor this will work to merge.

Steps to merge accounts is to have one account the name you want it to be and then edit and change the name on the other account to the name of the account you want. A screen will pop up and say this account name is already in use would you like to merge them and you say yes then it combines them for you.

If you have any questions, please email me at soswill@outlook.com.

Cristie

Handy Quick Reference Cheat Sheets
Chart of Accounts

Adding a New Account
5. Go to Menu Bar at the top of the screen, click on lists then click on Chart of Accounts
6. Click on the Account button at the bottom left of the screen and choose New.
7. Choose the Account type that you are wanting to set up and click continue.
8. Enter account information and when done click save and close.

Editing an Account
5. Go to Menu Bar at the top of the screen, click on lists then click on Chart of Accounts.
6. Click once on the account you want to edit to highlight the account.
7. Click on the Account button at the bottom left of the screen and choose Edit Account.
8. The account you had highlighted to edit opens up. Edit the information then click save and close.

Delete or Inactivate an Account
5. Go to Menu Bar at the top of the screen, click on lists then click on Chart of Accounts.
6. Click once on the account you want to delete or inactivate to highlight the account.
7. Click on the Account button at the bottom left of the screen and click on Delete Account or Make Account Inactive.
8. Click OK to confirm any deleted account. If you chose to make account Inactive it will just disappear from your list, but it's just inactive and can be made active again anytime.

Handy Quick Reference Cheat Sheets
Customers

Accessing Customer Center
- Go to Menu Bar at the top of the screen, click on Customers, then click on Customer Center

Adding a New Customer
1. Click the Customers & Jobs tab in the Customer Center once the Customer Center is opened.
2. Click on the tab just above the Customers & Jobs Tab that is named New Customer & Job.
3. Click on Add New Customer.
4. Enter all the necessary customer information on each tabbed section in the New Customer window then click OK when finished.

Adding a Job to a Customer
1. Click the Customers & Jobs tab in the Customer Center once the Customer Center is opened.
2. Highlight the existing customer that you want to add a job to.
3. Click on the tab just above the Customers & Jobs Tab that is named New Customer & Job then click on Add Job.
4. Give the job a name and go through the tabs entering the information about the job then click ok when finished.

Editing or Deleting a Customer
1. Click the Customers & Jobs in the Customer Center once the Customer Center is opened.
2. Highlight and double click on the Customer and/or Job you want to edit. Make necessary changes and click ok.
3. To delete a job, highlight the job and right click on the highlighted job then choose delete job.
4. To delete a Customer, highlight the Customer and right click on the highlighted Customer then choose Delete customer: job. (Note you cannot delete Customer or Job if linked to any transactions and if linked then Click on Inactivate.)

Handy Quick Reference Cheat Sheets
Employees

Accessing Employee Center
- Go to Menu Bar at the top of the screen, click on Employees, and then click on Customer Center.

Adding a New Employee
1. Click the New Employee tab in the Employee Center once the Employee Center is opened.
2. Fill in all the New Employee information and click OK.

Editing, Deleting or Inactivating an Employee

1. Once the Employee Center is open double click on the employee you want to edit.
2. Make the changes to the employee you are editing and click OK when done.
3. To delete an employee, highlight the employee you want to delete then right click on the employee and click on delete employee. (Note if employee is linked to any transactions you can only make them inactive).
4. To make employee inactive, highlight employee and right click on the employee and click on Make Employee Inactive.

Creating Custom Fields

Customers, Employees and Vendors
1. Click open the Customer, Employee or Vendor center to create the custom fields you want. Click open a customer or employee or Vendor and click on Additional Info Tab. Click Define Fields.
1.
2. Start Entering Field Names and place check mark in field to whether it's a customer, employee or vender or a combination of the three. Click Ok when done.

Handy Quick Reference Cheat Sheets
Vendors

Accessing Vendor Center
- Go to Menu Bar at the top of the screen, click on Vendors, and then click on Customer Center.

Adding a New Vendor
1. Click the New Vendor Button just above the Vendors Tab after opening the vendor center.
2. Click on New Vendor
3. Enter in all the Vendor Information. Be sure to go through the Tabs and enter what is necessary then click ok when finished.

Editing, Deleting or Inactivating a Vendor
1. Once Vendor Center is open double click on Vendor to edit.
2. After edits are made to your Vendor then click OK.
3. To Delete a Vendor, highlight vendor and right click on the highlighted Vendor and click on Delete Vendor. Click ok to confirm delete.
4. If the vendor has transactions linked to that Vendor then you have to make them inactive.
5. To make Vendor inactive, highlight Vendor and right click on the Vendor and Click on Make Vendor Inactive.
2.

Adding Fields to Vendors
1. Once Vendor Center is open double click on Vendor to edit.
2. Click on New Vendor just above Vendors Tab that is opened and then click on Add Multiple Vendors.
3. Click on Customize Columns.
4. The column that says available columns to the left can be added to your vendor information. You can add one or all or anything in-between. You customize to your business.

Handy Quick Reference Cheat Sheets
Managing List Items

Creating Item List Custom Fields
1. Go to the Menu Bar at the top of the screen and click on lists then click on Item List. Click on item list at bottom of screen, click New if adding new item or Click Edit if making changes to an item.
2. To customize fields to new items or edit items after opening item click on custom fields. If no fields are defined yet a screen will pop up saying no fields are defined yet and to define them click on the define fields, click ok then click define fields.
3. Enter Item Label name, click use & ok, enter values & ok.

Sorting Lists
1. Manual sort by click and drag the diamond next to the name.
2. Automatically sorting, click the column heading. You can sort by any column, so depending on your needs.
3. Remove the auto sort by clicking the new diamond to the left of the column heading.
4. Restore original sort order by selecting View from the top menu bar, then clicking on re-sort list then click ok.

Inactivating and Reactivating Items
1. Highlight Item and right click on the highlighted Item click Make Item Inactive.
2. To show all items including inactive items click on box, Include Inactive. Can also see all in lists by selecting all.
3. To reactivate show the inactive items within the list and click the X to change from inactive to active.

Renaming and Merging List Items
1. To rename open the item to rename it, type new name and click ok or save and close button to save changes.
2. To merge, change the name to the same as another item and choose yes when prompted to merge.

Handy Quick Reference Cheat Sheets
Sales Tax

Creating a Sales Tax Item or Group
1. First make sure in Preferences Sales Tax is turned on.
2. Select Lists then click on item lists.
3. Click on Item at the bottom of the screen and click on New.
4. Click on Sales Tax Item or Sales Tax Group from the list.
5. Enter tax item information and click ok.

Setting Default Sales Tax Preferences.
1. Go to edit on the Menu Bar at the top and click on Preferences then click on Sales Tax & Company Preferences.
2. Fill in all the necessary information and click ok.

Setting a Customer Taxable
1. Click Customers on top Menu, click on Customer Center.
2. Click the Customers & Jobs tab and the left side, double click name of the customer in the list, make changes, and click ok.

Sales Tax Settings for an Item
1. Click on Lists from the Menu Bar then click on Item List.
2. Highlight the item then click the item button and click edit.
3. Click Tax Code & choose appropriate selection & click ok.

Creating a Sales Tax Report
1. Click on Vendors on the Top Menu Bar, click Sales Tax, then Sales Tax Liability or Sales Tax Revenue Summary and change dates to the correct time period. Press Esc button to close report.
3.

Paying Sales Tax
1. Click Vendors from Top Menu Bar, Sales Tax then click pay sales Tax. Make selections for the Account and dates.
2. Click to select the Pay column for agencies to pay, click adjust button to make adjustments if necessary, click ok.
3. Click on Print Checks when ready to print the sales check you just created.

Handy Quick Reference Cheat Sheets
Inventory

Turning on Inventory in QuickBooks
1. Click on Edit then Preferences from the Top Menu Bar.
2. Click on Items & Inventory from the list.
3. Check the Inventory and purchase orders are active under the Company Preferences Tab, set rest of preferences & click ok.

Creating New Inventory Part Items
1. Click Lists then Item List from Top Menu Bar.
2. Click New from the Item Button on bottom of the screen.
3. Click Inventory part from the Type in the drop down menu.
4. Enter inventory part information and click ok.

Creating a Purchase Order
1. Click Vendors then click Create Purchase Orders from the Top Menu Bar.
2. Click the vendor from the vendor drop down list.
3. Enter Purchase Order information and click Save & Close or Save & New button, depending if creating more than one.

Creating Purchase Order Reports
1. Click lists then Chart of Accounts from the top Menu Bar.
2. Highlight purchase orders account, click reports button then click Quick Report: Purchase Orders from the menu.
3. You can access more detailed reports from the reports menu from the Top Menu Bar and click on Purchases.

Receiving Inventory with a Bill
1. Click Vendors, then Receive Items and Enter Bill from the top Menu Bar.
2. Click on the Vendor from the drop down list on the Bill entry.
3. Enter bill information and click the save & close button.

Handy Quick Reference Cheat Sheets
Inventory Continued

Creating an Item Receipt
1. Click Vendors then Receive Items from the top Menu Bar.
2. Choose the vendor from the Vendor drop down list.
3. Enter the receipt information and click the Save & Close button.

Matching a Bill to an Item Receipt
1. Click Vendors then Enter Bill for Received Items from the top Menu Bar.
2. Choose the vendor from the Vendor drop down list.
3. Choose the item receipt and click the ok button.
4. Enter the date when the bill was received in the Date field and click the Save & Close button.

Manually Adjusting Inventory
1. Click Vendors, then Inventory Activities then Adjust Quantity/Value on Hand from the top Menu Bar.
2. Choose the type of inventory adjustment to make from the Adjustment Type drop down list.
3. Make the necessary adjustments to the inventory.
4. Click the Save & Close button.

Handy Quick Reference Cheat Sheets
Other Items

Creating Other Items

Such as service, non-inventory parts, other charges, subtotals, groups, discounts and payments.

1. Click lists then Item List from the top Menu Bar.
2. Click New from the Item button from the bottom of the screen after opening the items list.
3. Choose the item type from the Type drop down list.
4. Enter the item information and click ok.

Changing Item Prices
1. Click Customers then Change Item Prices from the top Menu Bar.
2. Click the Item Type drop down to choose only items that match the item type you want.
3. Click the left column to check the item(s) you wish to change.
4. Adjust prices using the fields at the bottom.
5. Click the adjust button and then click ok.

Handy Quick Reference Cheat Sheets
Sales

Creating an Invoice or Sales Receipt
4. Click Customers then Create Invoices or click Customers then Enter Sales Receipts from the top Menu Bar.
5. Pick a template from the Template drop-down menu.
6. Choose the Customer: Job drop down list to select a customer.
7. Enter the invoice or receipt information and click save & close or save & new, depending on if you enter more than one invoice or receipt.

Finding Transactions
1. Open the form window for the type of transaction you need to find. For example, to find an invoice, open the Create Invoices window.
2. Click edit find, form type (such as invoices or bills), from the top Menu Bar.
3. Enter necessary information for values to find the transaction & click the Find button. Double click item to open it.

Previewing Invoices and Receipts
1. Click open the receipt or invoice for previewing.
2. Click the drop down arrow below the Print button in the Main tab of the Ribbon.
3. Choose the Preview from the drop down menu.

Printing Invoices and Receipts
1. Click open the sales form to print.
2. Click the Print button in the Main Tab of the Ribbon.
3. Set Preferred Printing Parameters.
4. Click the Print Button.

Handy Quick Reference Cheat Sheets
Price Levels

Creating New Price Levels
1. Click lists then Price Level List from the top Menu Bar.
2. Click the Price Level button and select New from the Pop up menu.
3. Type the name of the new price level into the Price Level Name field.
4. Enter the price level information
5. When finished entering information click ok.

Associating Defaults with a Customer
1. Click Customer the Customer Center from the top menu bar.
2. Double click on the customer on the Customers & Jobs tab of the customer center.
3. Choose the Payment Settings tab in the Edit Customer window.
4. Choose the appropriate price level from the Price Level drop-down menu.
5. When finished click ok.

Changing Line Item Rates
1. Choose the line item in the invoice or receipt.
2. Click into the Rate column.
3. Enter the Price Level.
4. Click Save & Close when done.

Handy Quick Reference Cheat Sheets
Billing Statements

Setting Finance Charge Preferences
1. Click edit then Preferences from the top Menu Bar.
2. Choose the Finance Charge icon to the left.
3. Enter your information on the Company Preferences tab and when finished click ok.

Entering State Charges
1. Click on the customer you want to highlight on the Customers & Jobs tab of the Customer Center.
2. Click on Customers then choose Statement Charges from the top Menu Bar.
3. Enter the charge & click Record Button then click the X or press Esc Button to exit out of screen.

Creating Statements
1. Click Customers then choose Create Statements from the top Menu Bar.
2. Choose statement options, customers and any other options you need.
3. Click Preview, Print, E-Mail or all three buttons to depending on your choice and the customer's preference as well.

Handy Quick Reference Cheat Sheets
Payment Processing

Recording a Payment in Full
1. Click Customers then choose Receive Payments from the top Menu Bar.
2. Choose the name of the customer from the Received From drop down list.
3. Enter the partial payment received information.
4. If you want to link the payment to any charge other than the oldest invoice, click the Un-apply Payment Button in the Main tab of the Ribbon.
5. Enter the amount received to apply to the correct invoice under the Payment column.
6. If an underpayment of the total amount due is entered, choose the Write off extra amount button to write off the remaining balance, of your choosing or Click on Leave this as an underpayment.
7. When finished click either the Save & Close or Save & New button, depending on if you have more than one payment to enter.

Applying One Payment to Multiple Invoices/Charges
1. Click Customers then choose Receive Payments from the top Menu Bar.
2. Select the name of the Customer from the Received from the Drop-Down List.
3. Enter the Payment Received Information.
4. Click the Un-apply Payment Button in the Main tab of the Ribbon, so you can apply the correct invoices directly to your payment received.
5. Enter the amount then start checking invoices to apply to the payment.
6. Click the Save & Close Button if you are done or if you have more payments to enter click Save & New Button.

Entering Overpayments
1. Click Customers then choose Receive Payments from the top Menu Bar.
2. Choose the name of the Customer from the Received from Drop down List.
3. Enter the Payment information received.
4. The Customers overpayment is shown as an overpayment at the bottom left corner. Select either the Leave the credit to be used later or the Refund the amount to the customer.
5. When finished Click Save & Close Button or if you have more payments to enter Click Save & New Button.

Entering Down Payments or Prepayments
1. Click Customers then choose Receive Payments from the top Menu Bar.
2. Choose the name of the Customer from the Received from drop down list.
3. Enter the payment amount received information.
4. The customer's down payment or prepayment amount is listed as an Overpayment in the bottom left corner. Select the Leave the Credit to apply to an invoice later.
5. Click Save & Close button if finished or if you have more payments to enter Click Save & New Button to continue.

Handy Quick Reference Cheat Sheets
Payment Processing Continued

Applying Customer Credits
1. Click Customers then choose Receive Payments from the top Menu Bar.
2. Choose the name of the customer from the Received from drop down list and choose the correct invoice to apply the customer's credit DO NOT mark it with a checkmark, but select it by Clicking on any other column available.
3. Click the Discounts & Credits button in the Main tab of the Ribbon.
4. On the Credits tab, click the checkmark column next to the credit in the Available Credits section.
5. To apply a partial credit you need to change the amount in the amount to use column.
6. Click the Done button and then either the Save & Close or the Save & New Button, depending on if you have more transactions to enter.

Making Deposits
1. Click banking then choose Make Deposits from the top Menu Bar.
2. Click to choose any payments to deposit in the Payments to Deposit Window then click ok.
3. In the make deposits screen select the bank account from the Deposit to Drop down list.
4. Enter the date of the deposit.
5. Click into the next row if you have any other payments going in this deposit.
6. Enter any Cash Back information if needed.
7. Click on the drop down arrow to the right of the toolbar's Print button and choose either Deposit Slip or Deposit Summary and then the Print button in the Print Box.
8. Click the Save & Close Button unless you have more separate deposits then Click Save & New.

Handling Bounced Checks
1. Click Customers, choose Receive Payments from the top Menu Bar.
2. Find the payment that contains the bounced check to display it in the Receive payments screen by using the Find button or the Previous and Next arrows.
3. Choose Record Bounced Check Button from Main tab in the Ribbon area. Enter Check Info then click next & finish.
4. Click the Save & Close button.

Refunding a Customers Purchases
1. Click Customers then choose Create Credit Memos/Refunds from the top Menu Bar.
2. Choose the customer from the Customer Job drop down list.
3. Enter the returned items in the line items area.
4. Choose Use Credit to Give Refund button in the Main tab of the Ribbon to issue a Refund check to the Customer.
5. Choose the correct account to issue funds for the refund check along with any other information necessary, click ok.
6. Click Save & Close button, Print check & credit memo.

Handy Quick Reference Cheat Sheets
Payment Processing Continued

Refunding Customer Payments
1. Click banking then choose Write Checks from the top Menu Bar.
2. Enter check Information then choose Accounts Receivable account on the Expenses Tab.
3. Click Save & Close button & print the check.
4. Click Customers then choose Receive Payments from the top Menu Bar then choose the customer from the Received from drop down list.
5. Click to choose the refund check you wrote and then click the Discounts & Credits button on the Main tab in the ribbon.
6. Choose the credit that matches the refund check amount on the Credits tab. Click Done, Save & Close Buttons.

Handy Quick Reference Cheat Sheets
Enter & Pay Bills

Entering Bills
1. Click Vendors, choose Enter Bills from the top Menu Bar.
2. Select a vendor from the Vendor drop down list.
3. Enter all the necessary bill information then Click the Save & Close button if you are done entering bills or Click Save & New Button if you have more bills to enter.

Paying a Bill
1. Click Vendors, choose Pay Bills from the top menu Bar.
2. Click the checkbox to the left of the bills to pay.
3. Change the amount to pay column if it's a partial payment.
4. When finished click the Pay Selected Bills button.

Apply Early Payment Discounts
1. Click Vendors, choose Pay Bills from top Menu Bar.
2. Click the checkbox to the left of the bill to pay then click Set Discount button.
3. Enter discount amount, click account then click done.
4. In the Pay Bills screen complete Bill Payment information and click the Pay Selected Bills Button.

Entering Vendor Credits
1. Click Vendors, choose Enter Bills from the top Menu Bar.
2. Choose the Credit option at the top of form.
3. Complete credit info and click the save and close button.

Applying Vendor Credits
1. Click Vendors, choose Pay Bills from the top Menu Bar.
2. Click the checkbox to the left of the bill to pay.
3. Click the Set Credits button.
4. If using only part of a credit, type the amount to apply in the Amount to use column then click the done button.
5. In the Pay Bills window, finish the bill payment information and click the Pay Selected Bills button.

Handy Quick Reference Cheat Sheets
Bank Accounts

Entering Transactions in the Register
1. Close out open screens you have open
2. Click Banking, choose Use Register from the top Menu Bar.
3. Choose the account from the drop down and click ok.
4. Record entry in the blank row and click the record button.

Write Checks Screen
1. Click Banking, choose Write Checks from the top Menu Bar.
2. Choose the correct checking account from the Bank Account drop down list.
3. Enter all the check information including the accounts/expenses to apply to check.
4. Click Save & Close button or if you have more checks to write click Save & New Button.

Writing Checks for Inventory Items
1. Click Banking, choose Write Checks from the top Menu Bar.
2. Enter the check information.
3. Choose the Items tab and select the inventory parts from the Item drop down and enter a quantity.
4. Click Save & close when finished.

Print a Single Check
1. Click Banking, choose Write Checks from the top Menu Bar.
2. Click on the arrows for previous or next or Find Button to display the check wanting to print.
3. Click the drop down arrow on the Print button in the Main tab of the Ribbon.
4. Choose Check from the drop down and then click ok.

Printing a Batch of Checks
1. Click Banking, choose Write Checks from the top Menu Bar.
2. Click the drop down arrow on the Print button in the Main tab of the Ribbon area and choose Batch.
3. Click to un-check any checks NOT to print.
4. Choose the correct bank account, enter a first check number and click ok.
5. Pick any other desired printing options in the Print Checks box and click the Print Button.

Transferring Funds
1. Click Banking, choose Transfer Funds from the top Menu Bar.
2. Enter the necessary transfer information.
3. Click Save & close unless you have more transfers then click save and new.

Handy Quick Reference Cheat Sheets
__Bank Accounts Continued__

Voiding Checks
1. Click Banking, choose Write Checks from the top Menu Bar.
2. Use the Find Button or the Previous or Next arrows to locate the check to display.
3. Choose Edit, then Void Check from the top Menu Bar.
4. Click Save & Close then Yes to Confirm changes.

Handy Quick Reference Cheat Sheets
Reports

Creating a QuickReport
1. Click an item in any list, open a transaction form, or display the information.
2. Press the Control Button and Q Button at the same time for a QuickReport to Display.
3. Press Esc to close the report when finished.

Quick Zooming a Report
1. Place your mouse over the information in the report you are wanting to see until a magnifying glass with a Z appears and then double click.
2. The information you are looking to see will appear on screen.
3. Close the screen when finished by press the Esc button or clicking on the X in right hand of the report.

Modifying Reports
1. Modifying a preset report, open report you want to use for modification, choose Customize Report button on toolbar.
2. Creating a new transaction detail or summary report from scratch you would choose reports then click Custom Reports from the top Menu Bar and then select Transaction Detail or Summary from the menu.
3. In the Modify Report Box make the needed changes on the Display, Filters, Header/Footer and Fonts & Numbers tabs.
4. Click Ok to modify the report settings.

Customizing Report Columns
1. Rearrange report columns by placing the mouse over the name of the column in the heading until the pointer turns into a hand icon. Click, drag and release to the location you want.
2. Resizing columns in a report, place the mouse to the right of the name of the column to resize, where the three dots are at, until the mouse changes into a thin vertical by a cross arrow.
3. Click, drag left or right and release to resize.

Memorizing Modified Reports
1. Click the memorize button in the toolbar at the top of the modified reports window.
2. Enter the report name in the Name field.
3. Check and choose a Memorized Report Group if you want and then click ok.

Printing Reports
1. Click the Print button in the toolbar of the report you want and select Report from the drop down list.
2. Set print options in the Print Reports screen.
3. Set the options you need and click the Print button.

Handy Quick Reference Cheat Sheets
Reports Continued

Batch Printing Forms
1. Click File, choose Print Forms from the top Menu Bar.
2. Click the type of form to print from the slide out menu to the right.
3. Set Printing options you need and click ok.

Handy Quick Reference Cheat Sheets
Estimating

Creating a New Job
1. Click Customers, choose Customer Center from the top menu bar.
2. Choose the customer in the Customers & Jobs list.
3. Click the New Customer & Job Button and select Add Job.
4. Enter your job name in the job name field.
5. Click on the Job Info tab and fill in all the necessary information.
6. When finished click ok.

Creating Estimates
1. Click Customers, choose Create Estimates from the top Menu Bar.
2. Choose the job from the Customer: Job drop down list.
3. Fill in the estimate information.
4. When done click Save & Close or Save & New if you have more estimates to enter.

Creating Invoices from Estimates
1. Click Customers, Create Invoices from the top Menu Bar.
2. Choose the job from the Customer: Job drop down list.
3. When the available estimates window appears choose the estimate you want to create an invoice from and click ok.
4. In the Create Progress Invoice Based on Estimate screen, choose an invoicing option and click ok.
5. When finished click save and close or save and new to continue invoicing from more estimates.

Making Estimate Inactive
1. Click Customers, Create Estimates from the top Menu Bar.
2. Use the Find button or the previous or next arrows to find the estimate you want to make inactive.
3. Click the Mark as Inactive button on the Main tab of the Ribbon, then click save & close button.

Purchases for a Job
1. Click Vendors, choose Click Purchase Orders from the top Menu Bar. You can also make a purchase using Enter bills, write checks or enter Credit Card Charges as well.
2. Enter the vendor information that you are making the purchases from.
3. Enter the first Item for the expense for the job in the line items area.
4. For each line item you need to use the drop down list to select the Customer: Job to be billed.
5. When finished Click the Save & Close unless you have more purchases then you Click Save & New button.

Handy Quick Reference Cheat Sheets
Estimating Continued

Invoicing Job Costs
1. Click Customers, choose Create Invoices from the top Menu Bar.
2. Choose the job from the Customer: Job drop down list.
3. In the Billable Time/Costs screen click the Select the outstanding billable time and costs to add to this invoice option button and then click ok.
4. Click the left column to select expense to bill out.
5. Enter all billable items and expenses then click ok.
6. When invoice finished select Save & New if need to do more invoicing or select Save & Close button if you are finished.

Creating Job Reports
1. Click Reports, then Jobs, Time & Mileage from the top Menu Bar.
2. Click the report name in the menu.
3. Select dates then hit the refresh Button.
4. You can of course customize to what you need.
5. Print if you need or save as a PDF.
6. When finished Press Esc button or click on the X in the top right hand corner of the report.

Handy Quick Reference Cheat Sheets
Time Tracking

Printing Blank Weekly Timesheets
1. Click Employees, choose Enter Time then select Use Weekly Timesheet from the top Menu Bar.
2. Click the drop down arrow to the right of the Print button and choose Print Blank Timesheet.
3. Click the Print Button enter the number of time sheets you want to print. Press Esc button or Click on X to exit.

Using Weekly Timesheets
1. Click Employees, choose Enter Time then Use Weekly Timesheet from the top Menu Bar.
2. Choose a name and date at the top of the screen.
3. Enter the timesheet information in the columns.
4. Click either Save & Close if you have finished entering timesheet information or Save & New if you need to enter more timesheets.

Entering Single/Time Activity
1. Click Employees, choose Enter Time then Enter Single Activity from the top Menu Bar.
2. Enter the employee activity information and click either Save & Close if finished entering time or Save & New if you need to enter more time.

Invoicing A Customer for Time/Services
1. Click Customers, create Invoices from the top Menu Bar.
2. Use the Customer: Job drop down list to choose the customer: Job to bill.
3. In the Billable Time/Costs screen click the Select the outstanding billable time and costs to add to this invoice option and click ok.
4. In the Choose Billable Time & Costs screen click the Time tab and choose hours to bill the customer by clicking the line items left column. Click ok, save & Close or Save & New.

Displaying Time Tracking Reports
1. Click Reports, choose Jobs, Time & Mileage from the top Menu Bar.
2. Click to choose the Report name in the menu in the slide out menu to your right.
3. Fill in dates needed and hit the refresh button and print if needed.
4. Press the Esc button when done.

Handy Quick Reference Cheat Sheets
Time Tracking Continued

Entering Vehicle Mileage
1. Click Company, choose Enter Vehicle Mileage from the top Menu Bar.
2. Enter all vehicle, job and mileage information necessary.
3. Entering mileage rates, click the Mileage Rates button at the top of the window, enter the rate then click the close button.
4. Click Save & Close if you are done or Save & New if you are entering more than one entry.

Invoicing Customers for Mileage
1. Click Customers, choose Create Invoices from the top Menu Bar.
2. Click on the Customer: Job drop down list to choose the name you have billable mileage to invoice out.
3. In the Billable Time/Costs screen click the Select outstanding billable time and costs to add to this invoice option and click ok.
4. Click the Mileage tab in the Choose Billable Time/Costs screen, then select the mileage to bill out by clicking the line item's left column.
5. Click ok
6. Click Save & Close if you are finished with invoicing for mileage or if you have more Click Save & New.

Handy Quick Reference Cheat Sheets
Payroll

Creating and Viewing Payroll Items
1. To look at your current set of payroll items you need to Click Lists, choose Payroll Item List from the top Menu Bar.
2. Click the Payroll Item button in the lower left corner of the payroll item list to add a new payroll item then select New.
3. In the Add new Payroll item screen answer the questions and click the next button on each screen until the new item is set up.
4. Click Finish.

Setting Employee Payroll Defaults
1. Click Employees, choose Employee Center from the top Menu Bar.
2. Click the Manage Employee Information button in the toolbar & select the Change New Employee default settings.
3. Enter employee default information and click ok.

Employee Payroll Information Set Up
1. Click Employees, choose Employee Center from the top Menu Bar.
2. Click the New Employee button to open the New Employee screen or double click an existing employee on the Employees tab to open the Edit Employee screen.
3. Click the Payroll Info tab and enter all the employee's payroll information and then click ok.

Payroll Schedules
1. Click Employees, choose Add or Edit Payroll Schedules from the top Menu Bar.
2. Create a New Schedule, click the Payroll Schedule button, and choose New. Enter the schedule info and click ok.
3. Editing schedules click to choose the schedule in the Payroll Schedule list screen. Click the Payroll Schedule button, Edit Payroll Schedule. Enter the Schedule info and click ok.

Creating Scheduled Paychecks
1. Click Employees, choose Pay Employees then select Scheduled Payroll from the top Menu Bar.
2. In the Pay Employees section, select the name of the payroll schedule and click the Start Scheduled Payroll button.
3. To make changes to a paycheck, click the linked employee name in the list to open the paycheck in the Preview Paycheck screen. Edit the employee information and click Save & Close button.
4. Click the continue button.
5. Review the summary and select check options.
6. Click the Create Paychecks button.
7. Click the Print Paychecks and print Paystubs buttons when needed.
8. Click the Close button when finished.

Handy Quick Reference Cheat Sheets
Payroll Continued

Creating Unscheduled Paychecks
1. Click Employees, choose Pay Employees then Unscheduled Payroll from the top Menu Bar.
2. Enter the payroll information, and click to place a checkmark next to the names of employees to pay.
3. Click the Continue button.
4. Review the Summary and choose Check Options.
5. Click on the linked name of any employee shown in the list if editing is needed and click Save & Close after editing.
6. Click the Create Paychecks button.
7. Click the Print Paychecks and print Paystubs buttons as needed and click Close when finished.

Creating Employee Termination Paychecks
1. Click Employees, choose Pay Employees then select Termination Check from the top Menu Bar.
2. Enter the payroll information and click to place a checkmark next to the names of employees to pay for termination.
3. In the Release Date column, enter the employee's release date and then click the Continue button.
4. Click either the Make Inactive or Keep as Active button to continue.
5. Review the Summary and select check options.
6. Click on the linked name of the employee in the list to edit the payroll information if necessary then click Save & Close.
7. Click the Create Paychecks button.
8. Click the Print Paychecks and Print Paystubs buttons when needed and then click when finished.

Handy Quick Reference Cheat Sheets
Credit Cards

Creating Credit Card Accounts
1. Click Lists, choose Chart of Accounts from the top Menu Bar.
2. Click the Account button & choose New.
3. Select the Credit Card option and click Continue.
4. Enter the account information and click Save & Close or Save & New if you need to enter other accounts.

Entering Credit Card Charges
1. Click Banking, choose Enter Credit Card Charges from the top Menu Bar.
2. Choose the card from the Credit Card drop down list.
3. Enter all credit card charge information and click Save & Close or Save & New.

Reconciling Credit Card Accounts
1. Click Banking, choose Reconcile from the top Menu Bar.
2. Select the account from the Account drop down list.
3. Enter the credit card statement date, ending balance, and any finance charges, then click the Continue button.
4. Click the checkmark column to mark cleared transactions.
5. Click the Reconcile Now button.
6. Select an option to either write a check or enter a bill to pay the credit card bill and click ok.
7. Select an option in the Select Reconciliation Report box. Click Display, Print or Close.
8. Select the Bank or credit card company to pay in the Write Checks or Enter Bills window and click Save & Close when finished.

Handy Quick Reference Cheat Sheets
Loan Manager

Working with the Loan Manager
6. Adding a Loan to the Loan Manager, click Banking, choose Loan Manager from the top Menu Bar.
7. Click the Add a Loan button.
8. Enter the loan information on each screen and click next until the wizard is completed.
9. Click the Finish button when done.

Editing a Loan in Loan Manager
4. Click Banking, choose Loan Manager from the top Menu Bar.
5. Click the loan name in the Loan List.
6. Click the Edit Loan Details button to return to the wizard to edit the loan or click the Remove Loan Button and Yes to remove if wanting to delete loan.

Handy Quick Reference Cheat Sheets
Company Information

Updating Company
1. Click Company, choose My Company from the top Menu Bar.
2. Click the Edit button.
3. Edit the company information and when finished click ok.

Reminders & Setting Preferences
1. Click Edit, choose Preferences from the top Menu Bar.
2. Click Reminders from the box at the left.
3. Click the My Preferences tab, and select Show Reminders List when opening a Company file.
4. When finished Click ok.

General Journal Entries
1. Click Company, choose make General Journal Entries from the top Menu Bar.
2. Click to select the accounts involved in the transaction and enter the credit and debit amounts.
3. When finished Click Save & Close to post the transaction.

QuickBooks Super Shortcuts

General

General action	Shortcut
To start QuickBooks without a company file	Ctrl (while opening)
To suppress the desktop windows (at Open Company window)	Alt (while opening)
Display product information about your QuickBooks version	F2
Close active window	Esc or Ctrl + F4
Save transaction	Alt + S
Save transaction and go to next transaction	Alt + N
Record (when black border is around OK, Save and Close, Save and New, or Record)	Enter
Record (always)	Ctrl + Enter

QuickBooks Super Shortcuts

Dates

In date fields, press the key for the symbol shown to quickly enter the date you want.

To change to	Shortcut key
Next day	+ (plus key)
Previous day	- (minus key)
Today	T
Same date in previous week	[(left bracket)
Same date in next week	] (right bracket)
Same date in last month	; (semicolon)
Same date in next month	' (apostrophe)
First day of the **W**eek	W
Last day of the wee**K**	K
First day of the **M**onth	M
Last day of the mont**H**	H
First day of the **Y**ear	Y
Last day of the yea**R**	R
Date calendar	Alt + down arrow

QuickBooks Super Shortcuts

Editing

Editing	Shortcut
Edit transaction selected in register	Ctrl + E
Delete character to right of insertion point	Del
Delete character to left of insertion point	Backspace
Delete line from detail area	Ctrl + Del
Insert line in detail area	Ctrl + Ins
Cut selected characters	Ctrl + X
Copy selected characters	Ctrl + C
Paste cut or copied characters	Ctrl + V
Increase check or other form number by one	+ (plus key)
Decrease check or other form number by one	- (minus key)
Undo changes made in field	Ctrl + Z

QuickBooks Super Shortcuts

Activities

Ctrl + O Copy check transaction in register	Ctrl + I Create invoice
Ctrl + D Delete check, invoice, transaction, or item from list	Ctrl + F Find transaction
Ctrl + G Go to register of transfer account	Ctrl + H History of A/R or A/P transaction
Ctrl + M Memorize transaction or report	Ctrl + N New invoice, bill, check or list item in context
Ctrl + A Open account list	Ctrl + J Open Customer Center (Customers & Jobs list)
F1 Open Help for active window	Ctrl + L Open list (for current drop-down menu)
Ctrl + T Open memorized transaction list	Ctrl + R Open split transaction window in register
Ctrl + Y Open transaction journal	Ctrl + V Paste copied transaction in register
Ctrl + P Print	Ctrl + Q QuickReport on transaction or list item
Enter = QuickZoom on report	Ctrl + S Show list
Ctrl + U Use list item	Ctrl + W Write new check

QuickBooks Super Shortcuts

Moving Around in a Window

Moving around a window	Shortcut
Next field	Tab
Previous field	Shift + Tab
Beginning of current field	Home
End of current field	End
Line below in detail area or on report	Down arrow
Line above in detail area or on report	Up arrow
Down one screen	Page Down
Up one screen	Page Up
Next word in field	Ctrl + Right arrow
Previous word in field	Ctrl + Left arrow
First item on list or previous month in register	Ctrl + Page Up
Last item on list or next month in register	Ctrl + Page Down
Close active window	Esc or Ctrl + F4

NOTES

NOTES

NOTES

NOTES

NOTES

Cristie Will, BBA, CHC, CIC, Author

Cristie was born and raised in Hobbs, New Mexico. She grew up in the Construction Industry. Her granddad started Walton Construction Company and her parents took over when he died. The Company was in the Family for 60 years before selling. Also, grew up with a family Restaurant called Pantastix. She moved to Colorado 18 years ago and still living there loving all the beauty Colorado has to offer. She has a daughter Lauren and a son Josh along with beautiful grandchildren. She has been an accountant the last 30 years. Not only an accountant and Health Coach but a teacher as well, teaching QuickBooks, cooking, detoxing and weight loss classes too! She still has her accounting business and teaching QuickBooks.

In 2012, she lost her husband to lung cancer. After losing her husband to lung cancer she needed to make changes in her own health, so she did. Cristie went through a life transformation losing 200 pounds and went back to school to become a Nutritional Heath Coach adding Cleansing Intensive certification. She obtained her education from Institute of Integrative Nutrition for her Health Coaching. Her education for the Cleansing Intensive education was under Dr. Terry Willard CIH, PHD at the Wild Rose College. She is currently studying to add FDN, Functional Diagnostic Nutritionist to her skills to be able to help even more people.

Additional Resources & References

http://quickbooks.intuit.com/
QuickBooks Main Website

http://www.soswill.com/
My Accounting Website for additional Information, Books and Client Testimonials

www.cbwill.com
My Author Website for more information about me.

Made in the USA
Columbia, SC
05 November 2020